Lab Manual for CCNP Guide to Advanced Cisco Routing

Michael Grice

THOMSON

COURSE TECHNOLOGY

Australia • Canada • Mexico • Singapore • Spain • United Kingdom • United States

THOMSON
™
COURSE TECHNOLOGY

Lab Manual for CCNP Guide to Advanced Cisco Routing

is published by Course Technology

Associate Publisher:
Steve Elliot

Technical Editor:
Michael Hogan

Editorial Assistant:
Nick Lombardi

Acquisitions Editor:
William Pitkin, III

Senior Manufacturing Coordinator:
Laura Burns

Cover Design:
Abby Scholz

Product Manager:
Charles Blum

Product Marketing Manager:
Jason Sakos

Text Designer:
GEX Publishing Services

Production Editor:
Brooke Booth

Associate Product Manager:
Tim Gleeson

Compositor:
GEX Publishing Services

Disclaimer
Course Technology reserves the righ
revise this publication and make
changes from time to time in its co
without notice.

ISBN 0-619-13086-5

TABLE OF CONTENTS

INTRODUCTION

Hands-on learning is the best way to master the networking skills necessary for both the CCNP exam and a career in wide-area networking. This book contains more than 40 hands-on exercises that apply networking concepts, such as OSPF, route filtering and policy routing, and EIGRP as they would be applied on Cisco equipment in the real world and on CCNP Exam #640-603. In addition, each chapter offers multiple review questions to reinforce mastery of the CCNP topics.

The organization of this lab manual follows the same organization as Course Technology's *CCNP Guide to Advanced Cisco Routing*, and using the two together will provide a substantial, effective learning experience.

This book is suitable for use in any Cisco CCNP course that prepares students for Cisco Exam #640-603. As a prerequisite, students should have basic networking knowledge as well as the CCNA certification or equivalent knowledge. This book is best used when accompanied by Course Technology's textbook *CCNP Guide to Advanced Cisco Routing*.

FEATURES

In order to ensure a successful experience for instructors and students alike, this book includes the following sections for each lab:

- **Objectives:** Every lab has a brief description and list of learning objectives.
- **Materials Required:** Every lab includes information on hardware, software, and other materials you will need to complete the lab.
- **Estimated Completion Time:** Every lab has an estimated completion time so that you can plan your activities more accurately.
- **Activity:** The actual lab activity is presented in this section. Logical and precise step-by-step instructions guide you through the lab.
- **Certification Objectives:** Each chapter lists the relevant objectives from Cisco's CCNP Exam #640-603.
- **Review Questions:** Questions help reinforce concepts presented in the lab.

HARDWARE REQUIREMENTS

The following is a list of hardware required to complete all the labs in the book. The hardware requirements for many of the individual labs are less than what is listed. The hardware required is as follows:

- A laptop or a personal computer (PC) with a terminal emulation program such as Hyperterminal
- A rollover console cable to connect the laptop or PC to the routers
- Transceivers for the router Ethernet ports if these Ethernet ports use an AUI connection instead of RJ-45
- Three Cisco routers with at least one serial interface and at least one Ethernet interface
- One Cisco router with at least two Ethernet interfaces
- One Cisco router with at least two serial interfaces and at least one Ethernet interface
- Power cables for all routers
- One hub or switch with power cable
- Three V.35 DTE cables (male) with serial end to match serial interface on routers
- Three V.35 DCE cables (female) with serial end to match serial interface on routers
- Four Category 5 crossover cables
- Three Category 5 straight-through cables
- Six Ethernet 10BaseT UTP to AUI transceivers (unnecessary if the Ethernet interfaces on the routers are RJ-45 transceivers)

ACKNOWLEDGEMENTS

I would like to thank Charlie Blum for his hard work and for keeping me on track. Thanks also to all of the reviewers who worked under exceptionally tight deadlines and gave consistently great feedback. Finally, I'd like to thank my wife Nancy for bearing with me, and for just being herself.

CHAPTER ONE

MAKING NETWORKS SCALABLE

Labs included in this chapter

- ◆ Lab 1.1 Configuring RIP
- ◆ Lab 1.2 Configuring IGRP
- ◆ Lab 1.3 Mapping the Network

Cisco CCNP Exam #640-603 Objectives	
Objective	Lab
Compare distance vector and link-state protocol operation	1.1 and 1.2
Describe the use of the fields in a routing table	1.3
Analyze a routing table, and test connectivity using accepted troubleshooting techniques	1.3

Lab 1.1 Configuring RIP

Objectives

The goal of this lab is to configure RIP in a network. Additionally, you will review basic interface configuration.

Materials Required

This lab will require the following:

➤ Three Cisco routers with Ethernet or Fast Ethernet interfaces, cabled as shown in Figure 1-1. The interfaces should not be configured with IP addresses. Known telnet and enable passwords for the routers are needed, along with the router configured to require telnet logins

➤ A rollover console cable

➤ A laptop or a PC running a terminal emulation program such as Hyperterminal

➤ Two crossover Category 5 cables

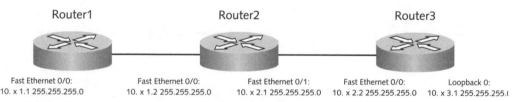

Router1	Router2	Router3

Fast Ethernet 0/0:   Fast Ethernet 0/0:   Fast Ethernet 0/1:   Fast Ethernet 0/0:   Loopback 0:
10. x 1.1 255.255.255.0   10. x 1.2 255.255.255.0   10. x 2.1 255.255.255.0   10. x 2.2 255.255.255.0   10. x 3.1 255.255.255.(

Figure 1-1   Network diagram for Lab 1.1, showing cabling and addressing

Estimated completion time: **20 minutes**

Activity Background

RIP is an example of a distance vector routing protocol. Routers using distance vector routing protocols periodically send routing updates to each of their neighbors. Each update contains a complete list of the routes known by the router and each route's metric. If a router does not receive a routing update from one of its neighbors by the time the invalid timer expires, it will declare that neighbor unreachable. A router will also send a flash update after a network topology change, such as a serial interface failing.

Distance vector routing protocols use a variety of techniques to prevent routing loops. In split horizon, a router will not advertise a route it learns from one interface out that same interface. Distance vector routing protocols require a router to mark a route as unreachable when its metric is too high. When a router knows that a particular route is down, it will advertise that route with an unreachable metric. Without poison reverse updates, other routers might continue to propagate the failed route. After receiving a poison reverse update, a router will not install a new route (unless the metric is better than the original metric) until the holddown timer expires. Finally, a router will not flush, or completely remove, a route from its routing table until after the flush timer expires. This prevents a router from flushing a failed route, learning the failed route from a neighbor, and then reinstalling the failed route.

Like other distance vector routing protocols, RIP is slow to converge. Additionally, the maximum number of hops allowed by RIP version 1 is 15. However, RIP is still used in many networks. Because of its simplicity, for instance, RIP is quite easy to configure. Additionally, RIP is also the only routing protocol understood by many devices.

In this lab, you will create a loopback or virtual interface. Although it is not a physical interface, the router will advertise it in its routing table and forward packets to it. Loopback interfaces can be useful for testing. Loopback interfaces are also used by some routing protocols for stability (since they do not go down unless the whole router goes down).

ACTIVITY

1. Power on all three routers. Power on the PC or laptop and open the terminal emulation program.

2. Make sure that the routers are cabled, as in Figure 1-1. Plug the RJ-45 end of the console cable into the console port on Router1, and attach the other end to the serial port on the PC or laptop.

3. In the terminal emulation program, type **enable** at the Router1> prompt and enter the enable password when prompted. The prompt changes to Router1#.

4. Type **config term** and press **Enter** to enter global configuration mode. The router prompt changes to Router1(config)#.

5. Type **int fast 0/0** and press **Enter** to enter interface configuration mode. The router prompt changes to Router1(config-if)#. If necessary, substitute the appropriate interface name and number.

6. Type **ip address 10.x.1.1 255.255.255.0**, where x is the number of your lab group as assigned by your instructor. Use 1 for x if you are working alone or if you are the only lab group. Press **Enter**. This configures interface Fast Ethernet 0 with an IP address of 10.x.1.1 and a subnet mask of 255.255.255.0.

7. Type **no shut** and press **Enter**. This turns on the interface if it was in the administratively down state (and does not hurt if the interface is up).

8. Type **exit** and press **Enter**. This will take you out of interface configuration mode without exiting from configuration mode. (In this case, typing exit again would also take you out of configuration mode.)

9. Type **router rip** and press **Enter**. The router enters router configuration mode.

10. Type **network 10.0.0.0** and press **Enter**. The router is now configured to run RIP, and will advertise routes for all subnetworks of the class A network 10.0.0.0.

11. Press **Ctl-Z** to exit configuration mode.

12. Now remove the end of the console cable from Router1 and plug it into the console port on Router2. Type **enable** and press **Enter** to enter enable mode.

13. Type **config term** and press **Enter**.

14. Type **int fast 0/0** and press **Enter**.

15. Type **ip address 10.x.1.2 255.255.255.0** and press **Enter**.

16. Type **no shut** and press **Enter**.

17. Type **exit** and press **Enter**.

18. Type **int fast 0/1** and press **Enter**.

19. Type **ip address 10.x.2.1 255.255.255.0** and press **Enter**.

20. Type **no shut** and press **Enter**.

21. Repeat Steps 9 through 11.

22. Unplug the console cable from Router2 and plug it into the console port on Router3.

23. Type **enable** and press **Enter**.

24. Type **config term** and press **Enter**.

25. Type **int fast 0/0** and press **Enter**.

26. Type **ip address 10.x.2.2 255.255.255.0** and press **Enter**.

27. Type **no shut** and press **Enter**.

28. Type **int loopback 0** and press **Enter**. This creates a loopback interface named Loopback 0.

29. Type **ip address 10.x.3.1 255.255.255.0** and press **Enter**.

30. Repeat Steps 9 through 11.

31. Now all three routers are configured for RIP. Type **show ip route** to see the routing table. You should see routes for 10.x.1.0/24, 10.x.2.0/24 and 10.x.3.0/24. If not, wait a minute or two and repeat this step until you do.

32. Type **debug ip rip** and press **Enter**. After a few seconds, debugging output appears. Based on the debugging output, which routes is the router receiving?

_____

33. Type **undebug all** and press **Enter**. This turns off all debugging. Since debugging can have a significant effect on router performance, you should get in the habit of always turning off debugging when you are done.

34. Type **telnet 10.x.1.1** to connect to Router1. Enter the telnet password at the Password: prompt.

35. Type **show ip route** to show Router1's routing table. Check to see if it has the same routes in its routing table as Router3. If not, repeat this step until it does.

Certification Objective

Objective for Cisco Exam 640-603: Routing

➤ Compare distance vector and link-state routing protocol operation

Review Questions

1. RIP is said to converge slowly. What does this mean?

   a. RIP adapts quickly to network topology changes.

   b. RIP does not adapt to network topology changes.

   c. RIP adapts slowly to network topology changes.

   d. RIP only allows routers to forward packets slowly.

2. Which of the following are properties of a distance vector routing protocol like RIP? (Choose all that apply.)

   a. The entire routing table is sent in each routing update.

   b. Only changes are sent in a routing update.

   c. Routers keep track of the topology of the entire network.

   d. Routers consider a route unreachable if it is too many hops away.

3. Which of the following are advantages of RIP? (Choose all that apply.)

   a. RIP is easy to configure.

   b. RIP converges quickly.

   c. RIP uses a minimum of bandwidth for its routing updates.

   d. RIP is often the only routing protocol supported by many devices.

4. When might you use a loopback interface? (Choose all that apply.)

   a. for testing

   b. to aid in stability with some routing protocols

   c. for load-balancing with a physical interface

   d. to use IP addresses more efficiently

5. Which of the following commands would configure RIP on a router with the interface 172.16.1.3?

   a. router rip

   b. router rip

      network 172.16.0.0

   c. router rip 1

      network 172.16.0.0

   d. rip router

      network 172.16.0.0

LAB 1.2 CONFIGURING IGRP

Objectives

The goals of this lab are to configure IGRP on a network, and debug a link failure.

Materials Required

This lab will require the following:

➤ Three Cisco routers connected and configured with IP addresses, as shown in Figure 1-1 (substituting the lab group number assigned by your instructor for *x*, or 1 if you are working alone, or are in the only lab group), but without any routing protocols configured

➤ Known telnet and enable passwords for the routers

➤ A rollover console cable

➤ A laptop or a PC running a terminal emulation program such as Hyperterminal

➤ Two crossover Category 5 cables

➤ A watch or clock

Estimated completion time: **30 minutes**

Activity Background

Cisco designed IGRP as a distance vector routing protocol, but with some improvements over RIP. As a result, IGRP is easy to configure, has an improved metric, and allows networks larger than 15 hops. However, routers running IGRP still broadcast their entire routing table at each update, and IGRP still converges slowly. One other disadvantage of IGRP is that since the protocol is proprietary to Cisco, only Cisco routers understand it.

Link-state routing protocols, such as Open Shortest Path First (OSPF), were designed to improve on IGRP by reducing the shortcomings of distance vector routing protocols. In a link-state routing protocol, each router builds a database of each link on the network. Whenever a link attached to a router goes down, the router transmits this information to every router on the network. As a result, each router has complete knowledge of the network topology, and can converge quickly after a link fails. Additionally, link-state routing protocols only send routing updates after a change. As a result, link-state routing protocols use much less bandwidth to send routing updates than distance vector routing protocols.

ACTIVITY

1. Power on all three routers. Power on the PC or laptop and open the terminal emulation program.

2. Plug the RJ-45 end of the console cable into the console port of Router1, and attach the other end to the serial port of the PC or laptop.

3. At the Router1> prompt, type **enable** and press **Enter**. The prompt changes to Router#.

4. Type **config term** and press **Enter**. The router prompt changes to Router(config)#.

5. Type **router igrp 1** and press **Enter**. The prompt changes to Router1(config-router)#. The 1 at the end of the command is the Autonomous System number, which must be the same for all routers on the network.

6. Type **network 10.0.0.0** and press **Enter**.

7. Press **Ctl-Z** to exit configuration mode.

8. Now type **show ip protocol** and press **Enter**. The output of the command shows that IGRP is now configured on the router.

9. Repeat Steps 2 through 8 for Router2 and Router3.

10. Plug the RJ-45 end of the console cable back into the console port of Router1.

11. Type **show ip route** and press **Enter**. You should see routing table entries for each of the networks in Figure 1-1 (10.x.1.0/24, 10.x.2.0/24, and 10.x.3.0/24). If not, repeat this step every 90 seconds until the network has converged and you see all of these networks in the routing table. According to the routing table, what is the next hop that Router1 will use when forwarding packets to the 10.x.3.0/24 network?

_____

12. To verify that the router can reach the 10.x.4.0/24 network, type **ping 10.x.3.1** and press **Enter**. Five exclamation points appear, indicating that five ICMP echo reply packets were received. Sometimes a period followed by four exclamation points appears. This happens when the router must make an Address Resolution Protocol (ARP) request first, and the initial ICMP echo reply packet arrives too

late. If this happens, repeat this step, and you should see five exclamation points in the command output, as shown in Figure 1-2.

13. Turn on debugging by typing **debug ip igrp events** and pressing **Enter**. Debugging output appears within a minute. The router displays additional debugging output after each routing update it sends, and after each routing update it receives.

```
Router1#ping 10.1.3.1
Sending 5, 100-byte ICMP Echos to 10.1.3.1, timeout is 2 seconds:
.!!!!
Success rate is 80 percent (4/5), round-trip min/avg/max = 1/1/4 ms
Router1#ping 10.1.3.1

Type escape sequence to abort.
Sending 5, 100-byte ICMP Echos to 10.1.3.1, timeout is 2 seconds:
!!!!!
Success rate is 100 percent (5/5), round-trip min/avg/max = 1/2/4 ms
Router1#
```

Figure 1-2   Output of the ping command

14. Now you will watch what happens when an interface goes down for an extended period of time. Disconnect the cable connecting Router2 and Router3. Record the time.

_____

15. After the next time the debugging output indicates that the router sent or received a routing update, type **show ip route** and press **Enter**. The routing table will show that the routes to the 10.x.2.0/24 and 10.x.3.0/24 networks might be down. See Figure 1-3 for an example of debugging output, followed by the output of the show ip route command.

16. Repeat the previous step until the router flushes the routes to the 10.x.2.0/24 and 10.x.3.0/24 networks. Record the time at which these networks were flushed, and the total time it took to flush them.

_____

17. Replace the cable connecting Router2 and Router3.

18. After the debugging output indicates that Router1 received or sent a routing update, type **show ip route** and press **Enter**. Repeat this step until all three routes are back in the routing table and the network has converged.

19. Now you will watch what happens when an interface goes down briefly. Disconnect the cable between Router2 and Router3. Record the time.

_____

20. When Router1 sends or receives its next routing update, type **show ip route** and press **Enter**. Repeat until the routes to 10.x.2.0/24 and 10.x.3.0/24 are marked as possibly down. Record the time. How long did it take for Router1 to change its routing table?

_____

21. Replace the cable connecting Router2 and Router3. Record the time.

_____

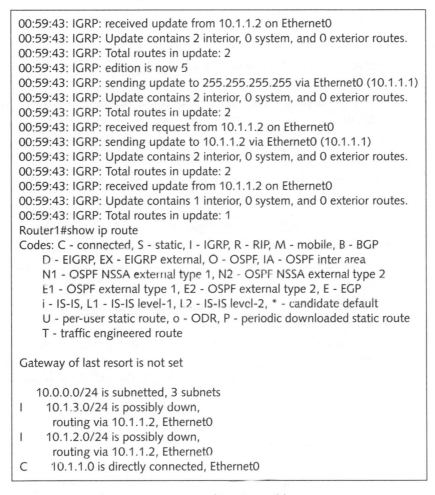

```
00:59:43: IGRP: received update from 10.1.1.2 on Ethernet0
00:59:43: IGRP: Update contains 2 interior, 0 system, and 0 exterior routes.
00:59:43: IGRP: Total routes in update: 2
00:59:43: IGRP: edition is now 5
00:59:43: IGRP: sending update to 255.255.255.255 via Ethernet0 (10.1.1.1)
00:59:43: IGRP: Update contains 2 interior, 0 system, and 0 exterior routes.
00:59:43: IGRP: Total routes in update: 2
00:59:43: IGRP: received request from 10.1.1.2 on Ethernet0
00:59:43: IGRP: sending update to 10.1.1.2 via Ethernet0 (10.1.1.1)
00:59:43: IGRP: Update contains 2 interior, 0 system, and 0 exterior routes.
00:59:43: IGRP: Total routes in update: 2
00:59:43: IGRP: received update from 10.1.1.2 on Ethernet0
00:59:43: IGRP: Update contains 1 interior, 0 system, and 0 exterior routes.
00:59:43: IGRP: Total routes in update: 1
Router1#show ip route
Codes: C - connected, S - static, I - IGRP, R - RIP, M - mobile, B - BGP
       D - EIGRP, EX - EIGRP external, O - OSPF, IA - OSPF inter area
       N1 - OSPF NSSA external type 1, N2 - OSPF NSSA external type 2
       E1 - OSPF external type 1, E2 - OSPF external type 2, E - EGP
       i - IS-IS, L1 - IS-IS level-1, L2 - IS-IS level-2, * - candidate default
       U - per-user static route, o - ODR, P - periodic downloaded static route
       T - traffic engineered route

Gateway of last resort is not set

     10.0.0.0/24 is subnetted, 3 subnets
I       10.1.3.0/24 is possibly down,
          routing via 10.1.1.2, Ethernet0
I       10.1.2.0/24 is possibly down,
          routing via 10.1.1.2, Ethernet0
C       10.1.1.0 is directly connected, Ethernet0
```

Figure 1-3 Debugging output and routing table

22. After the next routing update sent or received by Router1, type **show ip route** and press **Enter**. Repeat until the routes to 10.x.2.0/24 and 10.x.3.0/24 are no longer marked as down. How long did Router1 mark these routes as possibly down?

_____

Certification Objective

Objective for Cisco Exam 640-603: Routing

➤ Compare distance vector and link-state routing protocol operation

REVIEW QUESTIONS

1. What is the purpose of a poison reverse update?

   a. to prevent a router from reaching forbidden routes

   b. to allow a router to quickly install a new route

   c. to prevent a router from installing a bad route still advertised by one of its neighbors

   d. to allow a router to install an alternate route advertised by one of its neighbors

2. Which of the following are characteristics of a link-state routing protocol? (Choose all that apply.)

   a. Each router sends its entire routing table in each routing update.

   b. Each router sends routing updates only after network changes.

   c. Each router has complete knowledge of the network topology.

   d. Each router only knows about its neighboring routers.

3. Which of the following are true while the holddown timer is in effect for a route? (Choose all that apply.)

   a. The router continues to advertise the unreachable route, with an unreachable metric.

   b. The router will not accept other routes with the metric of the original route.

   c. The router will accept routes with metrics better than the original route.

   d. The router will accept any route.

4. Which of the following commands would configure IGRP on a router with an interface with an IP address of 192.168.154.1?

   a. router igrp

      network 192.168.154.0

   b. router igrp 1

      network 192.168.154.0 255.255.255.0

   c. router igrp 1

   d. router igrp 1

      network 192.168.154.0

5. Which of the following are advantages of link-state routing protocols over distance vector routing protocols such as RIP and IGRP? (Choose all that apply.)

   a. Link-state routing protocols send routing updates only after a change.

   b. Link-state routing protocols require a router to know the entire topology of the network.

   c. Link-state routing protocols require a router to send its entire routing tables with each update.

   d. After initialization, link-state routing protocols use much less bandwidth.

LAB 1.3 MAPPING THE NETWORK

Objective

The goal of this lab is to use information from the routing tables and Cisco Discovery Protocol (CDP) to map a network.

Materials Required

This lab will require the following:

> A functioning network consisting of three or more Cisco routers running a routing protocol such as RIP or IGRP. The example shown in Figure 1-4 could be used, or any other network consisting of three or more Cisco routers

> CDP running on each of the routers

> The routing protocol on the network has had sufficient time to converge

> A hub or switch with enough ports for each lab group, if the network in Figure 1-4 is used

> Known telnet passwords for the routers (the enable password is not required)

> A rollover console cable

> A laptop or a PC running a terminal emulation program such as Hyperterminal

> Paper and a pen or pencil

> Network diagramming software such as Visio (optional)

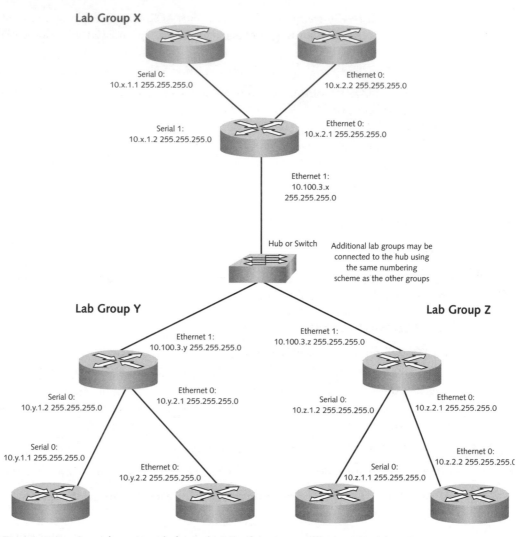

Figure 1-4   Sample network for Lab 1.3, showing cabling and addressing

Estimated completion time: **30 minutes**

Activity Background

A routing table shows you all the routes the router knows about, as well as which interface the router would use to forward packets for each route. Additionally, the routing table shows you the IP address of the next hop for non-connected networks. By using this information to identify the router's neighbors, you can map the network.

You can also get quite a bit of other information about a network from a routing table. For instance, each route in a routing table is marked with a brief code indicating the source of a route. R stands for RIP, I stands for IGRP, S stands for static, and so on. The routing table also contains information about the metric for the route, listed after the route itself. Finally, the routing table indicates whether or not the router has a default gateway or a default route (called a gateway of last resort).

Another tool you can use to map a network is CDP. CDP is a proprietary Cisco protocol used by Cisco devices to discover other Cisco devices. By default, a router sends CDP packets out each of its interfaces. Each CDP packet contains information about the router, including its name, hardware information, and the IP address of the interface sending the packet. Cisco switches also send CDP packets. As a result, you can use CDP to get Layer 2 information about a network.

In this lab, you will use the routing table, CDP, and other commands to make a map of a network.

ACTIVITY

1. Power on the PC or laptop and open the terminal emulation program.

2. Plug the RJ-45 end of the console cable into the console port of one of the routers. The router chosen does not matter, as you will perform the same process on each router.

3. Type **show interface** and press **Enter**. On the piece of paper, record the name and IP address of the router. Then record next to it the name of each active interface, along with the IP address and subnet mask.

4. Type **show version** and press **Enter**. The router prints information about the router, including its type, the version of Cisco IOS running, the amount of flash memory, and the amount of Random Access Memory (RAM). Record the router type on the piece of paper by the router's name.

5. Type **show ip route** and press **Enter**. For each connected network, record the network number and subnet mask next to the interface that it matches.

6. For each of the other networks, record the IP address of the next hop. Draw a line from this information to the name of the router you are currently logged onto. Record the network number and subnet mask of each network.

7. Type **show cdp neighbor detail** and press **Enter**. The router prints a list of neighboring routers or switches, along with additional details, including the IP address of the connected interface and the type of device. Look for the neighbors you already recorded in this output. If you find a new router, record its name and IP address and draw a line from this information to the name of the router you are currently logged onto.

8. Draw a circle around the information for the router you are currently logged onto.

9. Use the telnet command to log onto one of the router's neighbors. Repeat Steps 3 through 8 until you complete this for all routers.

10. On a clean sheet of paper (or using network diagramming software such as Visio), draw a diagram of the network containing the name and type of each router. Include the names, IP addresses, and subnet masks of each active interface. Draw lines between each connected router, and label each connection with its network number and subnet mask.

Certification Objectives

Objectives for Cisco Exam 640-603: Routing

➤ Describe the use of the fields in a routing table

➤ Analyze a routing table, and test connectivity using accepted troubleshooting techniques

REVIEW QUESTIONS

1. Which of the following information is not found in a routing table?

   a. the routing protocol through which the route was learned

   b. the next hop for each route

   c. the interface out of which a route will forward packets for each route

   d. the types of routers or switches to which a router is attached

2. How might you get information about the Layer 2 devices to which a router is attached?

   a. use its routing table

   b. use the Cisco Discovery Protocol

   c. look at its ARP table

   d. use flash updates

3. Which devices can use CDP?

   a. only Cisco devices

   b. all routers

   c. all switches

   d. all devices that support IP

4. What is the function of administrative distance?

   a. It allows you to quickly shut down an interface.

   b. It prevents routing loops.

   c. It allows a router to choose between routes from different sources of routing information.

   d. It allows a router to choose between routes from the same source of routing information.

5. In the routing tables in this lab, you should have seen that "the gateway of last resort is not set." What does this mean?

   a. The router has no default route.

   b. The router is not forwarding packets to any gateways.

   c. A default route must be configured before the router will forward packets.

   d. The default route is invalid.

MANAGING IP ADDRESSES AND BROADCASTS

Labs included in this chapter

➤ Lab 2.1 Discontiguous Subnets

➤ Lab 2.2 Variable-length Subnet Masks with a Classful Routing Protocol

➤ Lab 2.3 Configuring a Helper Address

➤ Lab 2.4 Allocating IP Addresses with Variable-Length Subnet Masks

Cisco CCNP Exam #640-603 Objectives	
Objective	Lab
Describe classful and classless routing protocols	2.1, 2.2
Configure an IP helper address to manage broadcasts	2.3
Use VLSMs to extend the use of IP addresses	2.4

LAB 2.1 DISCONTIGUOUS SUBNETS

Objective

In this lab, you will learn about the connectivity problems caused by discontiguous subnets in a classful routing protocol.

Materials Required

This lab will require the following:

➤ Three Cisco routers with Ethernet interfaces, cabled and configured, as shown in Figure 2-1

➤ Routing Information Protocol (RIP) version 1 configured on each router, and the network at convergence

➤ Known telnet and enable passwords for the routers

➤ A rollover console cable

➤ A laptop or a PC running a terminal emulation program such as Hyperterminal

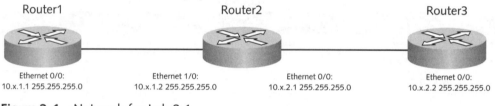

| Router1 | Router2 | Router3 |

Ethernet 0/0:   Ethernet 1/0:   Ethernet 0/0:   Ethernet 0/0:
10.x.1.1 255.255.255.0   10.x.1.2 255.255.255.0   10.x.2.1 255.255.255.0   10.x.2.2 255.255.255.0

Figure 2-1   Network for Lab 2.1

Estimated completion time: **20 minutes**

Activity Background

RIP version 1 is a classful routing protocol. Like all classful routing protocols, RIP version 1 cannot route between discontiguous subnets of the same classful network. Classful routing protocols summarize routes at classful network boundaries, even when subnets of a particular network are not connected. Connectivity problems result.

In this lab, you will use loopback interfaces to create discontiguous subnets on each end of a small RIP version 1 network. After confirming that you cannot reach both discontiguous subnets from all routers, you will configure each router to use RIP version 2. Although it has many of the same problems as the first version, RIP version 2 also has a number of improvements, including support for classless routing and Variable-Length Subnet Masks (VLSMs). After convergence, you will be able to reach both discontiguous subnets from all routers. You must, however, use the **no auto–summary** command in router configuration mode in order to prevent RIP version 2 from automatically summarizing routes along classful boundaries. RIP version 1 always automatically summarizes.

ACTIVITY

1. Power on the PC or laptop and open the terminal emulation program.

2. Plug the RJ-45 end of the console cable into the console port of Router1. Attach the other end of the console cable to the serial port on the laptop or PC. You may need to press **Enter** to bring up the Router1> prompt.

3. Type **enable** and press **Enter**. The router prompt changes to Router1#.

4. Type **config term** and press **Enter**. The router prompt changes to Router1(config)#.

5. Type **int loop 0** and press **Enter**. The router prompt changes to Router1(config-if)#.

6. Type **ip address 172.16.2.1 255.255.255.0** and press **Enter**.

7. Type **exit** and press **Enter**. The router prompt changes to Router1(config)#.

8. Now you will tell RIP to advertise this route. Type **router rip** and press **Enter**. The router prompt changes to Router1(config-router)#.

9. Type **network 172.16.0.0** and press **Enter**.

10. Click **Ctl-Z** to exit configuration mode.

11. Repeat Steps 2 through 10 on Router3, giving the loopback interface an IP address of 172.16.1.1 and a subnet mask of 255.255.255.0.

12. Wait one minute for RIP to converge.

13. Log onto Router1. Type **ping 172.16.1.1** and press **Enter**. The router prints five dots and indicates that the success rate was 0%.

14. Type **show ip route** and press **Enter**. According to the routing table, which interface will Router1 use to attempt to reach 172.16.1.1? *loopback*

_____

15. Log onto Router3. Type **ping 172.16.2.1** and press **Enter**. The router prints five dots and indicates that the success rate was 0%.

16. Type **show ip route** and press **Enter**. According to the routing table, which interface will Router1 use to attempt to reach 172.16.2.1?

_____

17. Log onto Router2.

18. Type **ping 172.16.1.1** and press **Enter**. The router prints some exclamation points and some dots and Us, indicating that the success rate was 40% or 60%. See Figure 2-2 for an example of what the output of this command might look like.

```
Router2#ping 172.16.1.1

Type escape sequence to abort.
Sending 5, 100-byte ICMP Echos to 172.16.1.1, timeout is 2 seconds:
U!.!U
Success rate is 40 percent (2/5), round-trip min/avg/max = 4/4/4 ms
Router2#ping 172.16.2.1

Type escape sequence to abort.
Sending 5, 100-byte ICMP Echos to 172.16.2.1, timeout is 2 seconds:
U!.!U
Success rae is 40 percent (2/5), round-trip min/avg/max = 4/4/4 ms
```

Figure 2-2   Partially successful ping command

19. Repeat the previous step, attempting to reach 172.16.2.1.

20. Type **show ip route** and press **Enter**. The routing table shows one route, 172.16.0.0/16. According to the routing table, which interface or interfaces would the router use to reach 172.16.1.1? Why do only some of the packets reach 172.16.1.1?

_____

21. Now you will configure RIP version 2 on each router in order to allow each router to reach the discontiguous subnets. On Router2, type **enable** and press **Enter**.

22. Type **config term** and press **Enter**.

23. Type **router rip** and press **Enter**.

24. Type **version 2** and press **Enter**. This configures the router to use RIP version 2.

25. Type **no auto-summary** and press **Enter**.

26. Click **Ctl-Z**.

27. Repeat Steps 22 through 26 on Router1 and Router3.

28. Now you will confirm that you can reach the discontiguous subnets from each router on the network. On Router1, type **ping 172.16.1.1** and press **Enter**. The router prints five exclamation points and indicates that the success rate was 100%. If you are unable to successfully ping this IP address, RIP did not yet converge. Wait 30 seconds and repeat this step until you can successfully ping 172.16.1.1.

29. Type **show ip route** and press **Enter**. How are the results of this command different from when the router was running RIP version 1?

_____

30. Repeat Steps 27 and 28 on Router3, pinging 172.16.2.1 instead.

31. Repeat Steps 27 and 28 on Router2, pinging both 172.16.1.1 and 172.16.2.1.

Certification Objective

Objective for Cisco Exam 640-603: Routing

➤ Describe classful and classless routing protocols

Review Questions

1. What is a classless routing protocol?

   a. a routing protocol that cannot route between discontiguous subnets

   b. a routing protocol that automatically summarizes at classful network boundaries

   c. a routing protocol that can communicate with other routing protocols

   d. a routing protocol that does not follow classful network boundaries

2. Why is RIP version 2 able to handle discontiguous subnets, while RIP version 1 is unable to handle them properly? (Choose all that apply.)

   a. RIP version 2 includes subnet masks in its routing updates, and RIP version 1 does not

   b. RIP version 1 includes subnet masks in its routing updates, and RIP version 2 does not

   c. RIP version 2 is a classless routing protocol, while RIP version 1 is not

   d. RIP version 1 is a classless routing protocol, while RIP version 2 is not

3. Which of the following are examples of a classless routing protocol?

   a. RIP version 1

   b. IGRP

   c. IGRP version 2

   d. OSPF

4. Where do classful routing protocols automatically summarize routes?

   a. Classful routing protocols don't summarize routes.

   b. Classful routing protocols summarize routes at the classful network boundaries.

   c. Classful routing protocols summarize all routes to fit a subnet mask of 255.255.255.0.

   d. Classful routing protocols summarize routes only when specifically configured to do so.

5. Which of the following are negative effects of route summarization? (Choose all that apply.)

   a. Routing tables may not have enough information to choose the best route.

   b. Routing tables may get too large.

   c. Route summarization may cause connectivity problems on networks with discontiguous subnets.

   d. Route summarization is not compatible with classful routing protocols.

LAB 2.2 VARIABLE-LENGTH SUBNET MASKS WITH A CLASSFUL ROUTING PROTOCOL

Objective

In this lab, you will learn how classful routing protocols handle Variable-Length Subnet Masks.

Materials Required

This lab will require the following:

➤ Three Cisco routers with Ethernet interfaces, cabled and addressed, as shown in Figure 2-3 (substituting the number of the lab group for the x in the IP addresses)

➤ RIP running and at convergence in the network

➤ Known telnet and enable passwords for the routers

➤ A rollover console cable

➤ A laptop or a PC running a terminal emulation program such as Hyperterminal

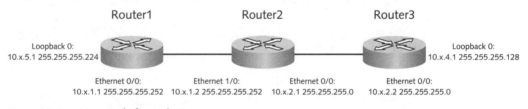

Router1   Router2   Router3

Loopback 0:   Loopback 0:
10.x.5.1 255.255.255.224   10.x.4.1 255.255.255.128

Ethernet 0/0:   Ethernet 1/0:   Ethernet 0/0:   Ethernet 0/0:
10.x.1.1 255.255.255.252   10.x.1.2 255.255.255.252   10.x.2.1 255.255.255.0   10.x.2.2 255.255.255.0

Figure 2-3   Network for Lab 2.2

Estimated completion time: **20 minutes**

Activity Background

As a classful routing protocol, RIP version 1 does not send the subnet mask of routes in its routing table when it sends routing updates. As a result, RIP version 1 routers only know the subnet masks of connected routes. They cannot directly discover the subnet mask of a remote route. If a remote route is a subnet of the same classful network as the IP of an attached interface, a RIP version 1 router will use the subnet mask of its attached interface. If a remote route is not, a RIP version 1 router will assume that the route's subnet mask is the same as the classful network it matches. If the subnet mask RIP version 1 uses does not match the actual subnet mask of a route, then the router will have problems reaching that router.

In this lab, you will attempt to configure VLSMs under RIP version 1 in order to verify that it does not handle VLSMs properly. Then (as in the previous lab) you will correct the problem by configuring the routers to use RIP version 2. RIP version 2 is a classless protocol. Routers running RIP version 2 include the subnet mask of each route in their routing updates.

ACTIVITY

1. Power on all three routers. Power on the PC or laptop and open the terminal emulation program.

2. Plug the RJ-45 end of the console cable into the console port of Router1. Connect the other end of the console cable to the laptop or PC. You may have to press the **Enter** key to bring up the Router1> prompt.

3. Now you will attempt to determine connectivity from one end of the network to the other by pinging the loopback interface at each end. Type **ping 10.x.4.1** and press **Enter**. Five dots appear, and the router indicates that the success rate was 0%.

4. Type **show ip route** and press **Enter**. Based on Figure 2-3, which routes are missing from Router1's routing table?

   _____

5. Log onto Router3 by repeating Step 2.

6. Type **ping 10.x.5.1** and press **Enter**. Five dots appear, and the router indicates that the success rate was 0%.

7. Type **show ip route** and press **Enter**. Based on Figure 2-3, which routes are missing from Router2's routing table?

   _____

8. Log onto Router2 by repeating Step 2.

9. Repeat Steps 3 and 6. Can you ping either of the loopback interfaces on Router1 and Router3?

   _____

10. Type **show ip route** and press **Enter**. Based on Figure 2-3, which routes are missing from Router2's routing table?

    _____

11. Now you will correct the problem by configuring each router to use a classless routing protocol, RIP version 2. Type **enable** and press **Enter**. The router prompt changes to Router2#.

12. Type **config term** and press **Enter**. The router prompt changes to Router2(config)#.

13. Type **router rip** and press **Enter**. The router prompt changes to Router2(config-router)#.

14. Type **version 2** and press **Enter**. Note that the no auto-summary command is not necessary since this network does not include discontiguous subnets.

15. Click **Ctl-Z** to exit configuration.

16. Repeat Steps 11 through 15 on both Router1 and Router3.

17. Log onto Router3 by repeating Step 2.

18. Type **ping 10.x.5.1** and press **Enter**. The router prints five exclamation points and indicates that the success rate is 100%. If the success rate is less than 100%, the network did not yet converge. Wait 30 seconds and repeat this step until it succeeds.

19. Type **show ip route** and press **Enter**. Based on Figure 2-3, are any of the routes you expect to see missing?

_____

20. Repeat the previous three steps on Router1, pinging 10.x.4.1.

Certification Objective

Objective for Cisco Exam 640-603: Routing

➤ Describe classful and classless routing protocols

Review Questions

1. You were unable to ping the loopback addresses at the other end of the network at the beginning of this lab. What are the most likely explanations for this? (Choose all that apply.)

   a. RIP version 1 does not include the subnet masks of the routes included in its routing updates.

   b. RIP version 1 summarizes routes along classful boundaries.

   c. RIP version 1 uses poison reverse updates to help prevent routing loops.

   d. RIP version 1 uses flash updates in order to send routing updates immediately after a change.

2. Why is RIP version 2 able to handle variable-length subnet masks, while RIP version 1 is unable to handle them properly? (Choose all that apply.)

   a. RIP version 2 includes subnet masks in its routing updates, and RIP version 1 does not.

   b. RIP version 1 includes subnet masks in its routing updates, and RIP version 2 does not.

   c. RIP version 2 is a classless routing protocol, while RIP version 1 is not.

   d. RIP version 1 is a classless routing protocol, while RIP version 2 is not.

3. How do VLSMs help in conserving IP addresses?

   a. Without VLSMs, the smallest possible subnet contains 254 usable IP addresses.

   b. VLSMs allow for better use of route summarization.

   c. VLSMs reduce routing table size.

   d. VLSMs require the use of link-state routing protocols.

4. In this lab, which of the following types of routes was guaranteed to be in each router's routing table?

   a. static

   b. default

   c. RIP

   d. connected

5. Which of the following are also strategies for conserving IP addresses? (Choose all that apply.)

   a. private addressing as defined in RFC 1918

   b. link-state routing protocols

   c. IP unnumbered links

   d. network address translation

LAB 2.3 CONFIGURING A HELPER ADDRESS

Objective

In this lab, you will learn how to configure a helper address.

Materials Required

This lab will require the following:

> ➤ A Cisco router with two Ethernet interfaces, which will be Router2

> ➤ A Cisco router with an Ethernet interface and a Cisco IOS feature set, such as IP Plus, which will function as a Dynamic Host Control Protocol (DHCP) server, which will be Router1

> ➤ A laptop or a PC with a network interface card cabled as shown in Figure 2-4, running Windows 98, Windows 2000, or Windows XP, a terminal emulation program such as Hyperterminal, and configured as a DHCP client

> ➤ Both routers, and the PC or laptop, cabled together, as shown in Figure 2-4, with the routers given the IP addresses shown

> ➤ RIP running on both routers and configured to advertise network 10.0.0.0

> ➤ Known telnet and enable passwords for the routers

> ➤ A rollover console cable

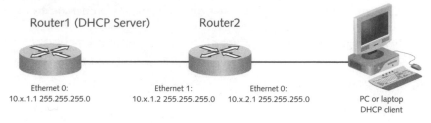

Figure 2-4   Network for Lab 2.3

Estimated completion time: **20 minutes**

Activity Background

By default, routers drop broadcasts. This helps keep broadcasts under control, and prevents them from propagating throughout the network and using too much of the available bandwidth. However, in some situations this can prevent some important network protocols from working. For instance, a host using DHCP broadcasts in order to find a DHCP server when it boots up. If the DHCP broadcasts must cross a router in order to reach the DHCP server, then the client will be unable to lease an IP address.

A router uses a helper address to cut down on broadcasts by converting certain broadcasts into unicast packets. It then forwards these packets to the IP address specified as the helper address. In order to allow the client in the previous example to lease an IP address, you would configure the router with the IP address of the DHCP server as its helper address. This way the router would forward the client's DHCP broadcasts to the DHCP server. At the same time, it would drop other broadcasts.

ACTIVITY

1. Power on both routers. Power on the PC or laptop and open the terminal emulation program.

2. Plug the RJ-45 end of the console cable into the console port on Router1, and connect the other end to the serial port on the PC or laptop. You may need to press **Enter** to bring up the Router1> prompt.

3. Now you will configure this router to be a DHCP server. Type **enable** and press **Enter**. The router prompt changes to Router1#.

4. Type **config term** and press **Enter**. The router prompt changes to Router1(config)#.

5. Type **ip dhcp pool POOL** and press **Enter**. This configures the router as a DHCP server, which assigns a pool of addresses named POOL.

6. Type **network 10.x.2.0 255.255.255.0** and press **Enter**. This configures the router to assign DHCP clients IP addresses on the 10.x.2.0 network with a

subnet mask of 255.255.255.0. You do not need to exclude addresses from this range, as the router will attempt to ping an address to verify that it is unused before assigning it. Excluding IP addresses is commonly performed to reserve IP addresses for hosts that need to keep the same IP addresses at all times.

7. Type **default–router 10.x.2.1** and press **Enter**. This configures the router to assign a default gateway of 10.x.2.1 to each client.

8. Now you will attempt to get an IP address from the DHCP server. Open a command prompt on the PC, type **ipconfig /release**. This releases any IP address that the PC might already have.

9. Type **ipconfig /renew** and press **Enter**. The PC attempts to lease an IP address from the DHCP server. An error message is printed, indicating that the DHCP client could not reach the DHCP server. Figure 2-5 shows an example of this on Windows 2000.

Figure 2-5 DHCP address renewal

10. Now you will configure Router2 with a helper address. Plug the console cable into Router2 as you did in Step 2. You may need to press **Enter** to bring up the Router2> prompt.

11. Type **enable** and press **Enter**.

12. Type **config term** and press **Enter**.

13. Type **int fast 0/0** and press **Enter** to place Router2 in interface configuration mode.

14. If you are using a router as the DHCP server, type **ip helper–address 10.x.1.1** and press **Enter**. If you are using the server at 10.x.1.3 as in Figure 2-4, type **ip helper–address 10.x.1.3** and press **Enter**. Because of the helper address you configured, Router2 will now forward DHCP requests to the DHCP server.

15. Repeat Steps 9 and 10. The PC leases an IP address from the DHCP server.

Certification Objective

Objective for Cisco Exam 640-603: Routing

➤ Configure an IP helper address to manage broadcasts

Review Questions

1. Which of the following are reasons why routers drop broadcast packets by default? (Choose all that apply.)

   a. Excessive broadcasts can use a significant amount of bandwidth.

   b. Both network servers and clients use broadcasts to perform important functions.

   c. Each host on a network must examine a broadcast packet to determine if it must process it further.

   d. Broadcasts should only be handled by switches.

2. Why are broadcasts useful for the proper function of a network? (Choose all that apply.)

   a. Some protocols require a server to communicate with every device on a network.

   b. Some servers use broadcasts to advertise their services.

   c. Routers must use broadcasts to advertise their routing tables.

   d. Some clients use broadcasts to find a server that can assign them an IP address.

3. Which of the following best describes the function of a helper address?

   a. The router forwards all broadcasts to the helper address.

   b. The router forwards specific broadcasts to the helper address.

   c. The router forwards specific broadcasts to the helper address, but only if a server at the helper address is listening.

   d. The router forwards specific broadcasts as unicast packets to the helper address.

4. Why does a DHCP client need to use a broadcast to find a DHCP server?

   a. The DHCP client does not know the address of the DHCP server when it boots up.

   b. The DHCP client must inform other hosts on the network that it does not have an IP address.

   c. The DHCP client knows the IP address of the DHCP server, but must give other DHCP servers a chance to answer.

   d. The DHCP client does not know the address of the router on its network segment.

5. What happens if a helper address is configured on a router, but there is no server configured with that address?

    a. The router will stop forwarding broadcasts to the helper address.

    b. The router will periodically ping the helper address to determine if the server is up.

    c. The router will continue to forward broadcast packets to the helper address.

    d. The router will answer the broadcast packets as necessary.

LAB 2.4 ALLOCATING IP ADDRESSES WITH VARIABLE-LENGTH SUBNET MASKS

Objective

In this lab, you will learn how to assign IP addresses.

Materials Required

This lab will require the following:

➤ Pencil and paper

➤ A calculator (or calculator program accessible in Microsoft Windows) capable of converting decimal numbers to binary

Estimated completion time: **30 minutes**

Activity Background

Using a Class C network with a standard subnet mask of 255.255.255.0 on a point-to-point link results in the waste of 252 usable addresses. You could subnet the Class C network into several smaller networks of the same size, but typically some of these will be too small and others too large. Ideally, you would allocate subnets based upon the number of hosts needed, regardless of the network class. Variable-Length Subnet Masking (VLSM) allows you to use different subnet masks as needed. For instance, you could allocate the network 192.168.12.4/30 for the point-to-point link, the network 192.168.12.64/26 for up to 62 hosts, and 192.168.12.128/27 for up to 126 hosts. As a result, you can allocate IP addresses more efficiently. However, you must use a routing protocol that supports the use of VLSM.

Another technique used in the allocation of IP addresses is Classless Interdomain Routing (CIDR). In CIDR, an address block, or route, is defined by a network number, or prefix, and the number of bits in the subnet mask, or the lengh of the prefix. For instance, one Class A network is 10.0.0.0 through 10.255.255.255. Only the first eight bits of the address are important. In CIDR terms, this is 10.0.0.0/8.

When allocating IP addresses, a useful technique is to find the largest subnet necessary and divide the block of IP addresses into subnets of that size. Any subnets that are not allocated are then divided into smaller subnets and allocated further. Any subnets still not allocated are divided into even smaller subnets, and so on. You can find the number of subnets of a given size possible in a block of IP addresses with the formula 2^n, where n is the prefix length of the desired subnet minus the prefix length of the subnet being divided. To find the number of Class C networks in a Class B network, you would find n by subtracting the length of the prefix of a Class B network (16 bits) from the length of the prefix of a Class C network (24 bits) to get eight. The result is $2^8 = 256$ possible Class C subnets in a Class B network.

Depending on your network environment, you may be assigned IP addresses in a number of ways. On a private network, you may use the private address space set aside by RFC 1918. This includes 10.0.0.0 to 10.255.255.255, 172.16.0.0 through 172.31.255.255, and 192.168.0.0 through 192.168.255.255. Alternately, you might be assigned a block of IP addresses by your Internet Service Provider (ISP), or by one of the Regional Internet Registries (RIRs). For instance, a block of IP addresses assigned by one of the RIRs might look like 207.116.0.0/20, where 207.116.0.0 is the prefix and 20 is the number of bits in the subnet mask, or its length. As a result, you have 12 bits available for your use. This particular assignment would allow you to allocate all the IP addresses from 207.116.0.0 through 207.116.15.255.

ACTIVITY

1. Look at the diagram in Figure 2-6. You have been asked to assign IP addresses for this network from the 192.168.212.0/22 block. You need to assign a subnet to each group of users in each location. For locations with two floors, you will assign one subnet for each floor. Additionally, each location has a group of servers, which will also be assigned its own subnet. Finally, you will assign a point-to-point subnet to each link. Table 2-1 summarizes the number of addresses needed for each location. How many Class C networks would it take to assign a network to each location and link in Table 2-1?

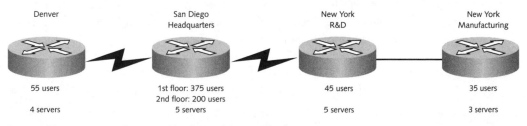

Figure 2-6   Network in need of IP address allocation

Table 2-1   IP addresses needed

Location or Link	Users	No. of Addresses Needed	Prefix Length	Subnet Mask	Addresses Allocated
San Diego, 1st floor	375	510	23	255.255.254.0	192.68.212.0 192.16c.213.255
San Diego, 2nd floor	200	254	24	255.265.255.0	192.168.214.0 192.K6.214.255
Denver	55	62	26	255.255.255.192	192.168.215.0 192.168.215.62
NY R&D, 2nd floor	45	62	26	255.255.255.192	192.165.215.64 192.168.215.127
NY Manufacturing	35	62	26	255.255.255.192	192.168.215.128 192.16c.215.191
New York R&D Servers	5	6	29	255.255.255.248	192.168.215.192 192.168.215.199
San Diego Servers	5	6	29	255.255.255.248	192.168.215.200 192.168.215.207
Denver Servers	4	6	29	255.255.255.248	192.168.215.208 192.168.215.215
NY Manufacturing Servers	3	6	29	255.255.255.248	192.168.215.216 192.168.215.223
Denver-San Diego Link	2	2	30	255.255.255.252	192.168.215.224 192.168.215.227
San Diego-NY R&D Link	2	2	30	255.255.255.252	192.168.215.228 192.168.215.231
NY R&D-NY Manufacturing Link	2	2	30	255.255.255.252	192.168.215.232 192.168.215.235

2. For each location and link, select the number of usable addresses in Table 2-2 that would allow you to assign an appropriate number of users. Enter these into Table 2-1, or onto a separate sheet of paper. For instance, for the users on the first floor in the San Diego office, you would select 512 usable addresses. For the links connecting each location, you would select two.

3. For each location and link, select the prefix length and subnet mask that would allow you to assign an appropriate amount of IP addresses. Enter this information in the appropriate column in Table 2-1, or on a separate sheet of paper.

Table 2-2 Prefix length, host bits, subnet mask, and number of usable addresses for a given prefix length

Prefix Length	Host Bits	Subnet Mask	Usable Addresses
16	16	255.255.0.0	65,534
17	15	255.255.128.0	32,766
18	14	255.255.192.0	16,382
19	13	255.255.224.0	8190
20	12	255.255.240.0	4094
21	11	255.255.248.0	2046
22	10	255.255.252.0	1022
23	9	255.255.254.0	510
24	8	255.255.255.0	254
25	7	255.255.255.128	126
26	6	255.255.255.192	62
27	5	255.255.255.224	30
28	4	255.255.255.240	14
29	3	255.255.255.248	6
30	2	255.255.255.252	2

4. Now take the largest block of addresses required and calculate the number of subnets this size into which the whole address block can be divided. The number of subnets the address block can be divided into is equal to 2^n, where n is the prefix length of the subnet minus the prefix length of the address block. For the first floor of the San Diego office, the prefix of the subnet is 23 bits long, while the prefix of the address block is 22 bits. As a result, the network can be divided into $2^1 = 2$ blocks with prefixes 22 bits long.

5. On a separate sheet of paper, draw two large boxes, one each for the number of address blocks this size into which the network can be divided. This will be your worksheet for allocating the addresses. At the top of the first box, write the address and prefix length of the subnet assigned in the previous step (192.168.212.0/23).

6. In Table 2-1 or on the sheet of paper where you are tracking address allocation, write 192.168.212.0/23 in the appropriate row in the Address Allocation column.

7. Now you will determine the network number of each block. On the calculator, convert each octet of the network number of the address block assigned (192.168.212.0) into binary and write it on the bottom of the separate sheet of paper. See Figure 2-7.

11000000 10101000 11010100 00000000
192   168   212   0

Figure 2-7   Network 192.168.212.0 in binary

8. Now convert the subnet mask you selected to binary and compare it to the network number in binary. Refer to Figure 2-8 to see what the subnet mask would look like in binary.

11111111 11111111 11111110 00000000

Figure 2-8   23-bit subnet mask in binary

9. Now you can determine the network numbers for all the possible subnets of 192.168.212.0/22 with 23-bit prefix lengths. To determine the possible network numbers, you fill the possible positions between the 23rd bit from the left to the 22nd bit from the left. The only possible options are where the 23rd position from the left is empty (see Figure 2-7) or contains a bit (see Figure 2-9).

11000000 10101000 11010110 00000000
192   168   214   0

Figure 2-9   Network 192.168.214.0 in binary

10. In the lower box on the worksheet, write 192.168.214.0/23. You will divide this block into smaller blocks to allocate the rest of the IP addresses.

11. Looking at Table 2-1, choose the next largest block of IP addresses to be assigned. This should be the second floor at the San Diego office, with 200 users. This would fit into a block of 254 users, with a prefix length of 24 and a subnet mask of 255.255.255.0.

12. Calculate the number of subnets with prefixes 24 bits long possible inside the 192.168.214.0/23 block. You should find that $2^1 = 2$ subnets are possible.

13. On the worksheet, divide the lower box labelled 192.168.214.0/23 into two halves. As you did in Steps 7 through 9, calculate the network numbers for these two subnets and write them in the two boxes you just made.

14. Assign the first 24-bit long subnet to the first floor of San Diego and write it both on the worksheet and in Table 2-1.

15. Now you will divide the remaining subnet into still smaller subnets in order to assign the remaining addresses. According to Table 2-1, the largest remaining blocks are between 55 and 35, which fit into a block with 62 usable addresses and a prefix 26 bits long.

16. Calculate the number of subnets with prefixes 26 bits long as you did in Steps 4 and 12.

17. On the worksheet, divide the remaining free block into the number of subnets you determined in the previous step.

18. Calculate the network numbers of these subnets, as you did in Steps 7 through 9, and write them on each open subnet on the worksheet.

19. Assign the appropriate address blocks in Table 2-1. You should have at least one subnet remaining.

20. Now you will divide one of the remaining subnets into smaller subnets for the server subnets. Determine the best subnet size for these, and record the prefix length.

21. Calculate the number of subnets possible, as you did in Steps 4 and 12, using the prefix length you determined in the previous step.

22. Divide the subnet into the number of smaller subnets you found in the previous step.

23. Calculate the network numbers of these subnets, as you did in Steps 7 through 9, and write them on each open subnet on the worksheet.

24. Assign the appropriate address blocks in Table 2-1. You should have at least one subnet remaining.

25. Now the links between routers remain. Each link (even the Ethernet or Fast Ethernet link) will be a point-to-point link, with only two IP addresses. A prefix with a length of 30 bits provides only two usable addresses and fits perfectly.

26. Repeat Steps 21 through 24 for the links between routers and record your address assignments in Table 2-1.

Certification Objective

Objective for Cisco Exam 640-503: Routing

➤ Use VLSMs to extend the use of IP addresses

Review Questions

1. You have a network that requires 2000 IP addresses to be on one network. Which type of classful network must be assigned to this network?

    a. Class A

    b. Class B

    c. Class C

    d. Class D

2. A RIR assigned your company the address block 14.0.0.0/18. How many usable addresses are contained within this block?

    a. 16,382

    b. 8190

2

    c. 32,766

    d. 65,534

3. How many subnets with a subnet mask of 255.255.255.248 can be allocated from within the subnet 172.25.128.16/26?

    a. 2

    b. 4

    c. 8

    d. 16

4. Four subnets with subnet masks of 255.255.255.224 are possible within the network block described by 192.168.1.0/25. What are their network numbers and prefix lengths?

    a. 192.168.1.0/28, 192.168.1.16/28, 192.168.1.32/28 and 192.168.1.48/28

    b. 192.168.1.0/27, 192.168.1.16/27, 192.168.1.32/27 and 192.168.1.48/27

    c. 192.168.1.0/27, 192.168.1.32/27, 192.168.1.64/27, 192.168.1.96/27

    d. 192.168.1.0/28, 192.168.1.32/28, 192.168.1.64/28, 192.168.1.96/28

5. Office A has 200 users, Office B has 100 users, and Office C has 89 users. How could you allocate 10.172.0.0/23 most efficiently so that each office has its own network?

    a. 10.172.0.0/24 to Office A, 10.172.1.0/24 to Office B, and 10.172.2.0/24 to Office C

    b. 10.172.0.0/25 to Office A, 10.172.0.128 to Office B, and 10.172.1.0/24 to Office C

    c. 10.172.0.0/24 to Office A, 10.172.1.0/26 to Office B, and 10.172.1.64/26 to Office C

    d. 10.172.0.0/24 to Office A, 10.172.1.0/25 to Office B, and 10.172.1.128/25 to Office C

CHAPTER THREE

OSPF

Labs included in this chapter

➤ Lab 3.1 Configuring OSPF on an Ethernet Network

➤ Lab 3.2 Designated Router Elections

➤ Lab 3.3 Troubleshooting Neighbor Problems

➤ Lab 3.4 Configuring Cost

➤ Lab 3.5 Configuring OSPF on an NBMA Network

Cisco CCNP Exam #640-603 Objectives	
Objective	Lab
Explain why OSPF is better than RIP in a single area	3.1
Explain how OSPF discovers, chooses and maintains routes	3.1, 3.2, 3.3, 3.4, and 3.5
Explain how OSPF operates in a single-area NBMA environment	3.4
Configure OSPF for proper operation in a single area	3.1, 3.4, 3.5
Verify OSPF operation in a single area	3.1, 3.2, 3.3, 3.4

LAB 3.1 CONFIGURING OSPF ON AN ETHERNET NETWORK

Objective

In this lab, you will learn how to configure Open Shortest Path First (OSPF) on an Ethernet network.

Materials Required

This lab will require the following:

➤ Three Cisco routers with Ethernet interfaces, cabled and configured with IP addresses, as shown in Figure 3-1

➤ No routing protocol running on any of the routers

➤ Known telnet and enable passwords for the routers

➤ A rollover console cable

➤ A laptop or a PC running a terminal emulation program such as Hyperterminal

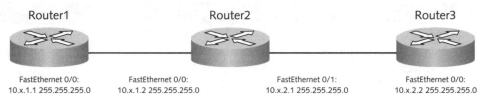

Router1	Router2		Router3
FastEthernet 0/0: 10.x.1.1 255.255.255.0	FastEthernet 0/0: 10.x.1.2 255.255.255.0	FastEthernet 0/1: 10.x.2.1 255.255.255.0	FastEthernet 0/0: 10.x.2.2 255.255.255.0

Figure 3-1   Network diagram for Lab 3.1, showing cabling and addressing

Estimated completion time: **20 minutes**

Activity Background

OSPF is a link-state routing protocol. Each router on an OSPF network builds a link-state database containing the topology of the entire network. This allows each router to run the Dijkstra or Shortest Path First algorithm, and quickly determine loop-free paths to all possible destinations. Additionally, this makes the hop limits used in RIP and IGRP unnecessary to prevent loops. Unlike RIP or IGRP, the only time that a router will exchange its full link-state database with another router is when it first comes online. OSPF typically requires a router to send routing updates only after topology changes. An OSPF router will also update a route after half an hour. While bandwidth usage is typically significantly less than in RIP, OSPF does require a router to use more memory and processor time.

Basic OSPF configuration is relatively straightforward. To activate OSPF, you run the **router ospf** command, specifying an OSPF process number. The process number does not need to be the same on neighboring routers. After activating OSPF, you must specify the networks that OSPF will advertise. You must specify the network with a network number and a mask. The wildcard mask indicates which bits in the network number are important, and works much like an access list. Then you must indicate to which area the networks will belong. In this chapter, you will add networks to Area 0. Area 0 is the backbone area in an OSPF autonomous system and all other areas must connect to it. OSPF areas will be covered in more detail in the next chapter.

In this lab, you will also configure each router with a loopback interface. The loopback interface's IP address is used as the router ID. If another interface's IP address were used, a router might need to change its router ID after an interface failure. This can cause instability. Configuring loopback interfaces as the router ID makes OSPF more stable, since the loopback interface will only go down if the entire router fails. Finally, you can prevent a router from becoming the DR or BDR at all by configuring it with an OSPF priority of 0.

ACTIVITY

1. Power on the routers and the PC or laptop and open the terminal emulation program.

2. Plug the RJ-45 end of the console cable into the console port of Router1. Attach the other end of the console cable to the serial port on the laptop or PC. You may need to press **Enter** to bring up the Router1> prompt.

3. Type **enable** and press **Enter**. The router prompt changes to Router1#.

4. Type **config term** and press **Enter**. The router prompt changes to Router1(config)#.

5. First you will configure the loopback interface. Type **int loop 0** and press **Enter**. The router prompt changes to Router1(config-if)#.

6. Type **ip address 10.100.x.1 255.255.255.255**, where x is the number of your lab group, and press **Enter**. A 32-bit subnet mask may be used for loopback interfaces to conserve IP addresses.

7. Type **exit** and press **Enter**. The router prompt changes to Router1(config)#.

8. Now you will configure OSPF on this router. Type **router ospf 1** and press **Enter**. The router prompt changes to Router1(config-router)#. The 1 is the OSPF process number, and its value may differ from router to router.

9. Type **network 10.0.0.0 0.255.255.255 area 0** and press **Enter**. This tells the router to advertise links for each interface whose IP address has a first octet of 10. Bits in the last three octets are ignored.

10. Press **Ctl-Z** to exit configuration mode.

11. Repeat Steps 2 through 10 on Router 2 and Router3, giving the loopback interface an IP address of 10.100.x.2 on Router2 and 10.100.x.3 on Router3.

12. Log into Router2. Type **show ip route** and press **Enter**. You should see routes for each of the loopback interfaces configured. If you do not, wait a few seconds and repeat this step until you do.

13. Type **show ip protocol** and press **Enter**. The router displays information about the OSPF protocol running on the router, including the networks advertised and sources of routing information (i.e., the router's neighbors).

14. Type **show ip ospf** and press **Enter**. The command output shows basic information about the OSPF process running on the router, including the number of times that the SPF algorithm executed, and the number of interfaces running OSPF.

15. Type **show ip ospf database** and press **Enter**. The command output shows a summary of the information in the router's link-state database.

16. Type **debug ip ospf events** and press **Enter**. Since the network is stable, at this point the router should only display information about hello packets received from neighboring routers.

17. Now you will turn off OSPF on Router2 and see how quickly it can rebuild the OSPF database. Type **config term** and press **Enter**. Note that you can still type when debugging output is scrolling down the screen. However, it may obscure what you typed. If this happens, press **Ctl-R** to instruct the router to reprint the line you are typing.

18. Type **no router ospf 1** and press **Enter**.

19. Press **Ctl-Z** to exit configuration mode.

20. Type **show ip route** and press **Enter**. You should only see routes for connected interfaces, and no routes for the loopback interfaces of the other routers.

21. Now you will reconfigure OSPF on Router2. Type **config term** and press **Enter**.

22. Type **router ospf 1** and press **Enter**.

23. Type **network 10.0.0.0 0.255.255.255 area 0** and press **Enter**. The router should display debugging information indicating that it is forming adjacencies with its two neighboring routers, that the designated router (DR) and the back-up designated router (BDR) are being elected on each network, and that it is exchanging link-state databases with its neighbors.

24. Press **Ctl-Z** to exit configuration mode.

25. Type **show ip route** and press **Enter**. The routing table should now contain the loopback interfaces of the other routers. If not, wait five seconds and repeat this step until these routes are in the routing table.

26. Type **undebug all** and press **Enter** to turn off all debugging on the router.

Certification Objectives

Objectives for Cisco Exam 640-603: Routing

➤ Explain why OSPF is better than RIP in a large internetwork

➤ Explain how OSPF discovers, chooses, and maintains routes

➤ Configure OSPF for proper operation in a single area

➤ Verify OSPF operation in a single area

Review Questions

1. Which of the following are reasons why OSPF uses bandwidth more efficiently than distance vector routing protocols like RIP and IGRP? (Choose all that apply.)

   a. OSPF routers maintain link-state databases containing the topology of the entire network.

   b. OSPF routers only send their entire link-state databases to their neighbors when they first come on-line.

   c. OSPF routers typically only send routing updates after topology changes.

   d. OSPF routers have no hop limits.

2. Which of the following commands will show you the number of times the SPF algorithm has run?

   a. show ip ospf database

   b. show ip ospf spf

   c. show ip ospf

   d. debug ip ospf events

3. Which of the following sets of commands would activate OSPF on an interface with an IP address of 172.16.1.3 and a subnet mask of 255.255.255.0? (Choose all that apply.)

   a. router ospf 1
      network 172.16.1.3 255.255.255.0 area 0

   b. router ospf 1
      network 172.16.0.0.0.0.0.255 area 0

   c. router ospf 1
      network 172.16.1.0 0.0.0.255 area 0

   d. router ospf 1
      network 172.16.0.0 0.0.255.255 area 0

4. Which of the following commands could you use to verify that OSPF is running? (Choose all that apply).

   a. show ip ospf

   b. router ospf 1

   c. show ip protocol

   d. debug ip ospf events

5. Which of the following commands could you use to look at all of the links in a router's link-state database?

a. show ip ospf database

b. show ip ospf link-state

c. show ip ospf

d. show ospf database

LAB 3.2 DESIGNATED ROUTER ELECTIONS

Objective

In this lab, you will examine the process in which designated and back-up designated router elections are made on a network.

Materials Required

This lab will require the following:

➤ Three Cisco routers with Ethernet or Fast Ethernet interfaces, and a hub or Layer 2 switch, cabled and configured as shown in Figure 3-2

➤ No routing protocol running on any of the routers

➤ Known telnet and enable passwords for the routers

➤ A rollover console cable

➤ A laptop or a PC running a terminal emulation program such as Hyperterminal

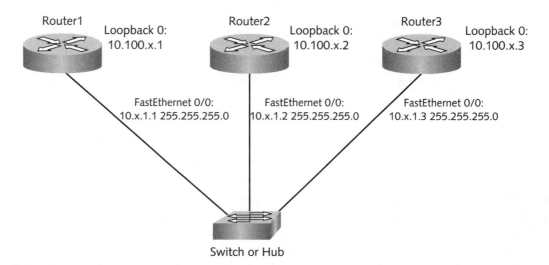

Figure 3-2   Network diagram for Lab 3.2, showing cabling and addressing

Estimated completion time: 20 minutes

Activity Background

The rules for determining whether or not a router will form an adjacency with neighboring routers depend on the type of network. On Ethernet networks, one router is elected the designated router (DR) and another is elected the back-up designated router (BDR). Each router on the network forms an adjacency with the DR and the BDR, and does not form adjacencies with other routers on the network. On networks with many routers, this saves bandwidth since a router will only have to exchange updates and link-state databases with the routers with which it forms adjacencies. For instance, on a network with 10 routers without the DR and BDR, each router must form adjacencies with 9 other routers. On networks with a DR and BDR, however, each router must form adjacencies with only the DR and BDR. Additionally, the DR and the BDR handle the flooding of link-state updates throughout the network after a topology change. The BDR takes over for the DR in case it fails.

The router whose interface has the highest OSPF priority is elected the DR, and the router with the interface with the second highest priority is elected the BDR. If no priority is configured, or the priority for each router is the same, the router with the highest router ID wins any ties. You can also make a router ineligible to become the DR or BDR by setting its priority to zero.

You should keep in mind, however, that adding a router with a higher priority to an existing OSPF network will not automatically make it the DR. When the existing DR fails, the existing BDR becomes the new DR, and the new router is elected the BDR. When the new BDR fails, the new router is promoted from BDR to DR.

ACTIVITY

1. Power on all the routers and the PC or laptop and open the terminal emulation program.

2. Plug the RJ-45 end of the console cable into the console port of Router1. Attach the other end of the console cable to the serial port on the laptop or PC. You may need to press **Enter** to bring up the Router1> prompt.

3. Type **enable** and press **Enter**. The router prompt changes to Router1#.

4. Type **config term** and press **Enter**. The router prompt changes to Router1(config)#.

5. Type **int fast 0/0** and press **Enter**. If necessary, substitute the appropriate interface name and number. The router prompt changes to Router1(config-if)#.

6. Now you will configure the OSPF priority so that Router1 is selected the designated router. Type **ip ospf priority 200** and press **Enter**. The priority may be any value between 0 and 255.

7. Type **exit** and press **Enter**.

8. Type **router ospf 1** and press **Enter**. The router prompt changes to Router1(config-router)#.

9. Type **network 10.0.0.0 0.255.255.255 area 0** and press **Enter**.

10. Press **Ctl-Z**. The router exits configuration mode.

11. Repeat Steps 2 through 10 with Router2. However, configure its interface with a priority of 150.

12. On Router3, repeat Steps 2 through 4 and 8 through 10 to configure OSPF on the router with the default priority on its Fast Ethernet interface.

13. While logged into Router3, type **show ip ospf int fast 0/0** and press **Enter**. The router displays information about OSPF for interface Fast Ethernet 0/0, including the router ID. Router1 is listed as the DR and Router2 is listed as the BDR.

14. Turn on debugging by typing **debug ip ospf events** and press **Enter**. Debugging output about hello messages received appears within 10 seconds.

15. Now pull the Ethernet cable connecting Router1 to the hub or switch. Watch the debugging output. After approximately 40 seconds, the dead interval will have passed without a hello packet from Router1. The debugging output indicates that a new DR and BDR were elected.

16. Reconnect the Ethernet cable from Router1 to the hub or switch. Debugging output on Router3 indicates that Router1 is forming an adjacency with Router3.

17. Type **show ip ospf int fast 0/0** and press **Enter**. The command output indicates that Router2 is the DR and Router3 is the BDR.

18. Now you will make Router1 the DR again. Start by removing the Ethernet cable connecting Router2 to the hub or switch. Watch the debugging output. Wait approximately 40 seconds for the dead interval to pass without a hello packet from Router2, and for the debugging output to indicate that a new DR and BDR were elected.

19. Now reconnect the Ethernet cable from Router2 to the hub or switch. Debugging output on Router3 indicates that Router2 is forming an adjacency with Router3.

20. Type **show ip ospf int fast 0/0** and press **Enter**. The command output indicates that Router3 is the DR and Router1 is the BDR. Since Router3 has a lower priority than Router1, why was Router3 elected the DR?

_____

21. Type **undebug all** and press **Enter**.

22. Move the console cable from Router3 to Router1. You may have to press **Enter** to bring up the Router# prompt.

23. Type **debug ip ospf events** and press **Enter**.

24. Pull the Ethernet cable connecting Router3 to the hub or switch. Watch the debugging output. Wait approximately 40 seconds for the dead interval to pass without a hello packet from Router3 and for the debugging output to indicate that a new DR and BDR were elected.

25. Type **show ip ospf int fast 0/0** and press **Enter**. The command output indicates that Router1 is the DR and Router2 is the BDR.

26. Type **undebug all** and press **Enter**.

Certification Objectives

Objectives for Cisco Exam 640-603: Routing

➤ Explain how OSPF discovers, chooses, and maintains routes

➤ Verify OSPF operation in a single area

Review Questions

1. Which of the following best describes the purpose of the back-up designated router?

   a. to route packets for any router on the network that does not have a designated route

   b. to take over for the designated router in case it fails

   c. to form adjacencies with all the routers in an area

   d. to keep a back-up copy of the link-state database

2. How do the designated router and back-up designated router reduce bandwidth used on a network?

   a. by reducing the number of hops a packet must go through

   b. by routing packets for other routers on the network

   c. by reducing the number of adjacencies each router in the network must form

   d. by reducing the number of copies of the link-state database kept by routers on the network

3. Which of the following routers on an Ethernet network would become the designated router at initialization?

   a. Router A, with a priority of 200 and a loopback address of 10.1.1.1

   b. Router B, with a priority of 100 and a loopback address of 10.1.1.1

   c. Router C, with a priority of 200 and a loopback address of 172.16.1.1

   d. Router D, with a priority of 0 and a loopback address of 172.16.1.1

4. The current designated router has a priority of 50 and a loopback address of 10.1.1.1. Which of the following routers would become the designated router if it failed?

   a. Router A, with a priority of 200 and a loopback address of 10.1.1.1

   b. Router B, with a priority of 100 and a loopback address of 10.1.1.1

   c. Router C, with a priority of 200 and a loopback address of 172.16.1.1

   d. Router D, the current BDR, with a priority of 1 and a loopback address of 172.16.1.1

5. Which of the following commands will show you the DR and BDR?

   a. debug ip ospf

   b. show ip ospf database

   c. show ip ospf

   d. show ip ospf int

LAB 3.3 TROUBLESHOOTING NEIGHBOR PROBLEMS

Objective

In this lab, you will learn to troubleshoot neighbor problems in OSPF.

Materials Required

This lab will require the following:

➤ Two Cisco routers with Fast Ethernet or Ethernet interfaces, cabled and configured, as shown in Figure 3-3

➤ No routing protocols configured on the routers

➤ Known telnet and enable passwords for the routers

➤ A rollover console cable

➤ A laptop or a PC running a terminal emulation program such as Hyperterminal

Router1   Router2

FastEthernet 0/0:   FastEthernet 0/0:
10.x.1.1 255.255.255.0   10.x.1.2 255.255.255.0

Loopback 0:   Loopback 0:
10.100.x.1 255.255.255.255   10.100.x.2 255.255.255.255

Figure 3-3   Network diagram for Lab 3.3, showing cabling and addressing

3

Estimated completion time: **20 minutes**

Activity Background

Establishing adjacencies between neighboring routers is an essential part of OSPF. Each OSPF router periodically sends hello packets, and waits to receive hello packets from its neighbors. If a router does not hear from its neighbor within an interval known as the dead interval, it declares that neighbor down, and begins flooding the status of the link. The dead interval is typically four times the hello interval. On multiaccess networks such as Ethernet, by default, the hello interval is 10 seconds and the dead interval is 40 seconds.

Problems in forming adjacencies can prevent OSPF from functioning at all. For instance, each hello packet contains a variety of information, including the hello and dead intervals and the area number. If these parameters (among others) in a hello packet received by a router do not match those configured on the router, then the two neighboring routers will not form adjacencies. Additionally, the network number and subnet mask must match. This is designed to prevent situations where critical timers and settings are different on neighboring routers. These situations can create problems that are very difficult to troubleshoot. Two routers on broadcast multiaccess networks such as Ethernet will also fail to form an adjacency if neither of them is eligible to become the DR.

ACTIVITY

1. Power on the routers and the PC or laptop and open the terminal emulation program.

2. Plug the RJ-45 end of the console cable into the console port of Router1. Attach the other end of the console cable to the serial port on the laptop or PC. You may need to press **Enter** to bring up the Router1> prompt.

3. Type **enable** and press **Enter**. The router prompt changes to Router1#.

4. Type **config term** and press **Enter**. The router prompt changes to Router1(config)#.

5. Type **int fast 0/0** and press **Enter**. If necessary, substitute the appropriate interface name and number.

6. Type **ip ospf priority 0** and press **Enter**. This makes Router1 ineligible to be the DR or BDR on any network attached to this interface (the 10.x.1.0/24 network in this case).

7. Type **exit** and press **Enter**.

8. Type **router ospf 1** and press **Enter**.

9. Type **network 10.0.0.0 0.255.255.255 area 0** and press **Enter**.

10. Type **Ctl-Z** to exit configuration mode.

11. Repeat Steps 2 through 10 on Router2 to configure OSPF on Router2 so that it is also ineligible to be the DR or BDR on the 10.x.1.0/24 network.

12. On Router1, type **clear ip route *** and press **Enter**. This ensures that you see only the most current routes in the routing tables.

13. Type **show ip route** and press **Enter**. The routing table shows only connected interfaces.

14. Repeat the previous two steps on Router2. Which routes are missing from the routing table?

---

15. On Router2, type **show ip ospf neighbor** and press **Enter**. The router prints that Router1 is in the 2WAY/DROTHER state.

16. Type **show ip ospf int fast 0/0** and press **Enter**. The router prints information about OSPF on that interface, indicating that the interface priority is 0, and that there is no DR or BDR on that network.

17. Repeat the previous step on Router1.

18. On Router1, type **debug ip ospf events** and press **Enter**.

19. Type **config term** and press **Enter**.

20. Type **int fast 0/0** and press **Enter**.

21. Type **ip ospf priority 1** and press **Enter**. Debugging output scrolls down the screen.

22. Press **Ctl-Z** to exit configuration mode.

23. Type **show ip ospf neighbor** and press **Enter**. The command output shows information about Router1's OSPF neighbor, Router2.

24. Type **show ip ospf int fast 0/0** and press **Enter**. The command output shows OSPF information about this interface. Which router is the DR, and why is there not a BDR?

---

25. Type **undebug all** and press **Enter**.

26. Repeat Steps 18 through 25 on Router2.

27. Now you will change the timers on Router2 to see how this affects the formation of an adjacency between the two routers. On Router2, type **config term** and press **Enter**.

28. Type **int fast 0/0** and press **Enter**.

29. Type **ip ospf hello-interval 500** and press **Enter**. This changes the hello interval on interface Fast Ethernet 0/0 to 500 seconds.

30. Type **exit** and press **Enter**.

31. Turn off OSPF by typing **no router ospf 1** and pressing **Enter**.

32. On Router1, type **config term** and press **Enter**.

33. Type **no router ospf 1** and press **Enter**.

34. Now you will reactivate OSPF on each router and see if they can develop an adjacency. On Router2 in configuration mode, type **router ospf 1** and press **Enter**.

35. Type **network 10.0.0.0 0.255.255.255 area 0** and press **Enter**.

36. Press **Ctl-Z** to exit configuration mode.

37. Repeat Steps 34 through 36 on Router1.

38. On Router1, type **show ip ospf neighbor** and press **Enter**. The command returns, indicating that the router has no neighbor.

39. Type **show ip ospf int fast 0/0** and press **Enter**. Information about OSPF on that interface appears. What is the value of the hello interval on Router1?

    _____

40. Repeat the previous two steps on Router2. What is the value of the hello interval on Router2?

    _____

41. On Router2, type **debug ip ospf adj** and press **Enter**. Debugging output appears, indicating that the two routers have mismatched parameters in their hello packets.

42. Type **undebug all** and press **Enter**.

43. On Router2, type **config term** and press **Enter**.

44. Type **int fast 0/0** and press **Enter**.

45. Type **no ip ospf hello-interval 500** and press **Enter**. This changes the hello interval on interface Fast Ethernet 0/0 back to the default (10 seconds).

46. Press **Ctl-Z** and press **Enter**.

47. Type **show ip ospf neighbor** and press **Enter**. The router prints information about its neighbor, Router2. If the router prompt returns without printing anything, wait a few seconds and repeat until it does.

48. Type **show ip ospf neighbor detail** and press **Enter**. What additional information is printed with this command?

    _____

Certification Objectives

Objectives for Cisco Exam 640-603: Routing

➤ Configure OSPF for proper operation in a single area

➤ Verify OSPF operation in a single area

Review Questions

1. Which of the following commands will allow you to see hello packets exchanged between two neighboring routers?

   a. show ip ospf neighbor

   b. show ip ospf int

   c. debug ip ospf

   d. debug ip ospf adj

2. Why won't two neighboring routers with different dead timers form an adjacency?

   a. Because they'll be unable to communicate with each other

   b. Because the OSPF protocol is designed to prevent them from becoming neighbors unless their timers match

   c. Because neither router is eligible to become the DR or BDR

   d. Because all routing protocols require matching timers

3. In OSPF, point-to-point links do not use a designated router or backup desig-nated router. What would be the effect of setting the priority of both ends of a point-to-point link to zero?

   a. none

   b. It would prevent the routers from becoming neighbors because neither router could become the DR or BDR.

   c. It would prevent the routers from becoming neighbors because the OSPF timers of the two routers would not match.

   d. None, because the router with the highest IP address automatically becomes the DR.

4. Which of the following commands will show you the hello timer?

   a. show ip ospf neighbor

   b. debug ip ospf neighbor

   c. debug ip ospf interface

   d. show ip ospf interface

5. You configured one router on a Fast Ethernet network with an OSPF priority of 1, and a second router with a priority of 0. Assuming that these are the only two routers on the network, what will happen? (Choose all that apply.)

   a. The routers will not form an adjacency.

   b. The routers will form an adjacency.

   c. The router with a priority of 1 will become the DR.

   d. The router with a priority of 0 will become the DR.

LAB 3.4 CONFIGURING COST

Objective

In this lab, you will learn to configure cost in OSPF.

Materials Required

This lab will require the following:

> ➤ Two Cisco routers with serial interfaces, cabled and configured, as shown in Figure 3-4

> ➤ A Cisco DTE/DCE serial crossover cable, or a Cisco DTE cable connected to a Cisco DCE cable

> ➤ A clock rate of 64000 configured on the serial interface attached to the DCE end of the serial cable

> ➤ OSPF running on both routers

> ➤ Known telnet and enable passwords for the routers

> ➤ A rollover console cable

> ➤ A laptop or a PC running a terminal emulation program such as Hyperterminal

Router1   Router2

Serial 0/0:   Serial 0/0:
10.x.3.1 255.255.255.0   10.x.3.2 255.255.255.0

Figure 3-4   Network diagram for Lab 3.4, showing cabling and addressing

Estimated completion time: **15 minutes**

Activity Background

Cost is the lone metric used by OSPF. In order for OSPF to determine the best path to all destinations, OSPF routers must be able to properly determine the cost of all links. Cisco's implementation of OSPF calculates the cost by dividing 100,000,000 by the bandwidth of the interface. There are three circumstances, however, where the bandwidth of the interface may be incorrectly determined. First, your network may contain routers from other vendors. The OSPF implementation of another vendor may use a different method to determine the cost, resulting in a different cost on the other end of the link. Since the cost on either end of the link should match, you should manually adjust the cost of the link on one side or the other. Second, Cisco routers assume serial links have a bandwidth of 1.544 Mbps.

Since a router cannot automatically determine the bandwidth of serial links, you must use the **bandwidth interface configuration** command to properly set the bandwidth. Third, the reference bandwidth of 100,000,000 used to calculate cost gives Fast Ethernet, Gigabit, and other links with over 100 Mbps bandwidth the same cost. As a result, you must change the reference bandwidth used with the **auto–cost reference-bandwidth** command in order for OSPF to distinguish between these links. For OSPF to work properly, this command should then be run on all routers in the network. However, with some older versions of IOS the **auto–cost reference-bandwidth** command is not available, and you must manually change the cost of interfaces.

You should keep in mind that changing the cost of a link forces flooding of link-state advertisements throughout the network and calculation of the Shortest Path First (SPF) algorithm. As a result, you should be cautious about doing this in production networks during business hours.

ACTIVITY

1. Power on the routers and the PC or laptop and open the terminal emulation program.

2. Plug the RJ-45 end of the console cable into the console port of Router1. Attach the other end of the console cable to the serial port on the laptop or PC. You may need to press **Enter** to bring up the Router1> prompt.

3. Type **show ip ospf int s0/0** and press **Enter**. If necessary, substitute the appropriate interface number. What is the cost of the interface?

   _____

4. Repeat the previous two steps for Router2.

5. Now you will change the cost of this router by changing the bandwidth seen by the router. On Router1, type **enable** and press **Enter**. The router prompt changes to Router1#.

6. Type **debug ip ospf spf** and press **Enter**. This will allow you to see when the router goes through the SPF calculation when the cost of a link changes.

7. Type **config term** and press **Enter**. The router prompt changes to Router1(config)#.

8. Type **int s0/0** and press **Enter**. The router prompt changes to Router(config-if)#.

9. Now you will configure the bandwidth of the interface in Kbps. (Note that this command only changes the bandwidth seen by the routing protocol, and has no effect on the actual bandwidth of the link.) Type **bandwidth 64** and press **Enter**. Debugging output appears, indicating that the router is running SPF for Area 0.

10. Press **Ctl–Z** to exit configuration mode.

11. Type **show ip ospf int s0/0** and press **Enter**. What is the cost now on the interface?

_____

12. Repeat Steps 5 through 11 on Router2.

3

13. Now you will change the bandwidth by changing the reference cost Cisco routers use to calculate the cost of the link. On Router1, type **config term** and press **Enter**.

14. Type **router ospf 1** and press **Enter**. The router prompt changes to Router1(config-router)#.

15. Type **auto-cost reference-bandwidth 10000** and press **Enter**. Debugging output appears, indicating that the router is running SPF for Area 0. The units of this command are Mbps.

16. Press **Ctl-Z** and press **Enter** to exit configuration mode.

17. Type **show ip ospf int s0/0** and press **Enter**. What is the cost of the interface now?

_____

18. Repeat Steps 13 through 17 on Router2.

19. Now you will override the cost calculated by the router with a manually configured cost. Type **config term** and press **Enter**.

20. Type **int s0/0** and press **Enter**.

21. Type **ip ospf cost 50** and press **Enter**.

22. Press **Ctl-Z** and press **Enter** to exit configuration mode.

23. Type **show ip ospf int s0/0** and press **Enter**. What is the cost now on the interface?

24. Repeat Steps 19 through 23 on Router1.

Certification Objectives

Objectives for Cisco Exam 640-603: Routing

➤ Explain how OSPF discovers, chooses, and maintains routes

➤ Configure OSPF for proper operation in a single area

Review Questions

1. What effect does changing the cost of an interface have on the network?

   a. It forces each router to run the SPF algorithm again.

   b. It causes each router to send its complete routing table to their neighbors.

   c. It forces the router to recalculate the cost on all its interfaces.

   d. It forces each router in the network to recalculate the costs on all interfaces.

2. Why is it sometimes desirable to change the reference bandwidth with the auto-cost reference-bandwidth command?

   a. Routers cannot automatically determine the bandwidth of serial links.

   b. With the default value, interfaces with 100 Mbps or less bandwidth have the same cost.

   c. With the default value, interfaces with 100 Mbps or more bandwidth have the same cost.

   d. With the default value, routers from other vendors cannot be used.

3. Which of the following commands can you use to find the cost of an interface?

   a. show ip ospf int

   b. debug ip ospf int

   c. show ip ospf adj

   d. show ip ospf neigh

4. What is the effect of manually configuring a bandwidth statement on an interface?

   a. none

   b. It allows a router to calculate the cost of the interface based on the actual bandwidth.

   c. It allows the router to forward packets at the speed configured.

   d. It prevents a router from being able to correctly calculate the cost for that interface.

5. Why might you need to manually configure the cost on an interface? (Choose all that apply.)

   a. Because Cisco routers do not automatically calculate cost for interfaces with more than 100 Mbps bandwidth

   b. Because routers from other vendors do not necessarily calculate cost in the same way as Cisco routers do

   c. Because older versions of Cisco IOS do not allow you to change the reference bandwidth, and you have interfaces faster than 100 Mbps

   d. Because you have interfaces faster than 100 Mbps, and you need each router to recalculate the cost of its interfaces

LAB 3.5 CONFIGURING OSPF ON AN NBMA NETWORK

Objective

In this lab, you will learn to configure OSPF on an NBMA network.

Materials Required

This lab will require the following:

> ➤ Three Cisco routers with serial interfaces, cabled and configured, as shown in Figure 3-5

> ➤ Two Cisco DTE/DCE serial crossover cables, or two pairs of Cisco DTE cable connected to Cisco DCE cables

> ➤ The DCE end of both serial cables attached to Router2

> ➤ A clock rate of 64000 configured on the serial interface attached to the DCE end of the serial cables

> ➤ Known telnet and enable passwords for the routers

> ➤ A rollover console cable

> ➤ A laptop or a PC running a terminal emulation program such as Hyperterminal

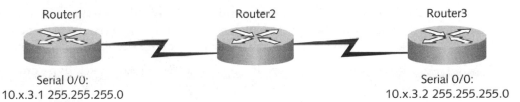

Router1   Router2   Router3

Serial 0/0:   Serial 0/0:
10.x.3.1 255.255.255.0   10.x.3.2 255.255.255.0

Figure 3-5   Network diagram for Lab 3.5, showing cabling and addressing

Estimated completion time: **20 minutes**

Activity Background

Because non-broadcast multiaccess (NBMA) networks do not support broadcasts or multicasts the way broadcast multiaccess networks do, OSPF routers cannot always automatically discover their neighbors. As a result, extra configuration must usually be performed to allow routers to find their neighbors. Cisco's implementation of OSPF has five possible modes on NBMA networks. Two of those modes, nonbroadcast or NBMA mode and point-to-multipoint mode, are defined in RFC 2328. Three more modes—point-to-point mode, point-to-multipoint nonbroadcast mode, and broadcast mode—are proprietary to Cisco routers. Which mode you use to configure your routers depends on several factors, including the topology of your network, and whether or not you need to include routers from other vendors.

In this lab, you will configure routers in the two RFC-compliant modes, NBMA mode and point-to-multipoint mode. NBMA mode requires you to explicitly configure each neighbor, while point-to-multipoint mode does not. NBMA mode works best in a fully meshed topology, and routers on a network in NBMA mode elect a DR and BDR. In contrast, point-to-multipoint mode works best in a partial mesh or star topology, while routers on a network in this mode do not elect a DR or BDR.

To perform this lab, you will configure one router as a frame-relay switch. Typically, this is done only for testing purposes. On the router that will be used as a frame-relay switch, you will first enable frame relay switching. Then you will configure frame-relay encapsulation on each interface, and configure permanent virtual circuits (PVCs) with frame-relay route statements. The frame-relay route statements tell the router which interface to use to send frame-relay packets from a particular Data Link Connection Identifier (DLCI). No IP address information is required. On the other routers, you will just configure frame-relay encapsulation on their serial interfaces. The routers will learn which DLCI to use dynamically through inverse Address Resolution Protocol (ARP). At this point, you will be able to configure the serial interface with an IP address and configure OSPF.

ACTIVITY

1. Power on the routers and the PC or laptop and open the terminal emulation program.

2. Plug the RJ-45 end of the console cable into the console port of Router2. Attach the other end of the console cable to the serial port on the laptop or PC. You may need to press **Enter** to bring up the Router2> prompt.

3. Now you will configure Router2 as a frame relay switch. Type **enable** and press **Enter**. The router prompt changes to Router2#.

4. Type **config term** and press **Enter**. The router prompt changes to Router1(config)#.

5. Type **frame-relay switching** and press **Enter**. This enables the router to be a frame relay switch.

6. Type **int s0/0** and press **Enter**. If necessary, substitute the appropriate interface number.

7. Type **encapsulation frame-relay** and press **Enter**. This configures the interface to use frame relay.

8. Type **frame-relay intf-type dce** and press **Enter**. This configures the interface to be a Frame Relay DCE.

9. Type **frame-relay route 100 interface s0/1 101** and press **Enter**. This configures the router to send traffic coming into interface Serial 0/0 with DLCI 100 and should be sent out interface Serial 0/1 with a DLCI of 101.

10. Type **exit** and press **Enter**.

11. Type **int s0/1** and press **Enter**.

12. Repeat Steps 7 and 8 for interface Serial 0/1.

13. Type **frame-relay route 101 interface s0/0 100** and press **Enter**. This configures the router to send traffic coming into interface Serial 0/1 with DLCI 101 and should be sent out interface Serial 0/1 with a DLCI of 100. In combination with the command you issued in Step 9, this allows Router1 and Router3 at the ends of the frame-relay links to communicate with each other.

14. Press **Ctl-Z** to exit configuration mode.

15. Type **show frame pvc** and press **Enter**. This command shows information about both of the PVCs you created. Since you did not yet configure the ends of each PVC, it indicates that both have a status of INACTIVE.

16. Now you will establish IP connectivity between routers. On Router1, type **enable** and press **Enter**.

17. Type **config term** and press **Enter**.

18. Type **int s0/0** and press **Enter**.

19. Type **ip address 10.x.3.1 255.255.255.0** (where x is the number of your lab group) and press **Enter**.

20. Type **encaps frame** and press **Enter**.

21. Press **Ctl-Z**. The router exits configuration mode.

22. Repeat Steps 16 through 21 on Router3, using an IP address of 10.*x*.3.2.

23. On Router3, type **ping 10.x.3.1** and press **Enter**. The router prints five exclamation points and indicates that the success rate was 100%.

24. On Router1, type **ping 10.x.3.2** and press **Enter**. The router prints five exclamation points and indicates that the success rate was 100%. Successful completion of this step and the previous step confirms that each router has IP connectivity with its neighbor.

25. Now you will configure the router in point-to-multipoint mode. On Router1, type **config term** and press **Enter**.

26. Type **int s0/0** and press **Enter**.

27. Type **ip ospf network point-to-multipoint** and press **Enter**.

28. Type **exit** and press **Enter**.

29. Type **router ospf 1** and press **Enter**.

30. Type **network 10.0.0.0 0.255.255.255 area 0** and press **Enter**.

31. Press **Ctl-Z** to exit from configuration mode.

32. Repeat Steps 25 through 31 for Router3.

33. On Router3, type **show ip ospf neighbor** and press **Enter**. The router prints details about Router2's neighbor, Router1, and indicates that it is in the FULL state.

34. Type **show ip ospf int s0/0** and press **Enter**. The router prints information about OSPF interface Serial 0/0. What is the network type listed?

_____

35. Now you will configure each router in NBMA mode. On Router 1, type **config term** and press **Enter**.

36. Type **int s0/0** and press **Enter**.

37. Type **ip ospf network non-broadcast** and press **Enter**. (Note that this command is the default, and is not necessary unless another OSPF network type has been configured.)

38. Type **exit** and press **Enter**.

39. Type **router ospf 1** and press **Enter**.

40. Type **network 10.0.0.0 0.255.255.255 area 0** and press **Enter**.

41. Type **neighbor 10.x.3.2** and press **Enter**.

42. Press **Ctl-Z** to exit configuration mode.

43. On Router3, repeat Steps 35 through 42. However, use a neighbor address of 10.*x*.3.1.

44. On Router3, type **show ip ospf neighbor** and press **Enter**. The router prints details about Router2's neighbor, Router1, and indicates that it is in the FULL state.

45. Type **show ip ospf int s0/0** and press **Enter**. The router prints information about OSPF interface Serial 0/0. What is the network type listed?

_____

Certification Objectives

Objectives for Cisco Exam 640-603: Routing

➤ Explain how OPSF operates in a single-area NBMA environment

➤ Configure OSPF for proper operation in a single area

➤ Verify OSPF operation in a single area

Review Questions

1. Why is neighbor discovery more complicated on NBMA networks?

   a. Routers cannot automatically discover their neighbors.

   b. NBMA networks prevent hello packets from being sent.

   c. NBMA networks effect the values of the OSPF timers.

   d. Routers cannot communicate properly with their neighbors.

2. What is a potential disadvantage of configuring Cisco routers in one of the proprietary Cisco NBMA modes?

   a. The routers may not be able to properly interact with other Cisco routers running OSPF.

   b. The routers may not be able to properly interact with other Cisco routers running other routing protocols.

   c. The mode may not be as well supported by Cisco.

   d. The routers may not be able to properly interact with routers from other vendors running OSPF.

3. Which of the following sets of commands would configure a Cisco router in NBMA mode?

   a. router ospf 1
      network 10.0.0.0 0.255.255.255 area 0

   b. router ospf 1
      network 10.0.0.0 0.255.255.255 area 0
      neighbor 10.1.1.1

   c. int fast 0/0
      ip ospf network point-to-multipoint
      network 10.0.0.0 0.255.255.255 area 0
      neighbor 10.1.1.1

   d. int fast 0/0
      ip ospf network point-to-multipoint
      network 10.0.0.0 0.255.255.255 area 0

4. Which of the following sets of commands would configure a Cisco router in point-to-multipoint mode?

   a. router ospf 1
      network 10.0.0.0 0.255.255.255 area 0

   b. router ospf 1
      network 10.0.0.0 0.255.255.255 area 0
      neighbor 10.1.1.1

   c. int fast 0/0
      ip ospf network point-to-multipoint
      network 10.0.0.0 0.255.255.255 area 0
      neighbor 10.1.1.1

   d. int fast 0/0
      ip ospf network point-to-multipoint
      network 10.0.0.0 0.255.255.255 area 0

5. Which of the following commands can you use to see the OSPF network type?

   a. show frame pvc

   b. show ip ospf int

   c. show ip ospf neighbor

   d. show ip ospf mode

CHAPTER FOUR

OSPF in Multiple Areas

Labs included in this chapter

♦ Lab 4.1 Configuring OSPF in Multiple Areas

♦ Lab 4.2 Route Summarization in OSPF

♦ Lab 4.3 Configuring Different Types of Areas

♦ Lab 4.4 Configuring Virtual Links

♦ Lab 4.5 Neighbor Issues on Multiple-Area OSPF Networks

Cisco CCNP Exam #640-603 Objectives	
Objective	**Lab**
Describe the issues with interconnecting multiple areas and how OSPF addresses each	4.1, 4.4
Explain the difference between the possible types of areas, routers, and LSAs	4.1, 4.3
Explain how OSPF operates in a multiple-area NBMA environment	4.1
Explain how OSPF supports the use of route summarization in multiple areas	4.2
Configure a multi-area OSPF network	4.1, 4.3, 4.4
Verify OSPF operation in multiple areas	4.1, 4.3, 4.4, 4.5
Explain how OSPF supports the use of VLSM	4.2

Lab 4.1 Configuring OSPF in Multiple Areas

Objective

In this lab, you will learn how to configure a multi-area OSPF network.

Materials Required

This lab will require the following:

➤ Four Cisco routers with the interfaces, IP addresses, and cabling as shown in Figure 4-1, with the interfaces attached to the DCE ends of the serial cables configured with a clock rate of 64000

➤ No routing protocol running on any of the routers

➤ Known telnet and enable passwords for the routers

➤ A rollover console cable

➤ A laptop or a PC running a terminal emulation program such as Hyperterminal

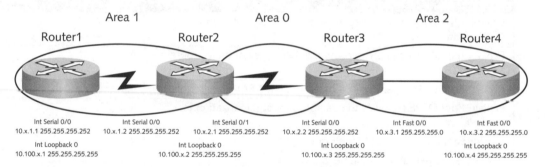

Figure 4-1   Network diagram for Lab 4.1, showing cabling and addressing

Estimated completion time: **20 minutes**

Activity Background

Using OSPF in a large autonomous system presents a number of problems. First, each router must have large link-state databases and routing tables in order to keep track of the topology of the entire autonomous system. Second, each router in the autonomous system must run through the SPF calculation each time a link anywhere in the autonomous system changes status. This limits the scalability of OSPF.

In OSPF, however, you can easily split your autonomous system into multiple areas. Routers in each area have complete knowledge of their individual areas, but do not necessarily have knowledge of other areas or external routes. Each area must be connected to Area 0, or the backbone area. The backbone area receives LSAs from all other areas and then propagates them through the autonomous system. In large networks, use of multiple areas in OSPF can decrease the frequency of SPF algorithm calculations, and the size of link-state databases and routing tables throughout the autonomous system.

Propagation of routes from one area into another is done by area border routers (ABRs). An ABR is simply a router that has an interface in at least two areas. Routers within an area send type 1 LSAs (describing a router's links within an area) and type 2 LSAs (describing the routers connected to a network). Area border routers send type 3 and type 4 LSAs for the links in their areas. These LSAs are called summary LSAs. Despite the name, the routes described by summary LSAs have not necessarily been summarized. A router that handles external routes is called an autonomous system border router (ASBR). An ASBR sends type 5 LSAs to advertise external routes.

Another benefit of using multiple OSPF areas is isolation of problems in one area. For instance, placing a flapping link in an NBMA network, such as frame relay, in an area outside the backbone reduces the number of times that the routers in the backbone must run through their SPF calculations.

ACTIVITY

1. Power on the routers and the PC or laptop and open the terminal emulation program.

2. Plug the RJ-45 end of the console cable into the console port of Router2. Attach the other end of the console cable to the serial port on the laptop or PC. You may need to press **Enter** to bring up the Router2> prompt.

3. Type **enable** and press **Enter**. The router prompt changes to Router2#.

4. Type **config term** and press **Enter**. The router prompt changes to Router2(config)#.

5. Type **router ospf 1** and press **Enter**. The router prompt changes to Router2(config-router)#.

6. Now you will configure interfaces Serial 0/1 and Loopback 0 in Area 0 and interface Serial 0/0 in Area 1 (substitute interface types and numbers as appropriate). Type **network 10.x.2.1 0.0.0.0 area 0** and press **Enter**.

7. Type **network 10.100.x.2 0.0.0.0 area 0** and press **Enter**.

8. Type **network 10.x.1.2 0.0.0.0 area 1** and press **Enter**. You have now configured Router2 as an area border router.

9. Press **Ctl-Z** to exit configuration mode.

10. On Router1, type **enable** and press **Enter**.

11. Type **config term** and press **Enter**.

12. Type **router ospf 1** and press **Enter**.

13. Now you will configure all of the interfaces on Router1 to be in Area 1. Type **network 10.0.0.0 0.255.255.255 area 1** and press **Enter**.

14. Press **Ctl-Z** to exit configuration mode.

15. On Router3, you will configure interfaces Serial 0/0 and Loopback 0 into Area 0, and interface Fast Ethernet 0/0 into Area 2. Repeat steps 3 and 4 on Router 3.

16. Type **router ospf 1** and press **Enter**.

17. Type **network 10.x.2.2 0.0.0.0 area 0** and press **Enter**.

18. Type **network 10.100.x.3 0.0.0.0 area 0** and press **Enter**.

19. Type **network 10.x.3.1 0.0.0.0 area 2** and press **Enter**.

20. Press **Ctl-Z** to exit configuration mode.

21. On Router 4, you will configure all interfaces in Area 2. Repeat steps 3 and 4 on Router 3.

22. Type **router ospf 1** and press **Enter**.

23. Type **network 10.0.0.0 0.255.255.255 area 2** and press **Enter**.

24. Press **Ctl-Z** to exit configuration mode.

25. Now all routers should be connected in a multi-area OSPF network. Type **show ip route** and press **Enter**. You should see routes for all of the loopback interfaces for each router. If you do not, wait five seconds and repeat this step until you do. See Figure 4-2 for an example of the output of this command. How many routes are marked with IA for intra-area OSPF routes?

```
router4#show ip route
Codes: C - connected, S - static, I - IGRP, R - RIP, M - mobile, B - BGP
       D - EIGRP, EX - EIGRP external, O - OSPF, IA - OSPF inter area
       N1 - OSPF NSSA external type 1, N2 - OSPF NSSA external type 2
       E1 - OSPF external type 1, E2 - OSPF external type 2, E - EGP
       i - IS-IS, L1 - IS-IS level-1, L2 - IS-IS level-2, * - candidate default
       U - per-user static route, o - ODR

Gateway of last resort is not set

     10.0.0.0/8 is variably subnetted, 7 subnets, 3 masks
C       10.1.3.0/24 is directly connected, Ethernet0
O IA    10.1.2.0/30 [110/74] via 10.1.3.1, 00:17:17, Ethernet0
O IA    10.1.1.0/30 [110/943] via 10.1.3.1, 00:17:17, Ethernet0
C       10.100.1.4/32 is directly connected, Loopback0
O IA    10.100.1.3/32 [110/11] via 10.1.3.1, 00:17:17, Ethernet0
O IA    10.100.1.2/32 [110/75] via 10.1.3.1, 00:17:17, Ethernet0
O IA    10.100.1.1/32 [110/944] via 10.1.3.1, 00:07:50, Ethernet0 router4#
```

Figure 4-2   Output of the show ip route command

26. Type **show ip ospf** and press **Enter**. Which areas are configured on this router? What kind of router is this?

_____

27. Type **show ip ospf database** and press **Enter**. How many link-state databases do you see on this router? Also, what are routes to intra-area destinations called?

_____

28. Repeat Steps 25 through 27 on the other three routers. Record how many areas are configured on each router and how many link-state databases you see on each router, as well as the type of each router.

_____

29. Now you will configure Router3 as an autonomous system border router. On Router3, type **config term** and press **Enter**.

30. First you will configure a second loopback interface. Type **int loop 1** and press **Enter**.

31. Type **ip address 172.16.1.1 255.255.255.0** and press **Enter**.

32. Type **exit** and press **Enter**.

33. Type **ip route 0.0.0.0 0.0.0.0 loopback 1** and press **Enter**. This configures a default route that will send all packets without a specific destination network in the routing table to interface Loopback 1. (As this interface is only a virtual interface, you configure this for testing purposes only).

34. Type **router ospf 1** and press **Enter**.

35. Type **default-information originate always** and press **Enter**. This configures OSPF on this router to propagate the default route. The always keyword tells it to propagate the route even when the next hop is unreachable.

36. Press **Ctl-Z** to exit configuration mode.

37. Type **show ip ospf** and press **Enter**. According to the command output, what kind of router is this?

_____

38. Type **show ip route** and press **Enter**. You see a route to 0.0.0.0/0 in the routing table. According to the routing table, what type of route is this?

_____

39. Repeat the previous step on Router1. According to the routing table, what type of route is this?

_____

40. On Router1, type **show ip ospf database** and press **Enter**. What type of LSA is the default route listed as?

_____

Certification Objectives

Objectives for Cisco Exam 640-603: Routing

➤ Describe the issues with interconnecting multiple areas and how OSPF addresses each

➤ Explain the difference between the possible types of areas, routers and LSAs

➤ Explain how OSPF operates in a multiple-area NBMA environment

➤ Configure a multi-area OSPF network

➤ Verify OSPF operation in multiple areas

Review Questions

1. Which of the following are reasons to configure an OSPF autonomous system into multiple areas? (Choose all that apply.)

   a. It decreases the complexity of configuration.

   b. It can decrease the size of link-state databases throughout the autonomous system.

   c. It can decrease the size of routing tables throughout the autonomous system.

   d. It can decrease the frequency of the SPF calculation.

2. Which of the following commands allows you to see the areas configured on a router?

   a. show ip ospf database

   b. show ip ospf

   c. show ip ospf link-state

   d. show ip ospf areas

3. Which of the following commands allows you to see the type of LSAs that are included in a router's link-state database?

   a. show ip ospf database

   b. show ip ospf

   c. show ip ospf link-state

   d. show ip ospf neighbor

4. Which of the following sets of commands would configure a router with interfaces with IP addresses of 10.1.1.1 and 172.16.1.1 as an ABR, with one interface in Area 1 and one interface in the backbone area? (Choose all that apply.)

   a. router ospf 1
      network 10.0.0.0 0.255.255.255 area 0
      network 172.16.0.0 0.0.0.0 area 1

b. router ospf 1
network 10.0.0.0 0.255.255.255 area 0
network 172.16.0.0 0.0.255.255 area 1

c. router ospf 1
network 10.0.0.0 0.255.255.255
network 172.16.0.0 0.0.255.255

d. router ospf 1
network 10.1.1.1 0.0.0.0 area 0
network 172.16.1.1 0.0.0.0 area 1

5. Which of the following routers would be both an ABR and an ASBR?

a. RouterA, which has interfaces in Area 0 and Area 1

b. RouterB, which has interfaces in Area 0

c. RouterC, which has interfaces in Area 0 and Area 1, and which propagates a default route

d. RouterD, which has an interface in Area 0, and which propagates a default route

LAB 4.2 ROUTE SUMMARIZATION IN OSPF

Objective

In this lab, you will configure route summarization in a multi-area OSPF network.

Materials Required

This lab will require the following:

➤ Four Cisco routers with the interfaces, IP addresses, and cabling as shown in Figure 4-3, with the interfaces attached to the DCE ends of the serial cables configured with a clock rate of 64000

➤ OSPF configured into areas as shown in Figure 4-3

➤ Known telnet and enable passwords for the routers

➤ A rollover console cable

➤ A laptop or a PC running a terminal emulation program such as Hyperterminal

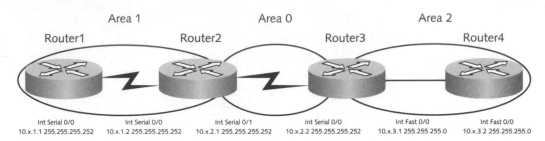

Figure 4-3   Network diagram for Lab 4.2, showing cabling and addressing

Estimated completion time: **20 minutes**

Activity Background

When using OSPF, you cannot summarize within an area because each router inside an area requires full knowledge of the network topology. Allowing route summarization within an area would hide knowledge of the topology from one or more routers, and OSPF would be unable to operate properly. However, you can configure route summarization between areas, or for external routes.

Configuring route summarization has two primary advantages. First, route summarization reduces the size of routing tables and link-state databases. This reduces the amount of memory used by routers and helps speed up convergence. Second, configuring an OSPF network into multiple areas does not completely isolate each area from another. After a link failure in one area, updated summary LSAs (which should not be confused with summary routes) are sent to routers in other areas. A flapping link in one area may cause a lot of LSA traffic and (depending on the network topology) SPF algorithm execution. After configuring route summarization, LSAs will not be sent to other areas unless all the routes summarized fail.

In OSPF, route summarization must be performed on area border routers or autonomous system border routers (ASBRs). While route summarization can reduce the size of routing tables and link-state databases, it can also result in poor path selection.

Finally, OSPF does not restrict how you may summarize routes. OSPF fully supports Variable-Length Subnet Masks (VLSMs), and you may advertise and summarize networks with any valid subnet mask.

ACTIVITY

1. Power on the routers and the PC or laptop and open the terminal emulation program.

2. Plug the RJ-45 end of the console cable into the console port of Router2. Attach the other end of the console cable to the serial port on the laptop or PC. You may need to press **Enter** to bring up the Router2> prompt.

3. First you will see what happens in one area when a link outage occurs in another area. Type **enable** and press **Enter**.

4. Type **config term** and press **Enter**.

5. Type **int loop 1** and press **Enter**.

6. Type **ip address 10.1.1.5 255.255.255.255** and press **Enter**.

7. Type **exit** and press **Enter**.

8. Type **router ospf 1** and press **Enter**.

9. Type **network 10.1.1.5 0.0.0.0 area 1** and press **Enter**.

10. Press **Ctl-Z** to exit configuration mode.

11. On Router4, type **show ip ospf** and press **Enter**. How many times was the SPF algorithm executed in Area 2?

_____

12. Type **debug ip ospf spf** and press **Enter**.

13. Disconnect the serial cable connecting Router1 and Router2. Debugging output appears after a few seconds on Router4, indicating that the router detected a change in an LSA, and will rebuild its routing table.

14. Reconnect the serial cable disconnected in the previous step. After a few seconds, debugging output appears indicating that OSPF is adding the route again. The router rebuilds its routing table.

15. Type **show ip ospf** and press **Enter**. The number of times the SPF algorithm was executed remains the same, even though the router rebuilt its routing table twice.

16. Type **show ip route** and press **Enter**. What is the subnet mask of the route to the 10.1.1.0 network? Is there a route to 10.1.1.5?

_____

17. Now you will configure route summarization to further isolate other areas from problems in Area 1. On Router 2, type **enable** and press **Enter**.

18. Type **config term** and press **Enter**.

19. Type **router ospf 1** and press **Enter**.

20. Type **area 1 range 10.x.1.0 255.255.255.0** and press **Enter**.

21. Press **Ctl-Z** to exit configuration mode.

22. On Router4, type **show ip route** and press **Enter**. What is the subnet mask of the route to the 10.1.1.0 network after route summarization is configured? Is there now a route to 10.1.1.5?

_____

23. Disconnect the serial cable connecting Router1 and Router2. No debugging output appears on Router4 to indicate that the router is rebuilding its routing table.

24. Type **ping 10.1.1.5** and press **Enter**. The router prints five exclamation points and indicates that the success rate is 100%.

25. Type **ping 10.1.1.1** and press **Enter**. The router prints a combination of Us and dots and indicates that the success rate is 0%.

26. Reconnect the serial cable connecting Router1 and Router2. No debugging output appears on Router4 to indicate that the router is rebuilding its routing table.

27. Type **undebug all** and press **Enter**.

Certification Objectives

Objectives for Cisco Exam 640-603: Routing

➤ Explain how OSPF supports the use of route summarization in multiple areas

➤ Explain how OSPF supports the use of VLSMs

Review Questions

1. Why is it impossible to summarize routes within an OSPF area?

   a. Each router would not have complete knowledge of the network topology.

   b. Route summarization in any routing protocol can only be done for external routes.

   c. Route summarization requires a complete link-state database to be effective.

   d. It would prevent routers in the area from becoming neighbors.

2. When does a router mark a summarized route as down?

   a. when any of the routes summarized go down

   b. This depends on the routing protocol.

   c. when all of the routes summarized go down

   d. never

3. Which of the following commands would summarize the routes 172.16.1.0/24, 172.16.2.0/24, and 172.16.4.0/24 into Area 1?

   a. Router(config-router)#area 1 range 172.16.0.0 255.255.255.0

   b. Router(config-router)#summary-route 172.16.0.0 255.255.0.0 area 1

   c. Router(config-router)#area 1 range 172.16.0.0 255.255.248.0

   d. Router(config-router)#area 1 range 172.16.0.0 0.0.7.255

4. You've summarized 192.168.1.0/29, 192.168.1.8/29, and 192.168.1.128/25 as 192.168.1.0/24. When would the router summarizing those routes mark the summarized route down?

   a. when 192.168.1.8/29 is marked as down

   b. when 192.168.1.0/29 and 192.168.1.8/29 are marked as down

   c. when 192.168.1.128/25 and 192.168.1.0/29 are marked as down

   d. when 192.168.1.0/29, 192.168.1.8/29, and 192.168.1.128/25 are marked as down

5. On which of the following types of routers can you perform summarization in OSPF? (Choose all that apply.)

   a. area border routers

   b. internal routers

   c. autonomous system border routers

   d. external border routers

LAB 4.3 CONFIGURING DIFFERENT TYPES OF AREAS

Objective

In this lab, you will learn how to configure different types of OSPF areas.

Materials Required

This lab will require the following:

> Three Cisco routers with the interfaces, IP addresses, and cabling, as shown in Figure 4-4

> No routing protocol running on any of the routers

> Known telnet and enable passwords for the routers

> A rollover console cable

> A laptop or a PC running a terminal emulation program such as Hyperterminal

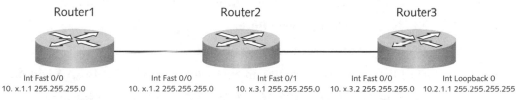

Router1	Router2	Router3
Int Fast 0/0	Int Fast 0/0 Int Fast 0/1	Int Fast 0/0 Int Loopback 0
10. x.1.1 255.255.255.0	10. x.1.2 255.255.255.0 10. x.3.1 255.255.255.0	10. x.3.2 255.255.255.0 10.2.1.1 255.255.255.255

Figure 4-4   Network diagram for Lab 4.3, showing cabling and addressing

Estimated completion time: **20 minutes**

Activity Background

Without having to manually configure route summarization, using stub areas or totally stubby areas can help reduce the number of routes and the size of link-state databases in an area. All routers inside any OSPF area must have complete knowledge of the topology inside that area. However, routers inside an OSPF area do not necessarily need to know much about the topology outside their own area.

In a stub area, routes outside of the OSPF autonomous system (sent in type 5 LSAs) are not propagated. An ABR propagates a default route, which routers inside the stub area use when they need to send packets outside of the OSPF autonomous system. Intra-area routes are still propagated throughout the stub area. In a totally stubby area, on the other hand, an ABR propagates a default route to reach any route outside of the totally stubby area. Type 3, type 4 and type 5 LSAs are not propagated. A stub area is configured with the **area** *number* **stub** command. This must be configured on each router in a stub area. A totally stubby area is configured by adding the **no–summary** keyword on an ABR. This tells the ABR not to advertise intra-area or external routes into the totally stubby area. While the **no–summary** keyword can be used on routers besides the ABR in a totally stubby area, it does not effect the configuration of the area.

One final type of area is the not-so-stubby area (NSSA). A not-so-stubby area allows you to redistribute limited amounts of routes, which would not be possible from within a stub or totally stubby area.

While stub, totally stubby areas, and not-so-stubby areas help reduce the size of routing tables and link-state databases, packets leaving these areas may not choose the best route. However, often these areas are designed so that they have only one, or at most two, exit points.

ACTIVITY

1. Power on the routers and the PC or laptop and open the terminal emulation program.

2. Plug the RJ-45 end of the console cable into the console port of Router3. Attach the other end of the console cable to the serial port on the laptop or PC. You may need to press **Enter** to bring up the Router3> prompt.

3. Type **enable** and press **Enter**.

4. Type **config term** and press **Enter**.

5. Now you will configure an external route. Type **int loop 1** and press **Enter**.

6. Type **ip address 172.16.1.1 255.255.255.0** and press **Enter**.

7. Type **exit** and press **Enter**.

4

8. Type **ip route 172.16.0.0 255.255.0.0 loop 0** and press **Enter**. This configures a static route, which would use interface Loopback 0 to reach any packets with destination addresses in the 172.16.0.0/16 network. (A loopback interface would not normally be used as the destination of a static route outside of a test lab.)

9. Type **router ospf 1** and press **Enter**.

10. Type **network 10.0.0.0 0.255.255.255 area 0** and press **Enter**.

11. Type **redistribute static** and press **Enter**. The router prints that only classful networks will be redistributed. (Redistribution will be covered in Chapter 7.)

12. Type **redistribute connected** and press **Enter**. The router prints that only classful networks will be redistributed.

13. Press **Ctl-Z** to exit configuration mode.

14. On Router2, type **enable** and press **Enter**.

15. Type **config term** and press **Enter**.

16. Type **router ospf 1** and press **Enter**.

17. Type **network 10.x.3.1 0.0.0.0 area 0** and press **Enter**.

18. Now you will configure the other interface on Router 2 in Area 1. Type **network 10.x.1.2 0.0.0.0 area 1** and press **Enter**.

19. Press **Ctl-Z** to exit configuration mode.

20. On Router1, type **config term** and press **Enter**.

21. Type **router ospf 1** and press **Enter**.

22. Type **network 10.0.0.0 0.255.255.255 area 1** and press **Enter**. You have now configured Area 1 as an ordinary area.

23. Press **Ctl-Z** to exit configuration mode.

24. Type **show ip route** and press **Enter**. Record the routes in the routing table that were learned from OSPF, along with the type of the route.

_____

25. Type **show ip ospf** and press **Enter**. What type of area is Area 1?

_____

26. Now you will configure Area 1 as a stub area. On router 1, type **config term** and press **Enter**.

27. Type **router ospf 1** and press **Enter**.

28. Type **area 1 stub** and press **Enter**.

29. Press **Ctl-Z** to exit configuration mode.

30. Repeat Steps 26 through 29 on Router2.

31. On Router1, type **show ip ospf** and press **Enter**. What kind of area is Area 1?

_____

32. Type **show ip route** and press **Enter**. The router prints the routing table, including inter-area routes and a default route. If the routing table does not contain this, wait five seconds and repeat until it does. What are the differences between the routes learned through OSPF in this routing table and the routes you recorded in Step 24?

_____

33. Now you will configure Area 1 as a totally stubby area. On Router2, type **config term** and press **Enter**.

34. Type **router ospf 1** and press **Enter**.

35. Type **area 1 stub no-summary** and press **Enter**. The no-summary keyword configures Area 1 as a totally stubby area.

36. Press **Ctl-Z** to exit configuration mode. Since Router1 is already configured to be in a stub area, no further configuration is necessary. Remember that the no-summary keyword is only necessary on the ABR.

37. On Router2, type **show ip ospf** and press **Enter**. What type of area is Area 1 now?

_____

38. On Router1, type **show ip route** and press **Enter**. What are the differences in the routing table between the routes learned through OSFP in this routing table and the routing table you recorded in Step 24?

_____

39. Now you will configure Area 1 as a NSSA. On Router1, type **config term** and press **Enter**.

40. Type **int loop 0** and press **Enter**.

41. Type **ip address 192.168.154.1 255.255.255.0** and press **Enter**.

42. Type **router ospf 1** and press **Enter**.

43. Type **redistribute connected subnets** and press **Enter**. This will configure Router1 to redistribute the 192.168.154.0/24 route.

44. Type **no area 1 stub** and press **Enter**.

45. Type **area 1 nssa** and press **Enter**.

46. Press **Ctl-Z** to exit configuration mode.

47. On Router2, type **config term** and press **Enter**.

48. Type **router ospf 1** and press **Enter**.

49. Type **no area 1 stub** and press **Enter**.

50. Type **area 1 nssa** and press **Enter**.

51. Press **Ctl-Z** to exit configuration mode.

52. On Router1, type **show ip ospf** and press **Enter**. What type of area is Area 1 listed as?

_____

53. Type **show ip route** and press **Enter**. Which types of routes do you see in Router1's routing table?

_____

54. Repeat Step 53 on Router3. You see a route for 192.168.154.0/24 as an external route.

Certification Objectives

Objectives for Cisco Exam 640-603: Routing

➤ Explain the difference between the possible types of areas, routers and LSAs

➤ Configure a multi-area OSPF network

➤ Verify OSPF operation in multiple areas

Review Questions

1. Which of the following are advantages of using stub areas? (Choose all that apply.)
   a. optimum path selection to areas outside the area
   b. Routers in stub areas do not have external or intra-area routers in their routing tables.
   c. Routers in stub areas do not have external routes in their routing tables.
   d. Stub areas do not need to be connected to the backbone.

2. Which of the following is a disadvantage of using a stub or totally stubby area?
   a. smaller link-state database
   b. Stub and totally stubby areas require connection to the backbone.
   c. Poor path selection is possible.
   d. Routers cannot reach external destinations.

3. What would be the effect of configuring Area 1 as a stub area on only one router in Area 1?
   a. no effect
   b. Area 1 would become a stub area.
   c. Area 1 would be unable to reach other areas.
   d. The one router would be unable to become part of the area.

4. Which of the following commands would configure Area 2 as a stub area?
   a. Router(config-router)#area 2 stub no-summary
   b. Router(config-router)#area 2 totally-stubby
   c. Router(config-router)#area 2 stub
   d. Router(config-router)#stub-area 2

5. Which of the following commands would configure Area 2 as a totally stubby area?

a. Router(config-router)#area 2 stub no-summary

b. Router(config-router)#area 2 totally-stubby

c. Router(config-router)#area 2 stub

d. Router(config-router)#stub-area 2

LAB 4.4 CONFIGURING VIRTUAL LINKS

Objective

In this lab, you will learn how to configure virtual links.

Materials Required

This lab will require the following:

➤ Four Cisco routers with the interfaces, IP addresses, and cabling, as shown in Figure 4-5

➤ No routing protocol running on any of the routers

➤ Known telnet and enable passwords for the routers

➤ A rollover console cable

➤ A laptop or a PC running a terminal emulation program such as Hyperterminal

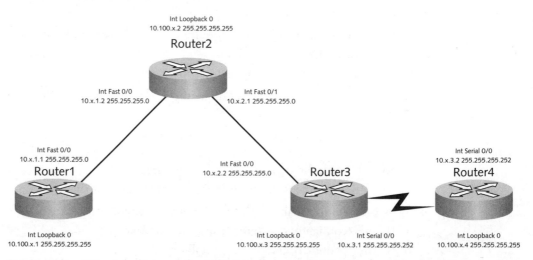

Figure 4-5   Network diagram for Lab 4.4, showing cabling and addressing

Estimated completion time: **20 minutes**

Activity Background

One of the requirements of using multiple OSPF areas is that each area must be connected to the backbone area. An area that is not connected to the backbone will not be able to share information with other areas, and will be isolated from them.

However, it is sometimes necessary to add an area to a network that is not attached to the backbone. Additionally, sometimes a link failure will cut off an area from its connection to the backbone. Even if the area still has a path to the backbone, it will be isolated if that path crosses through other areas. In these situations, you can configure a virtual link to attach the outlying area to the backbone. You configure the routers on each end of a virtual link with the transit area, or the area the link will be crossing, and with the router ID of the router on the opposite end.

While virtual links can be useful, they do add an additional layer of complexity to a network. To resolve problems with virtual links, for instance, you may need to troubleshoot both the virtual link itself and the transit area.

ACTIVITY

1. Power on the routers and the PC or laptop and open the terminal emulation program.

2. Plug the RJ-45 end of the console cable into the console port of Router1. Attach the other end of the console cable to the serial port on the laptop or PC. You may need to press **Enter** to bring up the Router1> prompt.

3. Type **enable** and press **Enter**.

4. Type **config term** and press **Enter**.

5. Type **router ospf 1** and press **Enter**.

6. Type **network 10.0.0.0 0.255.255.255 area 0** and press **Enter**.

7. Press **Ctl-Z** to exit configuration mode.

8. On Router2, type **enable** and press **Enter**.

9. Type **config term** and press **Enter**.

10. Type **router ospf 1** and press **Enter**.

11. Type **network 10.x.1.2 0.0.0.0 area 0** and press **Enter**.

12. Type **network 10.100.x.2 0.0.0.0 area 0** and press **Enter**.

13. Type **network 10.x.2.1 0.0.0.0 area 1** and press **Enter**.

14. Press **Ctl-Z** to exit configuration mode.

15. On Router3, type **enable** and press **Enter**.

16. Type **config term** and press **Enter**.

17. Type **router ospf 1** and press **Enter**.

18. Type **network 10.x.2.2 0.0.0.0 area 1** and press **Enter**.

19. Type **network 10.100.x.3 0.0.0.0 area 1** and press **Enter**.

20. Press **Ctl-Z** to exit configuration mode.

21. Now you will confirm that Area 0 and Area 1 were configured properly. Type **show ip route** and press **Enter**. You should see routes for 10.*x*.1.0/24, 10.*x*.2.0/24, and the three loopback addresses. If not, wait five seconds and repeat this step until the network has converged. Record the routes in the routing table.

_____

22. Now you will attempt to configure Area 2, which will not have a direct connection to the backbone area.

23. Type **config term** and press **Enter**.

24. Type **router ospf 1** and press **Enter**.

25. Type **network 10.x.3.1 0.0.0.0 area 2** and press **Enter**.

26. On Router4, type **enable** and press **Enter**.

27. Type **config term** and press **Enter**.

28. Type **router ospf 1** and press **Enter**.

29. Type **network 10.0.0.0 0.255.255.255 area 2** and press **Enter**.

30. Press **Ctl-Z** to exit configuration mode.

31. Type **show ip ospf neighbor** and press **Enter**. What is the status of Router4's neighbor relationship with Router3?

_____

32. Type **show ip route** and press **Enter**. Wait 30 seconds to make absolutely certain the network has had time to converge, and repeat. Which routes that you recorded in Step 20 are missing from this table?

_____

33. Now you will configure a virtual link to reconnect the backbone area. On Router3, type **config term** and press **Enter**.

34. Type **router ospf 1** and press **Enter**.

35. Type **area 1 virtual-link 10.100.x.2** and press **Enter**.

36. Press **Ctl-Z** to exit configuration mode.

37. On Router2, type **config term** and press **Enter**.

38. Type **router ospf 1** and press **Enter**.

39. Type **area 1 virtual-link 10.100.*x*.3** and press **Enter**.

40. Press **Ctl-Z** to exit configuration mode.

41. Type **show ip ospf virtual-links** and press **Enter**. The router displays information about the virtual link, including its status.

42. Repeat the previous step on Router3.

43. On Router4, type **show ip route** and press **Enter**. Do you see all the routes you recorded in Step 21?

Certification Objectives

Objectives for Cisco Exam 640-603: Routing

➤ Describe the issues with interconnecting multiple areas and how OSPF addresses each

➤ Configure a multi-area OSPF network

➤ Verify OSPF operation in multiple areas

Review Questions

1. Which of the following areas would require the configuration of a virtual link?

   a. Area 0, which is connected to Area 1, Area 2, and Area 3

   b. Area 1, which is connected to Area 0 and Area 1, but not Area 3

   c. Area 2, which is connected to Area 1 and Area 3, but not Area 0

   d. Area 3, which is connected to Area 0 and Area 2, but not Area 1

2. Which of the following commands can show you the status of a virtual link?

   a. show ip ospf virtual-link

   b. debug ip ospf virtual-link

   c. show ip ospf

   d. show ip ospf database

3. Which of the following sets of commands would configure a virtual link between RouterA with a router ID of 172.16.1.1 and RouterB with an ID of 172.25.128.1 through a transit area of Area 18?

   a. RouterA(config-router)#area 18 virtual-link 172.16.1.1

      RouterB(config-router)#area 18 virtual-link 172.25.128.1

   b. RouterA(config-router)#virtual-link 172.25.128.1 area 18

      RouterB(config-router)#virtual-link 172.16.1.1 area 18

    c. RouterA(config-router)#area 18 virtual-link

      RouterB(config-router)#area 18 virtual-link

    d. RouterA(config-router)#area 18 virtual-link 172.25.128.1

      RouterB(config-router)#area 18 virtual-link 172.16.1.1

4. In which of the following situations would you need to configure a virtual link? (Choose all that apply.)

    a. All areas are connected to Area 0.

    b. All areas but Area 1 are connected to Area 0.

    c. A link between two backbone routers has failed, but there is another path through Area 0.

    d. A link between two backbone routers has failed, but there is another path through Area 1.

5. Which of the following are disadvantages of using virtual links? (Choose all that apply.)

    a. They require all routers in an area to have the same virtual link flag.

    b. They require additional configuration on each router in the transit area.

    c. You have to troubleshoot the transit area in addition to the virtual link itself.

    d. Virtual links are not supported in NBMA networks.

Lab 4.5 Neighbor Issues on Multiple-Area OSPF Networks

Objective

In this lab, you will learn how to troubleshoot neighbor issues in OSPF networks with multiple areas.

Materials Required

This lab will require the following:

➤ Three Cisco routers with the interfaces, IP addresses, and cabling, as shown in Figure 4-6

➤ No routing protocol running on any of the routers

➤ Known telnet and enable passwords for the routers

➤ A rollover console cable

➤ A laptop or a PC running a terminal emulation program such as Hyperterminal

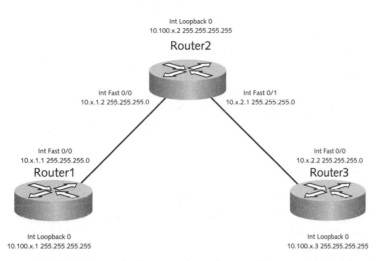

Figure 4-6   Network diagram for Lab 4.5, showing cabling and addressing

Estimated completion time: **15 minutes**

Activity Background

As with any other kind of routing protocol, OSPF will not work if routers do not share information. Because OSPF requires you to configure each interface in an area, activating an interface for OSPF is more complicated than most other routing protocols. A typo when configuring an area will prevent two routers from becoming neighbors.

Another factor making OSPF configuration more complicated is that each router in an area must be configured with the same area flags. If you configured an area to be a stub area on one router in your network, you must configure that area to be a stub area on all your routers. Otherwise not all of your routers will become neighbors.

When you activate OSPF on your routers, it pays to be careful when using the **network** command. Unless you have numerous interfaces on your router, it can often be helpful to specify the address of each interface in the **network** command. If you have many interfaces (and you do not wish to configure them in the same area), you should carefully use the address mask to select only the interfaces you want. For instance, the command **network 192.168.154.0 0.0.0.7 area 0** would match interfaces in networks 192.168.154.0/30 and 192.168.54.4/30, but the command **network 192.168.154.0 0.0.0.8 area 0** would not. When in doubt, use a calculator to check the bits used in the address mask.

When changing the area of an interface in OSPF, various versions of IOS respond differently. Versions of Cisco IOS after 12.0, for instance, typically allow you to change the area of an interface with the **network** command. Versions of Cisco IOS before 12.0, however, may require you to remove some or all network statements before you can change an interface's area.

ACTIVITY

1. Power on the routers and the PC or laptop and open the terminal emulation program.

2. Plug the RJ-45 end of the console cable into the console port of Router1. Attach the other end of the console cable to the serial port on the laptop or PC. You may need to press **Enter** to bring up the Router1> prompt.

3. Type **enable** and press **Enter**.

4. Type **config term** and press **Enter**.

5. Type **router ospf 1** and press **Enter**.

6. Type **network 10.0.0.0 0.255.255.255 area 0** and press **Enter**. This configures all interfaces in Area 0.

7. Press **Ctl–Z** to exit configuration mode.

8. On Router2, repeat Steps 2 through 5.

9. Type **network 10.0.0.0 0.255.255.255 area 1** and press **Enter**. This configures all interfaces in Area 1. The interfaces connecting Router1 and Router2 are now connected with interfaces in different OSPF areas.

10. Press **Ctl–Z** to exit configuration mode. Within 10 seconds you should see a console message indicating a mismatched area ID, and that it should be from a virtual link, but the virtual link cannot be found.

11. Type **show ip ospf neighbor** and press **Enter**. The Router2# prompt returns without printing anything.

12. Type **show ip ospf int fast 0/0** and press **Enter**. Which area is this interface in?

    _____

13. On Router1, type **show ip ospf int fast 0/0** and press **Enter**. Which area is this interface in?

    _____

14. Type **debug ip ospf events** and press **Enter**. Within 10 seconds you see a debugging message indicating that there is a mismatched area in the header.

15. Type **undebug all** and press **Enter**.

16. Now you will correct the problem. On Router2, repeat Steps 2 through 5.

17. Type **no network 10.0.0.0 0.255.255.255 area 1** and press **Enter**.

18. Type **network 10.1.1.2 0.0.0.0 area 0** and press **Enter**.

19. Type **network 10.1.2.1 0.0.0.0 area 1** and press **Enter**.

20. Press **Ctl–Z** to exit configuration mode.

21. Type **show ip ospf neighbor** and press **Enter**. You see Router1 listed as Router2's neighbor.

22. Now you will see what happens when an area type is not configured properly. On Router3, repeat Steps 2 through 5.

23. Type **network 10.0.0.0 0.255.255.255 area 1** and press **Enter**. All interfaces on Router3 are now configured to be in Area 1.

24. Type **area 1 stub** and press **Enter**. Area 1 on Router3 is now configured as a stub area.

25. Press **Ctl-Z** to exit configuration mode.

26. Wait 10 seconds and type **show ip ospf neigh** and press **Enter**. What state is Router2 in?

_____

27. Type **debug ip ospf events** and press **Enter**. Within 10 seconds, you see a debug message indicating that Router3 received a hello from Router2 with a mismatched Stub/Transit area option bit.

28. Type **undebug all** and press **Enter**.

29. Type **show ip ospf int fast 0/0** and press **Enter**. Does this command tell you which type of area Area 1 is?

_____

30. Type **show ip ospf** and press **Enter**. On Router3, what type of area is Area 1?

_____

31. To fix this, you will configure all routers in Area 1 as the same type of area. On Router2, repeat Steps 2 through 4.

32. Type **router ospf 1** and press **Enter**.

33. Type **area 1 stub** and press **Enter**.

34. Press **Ctl-Z** to exit configuration mode.

35. Type **show ip ospf neigh** and press **Enter**. What state is Router2 now in?

_____

Certification Objective

Objective for Cisco Exam 640-603: Routing

➤ Verify OSPF operation in multiple areas

Review Questions

1. Which of the following are reasons why two OSPF routers with adjacent interfaces might not become neighbors? (Choose all that apply.)

   a. The adjacent interfaces do not have a common subnet mask.

   b. The adjacent interfaces are not configured to be in the same area.

   c. The area on both routers is configured as a stub area.

   d. The area on one router is configured as a stub area, but not the other.

2. Which of the following commands will show you an area's type?

   a. show ip ospf database

   b. show ip ospf

   c. show ip ospf int

   d. show ip ospf area

3. Which of the following commands will show you if two adjacent interfaces were configured in different areas?

   a. show ip ospf

   b. show ip ospf area

   c. debug ip ospf

   d. debug ip ospf event

4. Which of the following sets of commands would configure an interface with an IP address of 172.20.125.1 and a subnet mask of 255.255.255.252 in Area 0, and an interface with an IP address of 172.20.125.5 and a subnet mask of 255.255.255.252 in Area 1? Use a calculator if necessary.

   a. network 172.20.125.0 0.0.0.255 area 0

      network 172.20.125.0 0.0.0.255 area 1

   b. network 172.20.125.0 0.0.0.4 area 0

      network 172.20.125.5 0.0.0.0 area 1

   c. network 172.20.125.1 0.0.0.0 area 0

      network 172.20.125.0 0.0.0.7 area 0

   d. network 172.20.125.0 0.0.0.3 area 0

      network 172.20.125.4 0.0.0.3 area 1

5. Which of the following are reasons why you might see errors indicating that packets requiring a virtual link have been seen, but no virtual link has been found? (Choose all that apply.)

   a. Only half of a virtual link was configured.

   b. A router interface was configured with the wrong virtual link.

   c. A router interface was configured in an area that does not match the interface on the other end of the link, and which is not connected to the backbone area.

   d. A router interface was configured in an area that does not match the interface on the other end of the link, but which is connected to the backbone area.

CHAPTER FIVE

EIGRP

Labs included in this chapter

➤ Lab 5.1 Configuring EIGRP

➤ Lab 5.2 Route Summarization in EIGRP

➤ Lab 5.3 Load Balancing in EIGRP

➤ Lab 5.4 EIGRP on NBMA Networks

➤ Lab 5.5 Troubleshooting Neighbor Issues in EIGRP

Cisco CCNP Exam #640-603 Objectives	
Objective	**Lab**
Describe EIGRP features and operation	5.1, 5.3
Explain how EIGRP discovers, chooses, and maintains routes	5.1, 5.3
Explain how EIGRP supports the use of VLSMs	5.2
Explain how EIGRP operates in an NBMA environment	5.4
Explain how EIGRP supports the use of route summarization	5.2
Describe how EIGRP supports large networks	5.2
Configure EIGRP	5.1
Verify EIGRP operation	5.1, 5.5

LAB 5.1 CONFIGURING EIGRP

Objectives

In this lab, you will learn how to configure EIGRP. You will also learn about its features and operation.

Materials Required

This lab will require the following:

➤ Four Cisco routers with the interfaces, IP addresses, and cabling, as shown in Figure 5-1 and the interfaces connected to the DCE ends of the serial cables configured with a clock rate of 6400

➤ No routing protocols running on any of the routers

➤ Known telnet and enable passwords for the routers

➤ A rollover console cable

➤ A laptop or a PC running a terminal emulation program such as Hyperterminal

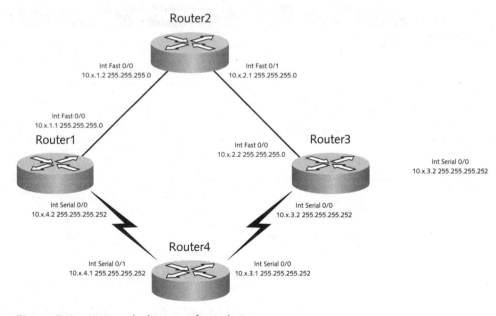

Figure 5-1   Network diagram for Lab 5.1

Estimated completion time: **20 minutes**

Activity Background

Enhanced Internet Gateway Routing Protocol (EIGRP) is a hybrid routing protocol. It combines some features of distance vector routing protocols such as IGRP, which it is based on, and some features of link-state routing protocols. Like distance vector routing protocols, EIGRP routers, which are changing routing information, only need to have knowledge of connected routers. Like a link-state routing protocol, however, EIGRP requires each router to keep track of some of the network topology. As a result, EIGRP is simpler to configure than OSPF, and uses fewer resources than OSPF, but converges faster than distance vector routing protocols.

EIGRP uses the Diffusing Update Algorithm (DUAL) to calculate its routing tables. In addition to its own routes, a router running EIGRP keeps track of the routes advertised by each neighboring router, and the metric advertised, or the advertised distance. To find the best route to a destination, a router calculates the feasible distance for each possible route by adding the advertised distance to the metric to reach the neighbor. The route with the lowest feasible distance, which will be free of routing loops, is known as the **successor**, and is added to the routing table. If they have the same feasible distance, multiple successors may be added to the routing table.

Alternate routes whose advertised distance is less than the feasible distance of the successor are known as **feasible successors**. If the current successor fails, then the best feasible successor is added to the routing table. If there are no feasible successors, the router sends query packets to its neighbors. If they know of another route to the destination, they send reply packets, and the router installs this route. If not, then the router removes the route from its routing table.

The EIGRP metric is based on five values: bandwidth, load, delay, reliability, and the maximum transmission unit (MTU). In order to calculate an EIGRP metric, each value is multiplied by a constant known as a K-value. By default, however, the K-values are set so that only the bandwidth of a link and its delay are used in the calculation of the EIGRP metric. Although Cisco recommends against it, EIGRP routers can be configured so that all five K-values are taken into account in the EIGRP metric. The EIGRP metric is equivalent to the IGRP metric multiplied by 256.

ACTIVITY

1. Power on the routers and the PC or laptop and open the terminal emulation program.

2. Plug the RJ-45 end of the console cable into the console port of Router1. Attach the other end of the console cable to the serial port on the laptop or PC. You may need to press **Enter** to bring up the Router1> prompt.

3. Type **enable** and press **Enter**. The router prompt changes to Router1#.

4. Type **config term** and press **Enter**. The router prompt changes to Router1(config)#.

5. Type **router eigrp 65000** and press **Enter**. The router prompt changes to Router1(config-router)#.

6. Type **network 10.0.0.0** and press **Enter**.

7. Press **Ctl-Z** to exit configuration mode.

8. Repeat Steps 2 through 7 for Router2, Router3, and Router4.

9. On Router4, type **show ip route** and press **Enter**. The router prints the routing table. You should see routes for 10.*x*.1.0/24, 10.*x*.2.0/24, 10.*x*.3.0/30, and 10.*x*.4.0/30.

10. Type **show ip prot** and press **Enter**. The router prints information about the EIGRP process running on the router, including the K-values and the networks advertised by EIGRP.

11. Type **show ip eigrp interfaces** and press **Enter**. The router prints a list of the interfaces activated for EIGRP.

12. Type **show ip eigrp topology** and press **Enter**. The router prints a list of all the EIGRP routes and their successors, including their state.

13. Type **show ip eigrp topology all-links** to look at all EIGRP links. On this network, this should be very similar to the output you saw in the previous step.

14. You can also see more detailed information about a particular route. Type **show ip eigrp topology 10.*x*.2.0 255.255.255.0** and press **Enter**. Note that the route and subnet mask must be an exact match for a route in the EIGRP topology table. You see information about the 10.*x*.2.0/24 route, including detailed information about the metric, the state of the route, and the hop count. What is the next hop for this route?

_____

15. Now you'll watch what happens when a route fails on EIGRP. On Router4, type **debug ip eigrp** and press **Enter**.

16. Type **config term** and press **Enter**.

17. Type **int s0/1** and press **Enter**.

18. Type **shut** and press **Enter**. Debugging output appears as the router runs the DUAL.

19. Press **Ctl-Z** to exit configuration mode.

20. After the debugging output stops, type **show ip route** and press **Enter**.

21. Repeat Steps 16 and 17.

22. Type **no shut** and press **Enter**. More debugging output appears as the router rebuilds its routing table.

23. Press **Ctl-Z** to exit configuration mode.

24. Type **undebug all** and press **Enter**.

Certification Objectives

Objectives for Cisco Exam 640-603: Routing

➤ Describe EIGRP features and operation

➤ Explain how EIGRP discovers, chooses, and maintains routes

➤ Verify EIGRP operation

Review Questions

1. Which of the following are advantages of EIGRP over traditional distance vector and link-state routing protocols? (Choose all that apply.)

   a. EIGRP configuration is less complex than link-state routing protocols.

   b. EIGRP requires less resources than link-state routing protocols.

   c. EIGRP converges faster than distance vector routing protocols.

   d. EIGRP has no topology requirements.

2. Which of the following commands would configure EIGRP on a router in autonomous system 313, and configure it to advertise a route to 172.16.1.1?

   a. Router(config)#router eigrp

      Router(config-router)#network 172.16.0.0

   b. Router(config)#router eigrp 313

      Router(config-router)#network 172.16.0.0 area 0

   c. Router(config)#router eigrp 313

      Router(config-router)#network 172.16.0.0

   d. Router(config)#router eigrp

      Router(config-router)#network 172.16.0.0 0.0.255.255

3. Which command can you use to look at information about every possible route stored in a router's EIGRP topology database?

   a. show ip eigrp

   b. show ip eigrp topology

   c. show ip eigrp database

   d. show ip eigrp topology all-links

4. Which command would show detailed information about the route to network 10.172.198.0/27 in autonomous system 100?

   a. show ip eigrp topology

   b. show ip eigrp topology 10.172.198.0 255.255.255.0

   c. show ip eigrp 100 topology 10.172.198.0 255.255.255.224

   d. show ip eigrp topology 10.172.198.0 255.255.255.224

5. Which command would you use to see the K-values used on a router?

   a. show ip eigrp

   b. show ip protocols

   c. show ip eigrp metrics

   d. show ip eigrp

5

LAB 5.2 ROUTE SUMMARIZATION IN EIGRP

Objective

In this lab, you will learn how to configure route summarization in EIGRP.

Materials Required

This lab will require the following:

➤ Four Cisco routers with the interfaces, IP addresses, and cabling, as shown in Figure 5-1, and the interfaces connected to the DCE ends of the serial cables configured with a clock rate of 6400

➤ EIGRP configured on each router with an autonomous system number of 65000 (as configured in Lab 5.1)

➤ Each router should be configured to allow the use of subnet zero with the **ip subnet-zero** command (this is the default in Cisco IOS 12.0 and up)

➤ Known telnet and enable passwords for the routers

➤ A rollover console cable

➤ A laptop or a PC running a terminal emulation program such as Hyperterminal

Estimated completion time: **20 minutes**

Activity Background

As in other routing protocols, route summarization in EIGRP can help you reduce the size of routing tables. Additionally, route summarization reduces the query scope. If a router receives a summary route from its neighbors and does not know the more specific routes within the summary, it will not send query packets for the more specific routes. Smaller routing tables and reduced query scope both help EIGRP become more scalable in large autonomous systems. Unlike OSPF, route summarization in EIGRP is not at all dependent on network topology. You may summarize however you need.

You should keep in mind, however, that EIGRP automatically summarizes along classful boundaries. For instance, if a router advertises it has interfaces with addresses on two different classful networks, such as 10.0.0.0/8 and 172.16.0.0/16, it will automatically summarize each network when advertised by an interface with an address on the other network. An interface with an IP address of 10.1.1.1 would summarize routes for 172.16.0.0/16, while an interface with an IP address of 172.16.1.1 would summarize routes for 10.0.0.0/8. This can cause connectivity problems on networks with discontiguous subnets. You can turn off this behavior with the **no auto-summary** command in router configuration mode. Despite its use of automatic summarization, EIGRP fully supports Variable-Length Subnet Masks.

Even with automatic summarization turned off, you should be careful when summarizing routes. In addition to poor path selection, you can also create connectivity problems with carelessly planned summarized routes, much in the same way that automatic summarization can cause connectivity problems with discontiguous subnets.

Route summarization in EIGRP is performed by configuring a summary address for an interface. When advertising routes, that interface will advertise the summary route instead of any subnets. The route itself will appear in the router's routing table as a null route, along with the more specific routes being summarized. For null routes, the next hop in the routing table is interface Null0. Packets whose destination addresses match the null route are dropped. The router uses the more specific routes whenever possible. Other routers only see the summarized route.

5

ACTIVITY

1. Power on the routers and the PC or laptop and open the terminal emulation program.

2. Plug the RJ-45 end of the console cable into the console port of Router1. Attach the other end of the console cable to the serial port on the laptop or PC. You may need to press **Enter** to bring up the Router1> prompt.

3. Type **enable** and press **Enter**.

4. Type **config term**, and press **Enter**.

5. First you will create some loopback interfaces, which you will summarize afterwards. Type **int lo 0** and press **Enter**.

6. Type **ip address 172.16.0.1 255.255.255.0** and press **Enter**.

7. Type **int lo 1** and press **Enter**.

8. Type **ip address 172.16.1.1 255.255.255.0** and press **Enter**.

9. Type **exit** and press **Enter**.

10. Now you will instruct EIGRP to advertise these routes. Type **router eigrp 65000** and press **Enter**.

11. Type **network 172.16.0.0** and press **Enter**.

12. Press **Ctl-Z** to exit configuration mode.

13. Type **show ip route** and press **Enter**. Which routes do you see for the loopback interfaces you configured, and which interface is the next hop for each of these routes?

_____

14. On Router3, type **show ip route** and press **Enter**. Compared to the previous step, which routes are missing from Router3's routing table?

_____

15. Now you will configure a loopback interface with another subnet of 172.16.0.0/16. Type **config term** and press **Enter**.

16. Type **int lo 0** and press **Enter**.

17. Type **ip address 172.16.2.1 255.255.255.0** and press **Enter**.

18. Type **int lo 1** and press **Enter**.

19. Type **ip address 172.16.3.1 255.255.255.0** and press **Enter**.

20. Type **exit** and press **Enter**.

21. Type **router eigrp 65000** and press **Enter**.

22. Type **network 172.16.0.0** and press **Enter**.

23. Press **Ctl-Z** to exit configuration mode.

24. Type **show ip route** and press **Enter**. Which routes exist to 172.16.0.0/16 and its subnets?

    _____

25. On Router2, type **show ip route** and press **Enter**. Which routes exist to 172.16.0.0/16 and its subnets?

    _____

26. Type **ping 172.16.0.1** and press **Enter**. What are the results of this attempt?

    _____

27. Type **ping 172.16.2.1** and press **Enter**. What are the results of this attempt?

    _____

28. Repeat the previous three steps on Router4.

29. Now you will turn off auto-summarization. On Router1, type **config term** and press **Enter**.

30. Type **router eigrp 65000** and press **Enter**.

31. Type **no auto-summary** and press **Enter**.

32. Press **Ctl-Z** to exit configuration mode.

33. Type **show ip protocols** and press **Enter**. The router prints out information about EIGRP, and indicates that automatic network summarization is not in effect.

34. Repeat the previous five steps on Router3.

35. On Router2, repeat Steps 25 through 27. How do these results differ from the previous attempts?

    _____

36. Repeat the previous step on Router4.

37. Now you will summarize the routes to the loopback interfaces on Router1 and Router3. On Router1, type **config term** and press **Enter**.

38. Type **int fast 0/0** and press **Enter**.

39. Type **ip summary-address eigrp 65000 172.16.0.0 255.255.254.0** and press **Enter**.

40. Type **int s 0/0** and press **Enter**.

41. Type **ip summary-address eigrp 65000 172.16.0.0 255.255.254.0** and press **Enter**.

42. Repeat Steps 37 through 41 on Router3, using a summary address and subnet mask of 172.16.2.0 255.255.254.0.

43. On Router2, type **show ip route** and press **Enter**. Which routes to subnets of 172.16.0.0/16 do you see in the routing table?

_____

44. Type **ping 172.16.0.1** and press **Enter**. The router prints five exclamation points and indicates that the success rate was 100%.

45. Type **ping 172.16.2.1** and press **Enter**. The router prints five exclamation points and indicates that the success rate was 100%.

46. Repeat Steps 43 through 45 on Router4.

Certification Objectives

Objectives for Cisco Exam 640-603: Routing

➤ Explain how EIGRP supports the use of VLSMs

➤ Explain how EIGRP supports the use of route summarization

➤ Describe how EIGRP supports large networks

Review Questions

1. Which of the following are advantages of route summarization in EIGRP? (Choose all that apply.)

    a. It reduces the size of routing tables in the autonomous system.

    b. It reduces the size of query scopes in the autonomous system.

    c. It is configured automatically for all kinds of routes.

    d. It uses a null interface.

2. A router is advertising a summary route of 192.168.16.0/20. If a packet comes in with a destination network and subnet mask that does not match a more specific route, what happens to the packet?

    a. The packet is sent out the router's default interface.

    b. The packet is sent out the router's default route.

    c. The packet matches a null route and is forwarded to its destination.

    d. The packet matches a null route and is discarded.

3. Which of the following sets of commands would allow you to configure a summary route of 192.168.16.0/20?

   a. Router(config)#router eigrp 212
     Router(config-router)# ip summary-address eigrp 212 192.168.16.0 255.255.240.0

   b. Router(config)#int fast 0/0
     Router(config-if)#ip summary-address eigrp 212 192.168.0.0 255.255.0.0

   c. Router(config)#int fast 0/0
     Router(config-if)# ip summary-address eigrp 212 192.168.16.0 255.255.240.0

   d. Router(config)#int fast0/0
     Router(config)#ip summary-address eigrp 212 192.168.16.0 255.255.240.0

4. RouterA is advertising routes for 172.16.12.0/24, 172.16.25.0/24, and others. However, RouterB sees only a route to 172.16.0.0/16, and you did not configure a summary route. What is a possible explanation for this?

   a. EIGRP was configured as a classful routing protocol.

   b. EIGRP is automatically summarizing at classful network boundaries.

   c. The more specific routes are unreachable.

   d. The metrics for the more specific routes are too high.

5. What does the **no auto-summary** command do?

   a. It disables route summarization of all kinds.

   b. It disables route summarization within an EIGRP area.

   c. It disables automatic route summarization along classless network boundaries.

   d. It disables automatic route summarization along classful network boundaries.

LAB 5.3 LOAD BALANCING IN EIGRP

Objective

In this lab, you will learn how to configure load balancing in EIGRP.

Materials Required

This lab will require the following:

➤ Four Cisco routers with the interfaces, IP addresses, and cabling, as shown in Figure 5-1, and the interfaces connected to the DCE ends of the serial cables configured with a clock rate of 6400

➤ EIGRP configured on each router with an autonomous system of 65000 (as configured in Lab 5.1)

➤ Known telnet and enable passwords for the routers

➤ A rollover console cable

➤ A laptop or a PC running a terminal emulation program such as Hyperterminal

Estimated completion time: **20 minutes**

Activity Background

Ordinarily, Cisco routers can perform load balancing over up to six paths with the same metric, using the **maximum-paths** command. However, you can configure a Cisco router running EIGRP to perform load balancing over a maximum of four different paths with unequal metrics.

The **variance** command allows you to perform unequal load balancing. A router will mark a route as feasible and add it to the routing table if two conditions are met. First, the feasible distance for the route (or the current best metric) must be greater than the advertised distance on the next hop router. Second, the feasible distance times the variance configured must be greater than or equal to the metric for the entire route through the next hop router. The default variance is 1, which does not allow load balancing over paths with unequal metrics.

For instance, suppose a router has a route with a feasible distance of 100. Neighboring routers advertise routes to the same destination with metrics of 190 and 210. The advertised distance of each route is less than 100. If the variance is configured at 2, then the route with the metric of 190 would be less than 2 $\times$ 100 = 200. Therefore, this route would be added to the routing table for load balancing. However, the route with a metric of 210 would not be added to the routing table. To add both routes to the routing table for load balancing, you could configure the variance at 3. Each route would have a metric less than 3 $\times$ 100 = 300.

ACTIVITY

1. Power on the routers and the PC or laptop and open the terminal emulation program.

2. Plug the RJ-45 end of the console cable into the console port of Router4. Attach the other end of the console cable to the serial port on the laptop or PC. You may need to press **Enter** to bring up the Router4> prompt.

3. Type **show ip route** and press **Enter**. Which interface is the next hop for the route to 10.*x*.2.0/30?

   _____

4. Type **trace 10.*x*.1.2** and press **Enter**. The router traces the path to 10.*x*.1.2. What is the path that the router uses to reach 10.*x*.1.2?

   _____

5. Type **show ip eigrp topology 10.*x*.1.0 255.255.255.0** and press **Enter**. The router prints detailed information about the two possible routes to 10.*x*.1.0. What are the feasible distances and the advertised distances for the two routes?

   _____

6. Type **show ip protocols** and press **Enter**. What is the EIGRP maximum metric variance?

_____

7. Now you will configure the router so that it will perform unequal load balancing between the two routes. At the router prompt, type **enable** and press **Enter**.

8. Type **config term** and press **Enter**.

9. Type **router eigrp 65000** and press **Enter**.

10. Type **variance 2** and press **Enter**.

11. Press **Ctl-Z** to exit configuration mode.

12. Type **clear ip route *** and press **Enter**. This will force the router to recalculate its routing table.

13. Type **show ip route** and press **Enter**. The router prints its routing table. If you do not see more than one route in the routing table to the 10.*x*.2.0/24 network, double the variance that is configured, and repeat Steps 8 through 12, until you do.

14. Type **show ip protocols** and press **Enter**. What is the EIGRP maximum metric variance?

_____

Certification Objectives

Objectives for Cisco Exam 640-603: Routing

➤ Describe EIGRP features and operation

➤ Explain how EIGRP discovers, chooses, and maintains routes

Review Questions

1. Which command would you use to configure load balancing over six multiple paths with the same metric?

a. maximum–paths 6

b. load–balancing 6

c. variance 6

d. ip load–balancing 6

2. Which of the following must be true in order for EIGRP to use a candidate route which does not have the best metric for unequal load balancing? (Choose all that apply.)

a. The feasible distance of the best route must be greater than the advertised distance of the candidate route.

b. The feasible distance of the best route must be greater than the feasible distance of the candidate route.

    c. The metric of the candidate route must be less than the variance times the feasible distance of the best route.

    d. The metric of the candidate route must be less than the feasible distance of the best route.

3. What does the command **clear ip route** * force a router to do?

    a. remove all routes from its routing table, and add them again

    b. remove all routes from its routing table, so that the router has no routes to forward packets

    c. clear all non-connected routes from its routing table

    d. clear all non-connected and non-static routes from its routing table

4. The advertised distance for each of the following routes is less than the feasible distance of the best route, 500. With a variance of 4, which of the following routes would be added to the routing table? (Choose all that apply.)

    a. a route with a metric of 2100

    b. a route with a metric of 1000

    c. a route with a metric of 1900

    d. a route with a metric of 3000

5. If the metric for the best route is 200, what would the variance have to be for a route with a metric of 1500 to be added to the routing table on an EIGRP router?

    a. 2

    b. 4

    c. 6

    d. 8

LAB 5.4 EIGRP ON AN NBMA NETWORK

Objective

In this lab, you will learn about some of the issues involved in configuring EIGRP on an NBMA network.

Materials Required

This lab will require the following:

> Three Cisco routers with the interfaces, IP addresses, and cabling, as shown in Figure 5-2, and the interfaces connected to the DCE ends of the serial cables configured with a clock rate of 6400

> No routing protocols running on any of the routers

> Serial interfaces attached to the DCE end of the serial cable, configured with the **clockrate 64000** command

➤ Known telnet and enable passwords for the routers

➤ A rollover console cable

➤ A laptop or a PC running a terminal emulation program such as Hyperterminal

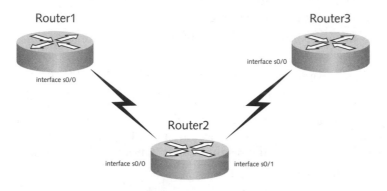

Figure 5-2   Network diagram for Lab 5.4

Estimated completion time: **20 minutes**

Activity Background

In general, configuration of EIGRP on an NBMA network is not as potentially complex as it is on an OSPF network. One complicating factor in configuring EIGRP on an NBMA network is that EIGRP limits the amount of routing update traffic allowed over an interface to 50% of the interface bandwidth. This prevents a momentary spike of routing update traffic from overwhelming a low-bandwidth link. Additionally, it reduces the chance that routing information will be lost because of dropped packets on a saturated link.

However, this can also cause potential problems. For instance, on a frame relay network, you might have many permanent virtual circuits (PVCs) with different committed information rates (CIRs) coming into the hub router on a multi-point subinterface. If the routers forward routing update traffic at 50% of the rate of the PVC with the highest CIR, then the PVC with the lowest CIR may become saturated. As a result, you may want to configure the subinterfaces with the highest CIRs with artificially low bandwidths.

Another potential problem is oversubscription. For instance, the physical interface on the hub router may not be able to handle the traffic that would result if each PVC forwarded traffic at its CIR. Even if routing update traffic on each individual PVC is limited to 50% of the total bandwidth, the physical interface may still be overwhelmed.

As a result, it is often useful to manipulate both the bandwidth on NBMA subinterfaces, and the percent of bandwidth used by EIGRP routing updates. You can configure the bandwidth used by EIGRP with the **bandwidth** command in interface configuration mode.

Remember that a Cisco router assumes a serial interface has a bandwidth of 1.544 Mbps, unless otherwise configured. To configure the maximum percentage of bandwidth used by EIGRP in routing updates, you can use the **ip bandwidth-percent eigrp** command in interface configuration mode.

ACTIVITY

1. Power on the routers and the PC or laptop and open the terminal emulation program.

2. Plug the RJ-45 end of the console cable into the console port of Router2. Attach the other end of the console cable to the serial port on the laptop or PC. You may need to press **Enter** to bring up the Router2> prompt.

3. Type **enable** and press **Enter**.

4. Type **config term** and press **Enter**.

5. Type **frame-relay switching** and press **Enter**.

6. Type **int s0/0** and press **Enter**.

7. Type **encaps frame** and press **Enter**.

8. Type **no ip address** and press **Enter**.

9. Type **frame-relay intf-type dce** and press **Enter**.

10. Type **frame-relay route 100 interface s0/1 101** and press **Enter**.

11. Type **exit** and press **Enter**.

12. Type **int s0/1** and press **Enter**.

13. Repeat Steps 7 through 9.

14. Type **frame-relay route 101 interface s0/0 100** and press **Enter**.

15. Press **Ctl-Z** to exit configuration mode.

16. Repeat Steps 2 through 4 on Router1.

17. Type **int s0/0** and press **Enter**.

18. Type **no ip address** and press **Enter**.

19. Type **encapsulation frame-relay** and press **Enter**.

20. Type **int s0/0.1 point-to-point** and press **Enter**.

21. Type **ip address 10.1.1.1 255.255.255.0** and press **Enter**.

22. Type **frame-relay interface-dlci 100** and press **Enter**.

23. Type **exit** and press **Enter**.

24. Type **router eigrp 65000** and press **Enter**.

25. Type **network 10.0.0.0** and press **Enter**.

26. Press **Ctl-Z** to exit configuration mode.

27. Repeat Steps 16 through 20 on Router3.

28. Type **ip address 10.1.1.2 255.255.255.0** and press **Enter**.

29. Type **frame-relay interface-dlci 101** and press **Enter**.

30. Repeat Steps 23 through 26 on Router3.

31. On Router3, type **show ip eigrp neighbors** and press **Enter**. You see the IP address of Router1 listed as Router3's neighbor.

32. Now you will configure the bandwidth on each interface, as well as the percentage of bandwidth to be used by EIGRP. Type **config term** and press **Enter**.

33. Type **int s0/0.1** and press **Enter**.

34. Type **bandwidth 25** and press **Enter**.

35. Type **ip bandwidth-percent eigrp 65000 120** and press **Enter**.

Certification Objective

Objective for Cisco Exam 640-603: Routing

➤ Explain how EIGRP operates in an NBMA environment

Review Questions

1. What is the effect of improperly configuring the bandwidth on interfaces on an NBMA network?

   a. It prevents EIGRP from properly calculating the maximum amount of routing update traffic to allow.

   b. It prevents EIGRP from properly calculating timer values.

   c. It keeps EIGRP routers from exchanging routing information.

   d. It reduces network throughput.

2. Which of the following is a situation where you might configure a subinterface with a bandwidth lower than its actual bandwidth?

   a. when you have several PVCs with the same CIR coming into a multi-point subinterface on the hub router, and your routing protocol is EIGRP

   b. when you have two PVCs with high CIRs and one PVC with a low CIR coming into a multi-point subinterface on the hub router, and your routing protocol is OSPF

   c. when you have two PVCs with high CIRs and one PVC with a low CIR coming into a multi-point subinterface on the hub router, and your routing protocol is EIGRP

   d. when you have several PVCs with the same CIR coming into a multi-point subinterface on the hub router, and your routing protocol is OSPF

3. Which of the following commands will allow you to change the maximum amount of bandwidth used by routing update traffic on an EIGRP interface in autonomous system 1000 on an NBMA network to 60%?

   a. bandwidth 60

   b. ip bandwidth-percent 60

   c. ip bandwidth-percent eigrp 60

   d. ip bandwidth-percent eigrp 1000 60

4. How does EIGRP use the **bandwidth** interface configuration command? (Choose all that apply.)

   a. in setting the metric for a route

   b. in setting the maximum bandwidth that will be used by a router for EIGRP routing updates on that interface

   c. in setting the maximum bandwidth used by the router on that interface

   d. in setting the EIGRP cost used for that link

5. In which of the following situations is the hub router oversubscribed?

   a. Two PVCs with 128 Kbps CIR and one PVC with 56 Kbps CIR are connected to a hub router with a subinterface with a CIR of 512 Kbps.

   b. Three PVCs with 256 Kbps CIR and one PVC with 56 Kbps CIR are connected to a hub router with a subinterface with a CIR of 1544 Kbps.

   c. Two PVCs with 512 Kbps CIR and one PVC with 128 Kbps CIR are connected to a hub router with a subinterface with a CIR of 1544 Kbps.

   d. Two PVCs with 128 Kbps CIR and one PVC with 56 Kbps CIR are connected to a hub router with a subinterface with a CIR of 256 Kbps.

LAB 5.5 TROUBLESHOOTING NEIGHBOR ISSUES IN EIGRP

Objective

In this lab, you will learn how to troubleshoot common neighbor issues with EIGRP.

Materials Required

This lab will require the following:

➤ Three Cisco routers with the interfaces, IP addresses, and cabling, as shown in Figure 5-3

➤ No routing protocols running on any of the routers

➤ Known telnet and enable passwords for the routers

➤ A rollover console cable

➤ A laptop or a PC running a terminal emulation program such as Hyperterminal

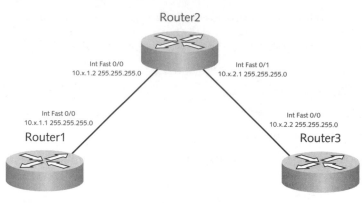

Figure 5-3   Network diagram for Lab 5-5

Estimated completion time: **20 minutes**

Activity Background

Unlike OSPF, EIGRP routers can have their timers set to different values. (You should keep in mind, however, that timers with different values on different routers could cause problems that are difficult to troubleshoot.) However, a different set of problems affects EIGRP neighbor issues.

One potential problem is the autonomous system number. Each EIGRP routing process in an autonomous system must be configured with the same autonomous system number. Neighboring routers with different autonomous system numbers are unable to exchange routing information.

Another potential problem is caused by the use of secondary IP addresses. A secondary IP address is an additional IP address configured on a router, used when an interface requires multiple IP addresses. Unexpectedly, use of secondary IP addresses can also prevent two neighboring EIGRP routers from exchanging routing information. The reason is that both neighboring EIGRP routers must be on the same network in order to share routing information. Cisco routers send an interface's main IP address and subnet mask in their EIGRP hello packets. If the network two routers share is configured with a secondary IP address on one router, then the other router will never see this information.

In addition to show and debug commands, another troubleshooting tool available for use with EIGRP is the **eigrp log-neighbor-changes** command in router configuration mode. This command tells the router to send a console message each time a neighbor changes state. This is especially useful if logged to another server using the syslog protocol, so that you can go back and examine the log at a later time.

ACTIVITY

1. Power on the routers and the PC or laptop and open the terminal emulation program.

2. Plug the RJ-45 end of the console cable into the console port of Router1. Attach the other end of the console cable to the serial port on the laptop or PC. You may need to press **Enter** to bring up the Router1> prompt.

3. Type **enable** and press **Enter**.

4. Type **config term** and press **Enter**.

5. Type **router eigrp 65000** and press **Enter**.

6. Type **network 10.0.0.0** and press **Enter**.

7. Repeat Steps 2 through 4 on Router2.

8. Now you will configure interface Fast Ethernet 0/0 with a secondary IP address to see how EIGRP handles this. Type **int fast 0/0** and press **Enter**.

9. Type **ip address 172.16.1.1 255.255.255.0** and press **Enter**.

10. Type **ip address 10.x.1.2 255.255.255.0 secondary** and press **Enter**.

11. Type **exit** and press **Enter**.

12. Type **router eigrp 65000** and press **Enter**.

13. Type **network 10.0.0.0** and press **Enter**.

14. Press **Ctl-Z** to exit configuration mode.

15. Type **show ip int fast 0/0** and press **Enter**. The router prints information about the interface, including the secondary IP address.

16. Type **show ip eigrp neighbor** and press **Enter**. Does Router1 appear as one of Router2's EIGRP neighbors?

   _____

17. Log onto Router1. Within 10 seconds, you should see a console message indicating that neighbor 172.16.1.1 is not on a common subnet.

18. Type **show ip eigrp neighbor** and press **Enter**. Does Router2 appear as one of Router1's EIGRP neighbors?

   _____

19. Now you will fix the problem. On Router2, type **config term** and press **Enter**.

20. Type **int fast 0/0** and press **Enter**.

21. Type **ip address 10.x.1.2 255.255.255.0** and press **Enter**.

22. Press **Ctl-Z** to exit configuration mode.

5

23. On Router1, type **show ip eigrp neighbor** and press **Enter**. Router2 now appears as one of Router1's EIGRP neighbors.

24. Now you will see what happens when you configure an incorrect autonomous system number when activating EIGRP on a router. On Router3, type **config term** and press **Enter**.

25. Type **router eigrp 1** and press **Enter**.

26. Type **network 10.0.0.0** and press **Enter**.

27. Press **Ctl-Z** to exit configuration mode.

28. Type **show ip eigrp neighbor** and press **Enter**. Does Router2 appear on Router3's list of neighbors?

    _____

29. Type **show ip prot** and press **Enter**. How does the command output list the autonomous system number?

    _____

30. Repeat the previous step on Router2.

31. Now you will fix the problem. On Router3, type **config term** and press **Enter**.

32. Type **no router eigrp 1** and press **Enter**.

33. Type **router eigrp 65000** and press **Enter**.

34. Type **network 10.0.0.0** and press **Enter**.

35. Press **Ctl-Z** to exit configuration mode.

36. Type **show ip eigrp neighbor**. The router prints a list of its EIGRP neighbors, which includes Router2.

37. Now you will configure a router to log neighbor changes. On Router2, type **config term** and press **Enter**.

38. Type **router eigrp 65000** and press **Enter**.

39. Type **eigrp log-neighbor-changes** and press **Enter**.

40. Unplug the Category 5 cable connecting Router2 to Router3. Within 40 seconds, you should see a console message indicating that neighbor 10.1.2.2 is down. Figure 5-4 shows this message.

```
3w2d: %DUAL-5-NBRCHANGE: IP-EIGRP 65000: Neighbor 10.1.2.2
(FastEthernet0/1) is down: holding time expired
```

Figure 5-4   Console message produced by the **eigrp log-neighbor-changes** command

41. Reconnect the cable connecting Router2 to Router3. Within 10 seconds, you should see a console message indicating that neighbor 10.1.2.2 is back up.

Certification Objective

Objective for Cisco Exam 640-603: Routing

➤ Verify EIGRP operation

Review Questions

1. Which of the following commands will show you the autonomous system an EIGRP routing process was configured to use? (Choose all that apply.)

   a. show ip protocol

   b. show ip route

   c. show ip eigrp topology

   d. show ip eigrp neighbor

2. Which of the following commands would configure a secondary IP address on an interface?

   a. Router(config-if)#ip address 172.16.1.1 255.255.255.0

   b. Router(config-if)#ip address 172.16.1.1 secondary

   c. Router(config-if)#ip address 172.16.1.1 255.255.255.0 secondary

   d. Router(config-if)#secondary ip address 172.16.1.1 255.255.255.0

3. Which of the following commands could you use to find a secondary IP address on an interface?

   a. show interface

   b. show ip interface

   c. show ip eigrp interface

   d. show ip eigrp topology

4. Which of the following situations would prevent two adjacent EIGRP routers from becoming neighbors and exchanging routing information? (Choose all that apply.)

   a. The two routers do not share a common network and subnet mask.

   b. The two routers do not share common timers.

   c. The two routers share a common network and subnet mask, but only with an IP address configured as a secondary address.

   d. The two routers do not share the same autonomous system number in their EIGRP routing processes.

5. What is the effect of using the **eigrp log-neighbor-changes** command in router configuration mode?

a. It causes the router to print a console message or send a syslog message when an EIGRP neighbor changes state.

b. It causes the router to re-exchange routing information with each of its neighbors.

c. It causes the router to print debugging output about neighbor state change events.

d. It causes the router to list all recent neighbor changes.

ROUTE FILTERING AND POLICY ROUTING

Labs included in this chapter

➤ Lab 6.1 Configuring Access Lists

➤ Lab 6.2 Configuring a Route Filter

➤ Lab 6.3 Configuring Passive Interfaces

➤ Lab 6.4 Configuring Administrative Distance

➤ Lab 6.5 Configuring Policy-Based Routing

Cisco CCNP Exam #640-603 Objectives	
Objective	Lab
Select and configure the different ways to control routing update traffic	6.1, 6.2, 6.3, 6.4
Configure policy-based routing using route maps	6.5
Configure policy-based routing and verify proper operation	6.5

LAB 6.1 CONFIGURING ACCESS LISTS

Objective

In this lab, you will learn how to configure standard and extended IP access lists.

Materials Required

This lab will require the following:

➤ Three Cisco routers with the interfaces, IP addresses, and cabling, as shown in Figure 6-1

➤ EIGRP configured on each router to advertise network 10.0.0.0 in autonomous system 65000

➤ Known telnet and enable passwords for the routers

➤ A rollover console cable

➤ A laptop or a PC running a terminal emulation program such as Hyperterminal

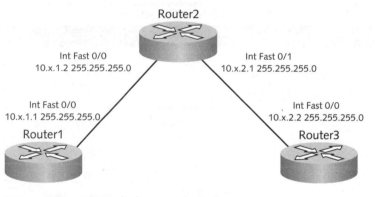

Figure 6-1   Network diagram for Lab 6.1

Estimated completion time: **20 minutes**

Activity Background

Access lists are used for a variety of purposes in Cisco routers. In addition to filtering packets, access lists are also used to select packets and routes for further processing by other parts of the Cisco IOS software. For instance, you use an access list to select the routes to be matched in a route filter (which you will learn about in more detail in Lab 6.2).

In general, access lists are interpreted in the same order that they were written. If a packet matches a statement, the packet is permitted or denied, as indicated by the matching statement. Any statements below the matching statement are skipped. If a packet reaches the end of the access list without matching a statement, it is automatically denied. This is known as **implicit denial**. Often the last statement in an access list permits all traffic in order to prevent the implicit denial from taking effect.

Numbered access lists are defined by a number. The number determines the type of access list. You cannot change the order of statements in a numbered access list, nor can you delete statements. Standard numbered IP access lists are identified with a number between 1 and 99. In a standard access list, you can only specify the source address of a packet. Extended numbered IP access lists, which are identified with a number between 100 and 199, allow you to specify the protocol and other parameters of a packet for both the source and destination addresses. For Transmission Control Protocol (TCP) packets, for instance, you can specify the source address, source port, destination address, and destination port. One other difference between standard and extended access lists is the use of the **log** keyword. In extended access lists, you can use the show access-lists command to see the number of packets matching any statements in the access list configured with the **log** keyword.

A named access list is defined by a name. Unlike a numbered access list, you can delete statements from a named access list. However, you still cannot change the order of statements in a named access list. While named access lists allow you to create more access lists and are easier to remember than numbered access lists, named access lists may not be usable in all areas where numbered access lists can be used.

ACTIVITY

1. Power on the routers and the PC or laptop and open the terminal emulation program.

2. Plug the RJ-45 end of the console cable into the console port of Router3. Attach the other end of the console cable to the serial port on the laptop or PC. You may need to press **Enter** to bring up the Router3> prompt.

3. Type **enable** and press **Enter**. The router prompt changes to Router3#.

4. Type **config term** and press **Enter**. The router prompt changes to Router3(config)#.

5. Now you will configure an access list on Router3 that will prevent Router1 or any host on the 10.x.1.0/24 network from reaching Router3. Type **access-list 1 deny 10.x.1.0 0.0.0.255** and press **Enter**. This will configure standard access list number 1. This line will deny traffic from any host with a source address inside 10.x.1.0/24.

6. Type **access-list 1 permit any** and press **Enter**. This line will ensure that traffic from other IP addresses is allowed.

7. Now you must apply the access list to the interface closest to Router1. Type **int fast 0/0** and press **Enter**.

8. Type **ip access-group 1 in** and press **Enter**.

9. Press **Ctl-Z** to exit configuration mode.

10. Type **show ip int fast 0/0** and press **Enter**. The router prints IP information about interface Fast Ethernet 0/0, including the number of the incoming access list.

11. On Router1, type **ping 10.1.2.2** and press **Enter**. The router prints a combination of Us and dots and indicates that the success rate is 0%.

12. On Router3, type **show access-list** and press **Enter**. Each access list configured on the router is shown. For extended access lists, the number of packets matched by each line configured with the log keyword is also shown.

13. Now you will try to connect to Router3 using another source address. On Router1, type **config term** and press **Enter**.

14. Type **int lo 0** and press **Enter**.

15. Type **ip address 10.100.*x*.1 255.255.255.255** and press **Enter**.

16. Press **Ctl-Z** to exit configuration mode.

17. Now you will attempt to ping Router3 using the extended ping command and the source address of interface Loopback 0. Type **ping** and press **Enter**.

18. The router prompts you with various options. You will enter input for only some of these. Press **Enter** at each option until the router prompt reads Target IP Address.

19. Type **10.1.2.2** and press **Enter**.

20. Press **Enter** until the router prompt reads Extended commands [n]:. Type **y** and press **Enter**.

21. The router prompt reads Source address or interface:. Type **lo 0** and press **Enter**. This tells the router to use the IP address of interface Loopback 0 as the source address on ICMP packets sent by the ping command.

22. Press **Enter** until the router indicates that it is sending five 100-byte ICMP Echos to 10.1.2.2, and that the success rate is 100%.

23. Now you will remove the access list from interface Fast Ethernet 0/0 on Router3. On Router3, type **config term** and press **Enter**.

24. Type **int fast 0/0** and press **Enter**.

25. Type **no ip access-group 1 in** and press **Enter**.

26. Press **Ctl-Z** to exit configuration mode.

27. Now you will configure an access list on Router2 that will block telnet access to Router3. On Router2, type **config term** and press **Enter**.

28. Type **access-list 100 deny tcp 10.*x*.1.0 0.0.0.255 host 10.*x*.2.2 eq 23** and press **Enter**. This will configure extended access list number 100. This line will

deny TCP traffic with a source address in the 10.x.1.0/24 network intended for host 10.x.1.2 with a destination port of 23 (corresponding to telnet).

29. Type **access-list 100 permit ip any any** and press **Enter**. This line will permit all other IP traffic.

30. Now you will apply the access list to interface Fast Ethernet 0/0 on Router2. Type **int fast 0/0** and press **Enter**.

31. Type **ip access-group 100 in** and press **Enter**.

32. Press **Ctl-Z** to exit configuration mode.

33. Type **show ip int fast 0/0** and press **Enter**. The router prints IP information about interface Fast Ethernet 0/0, including the number of the incoming access list.

34. On Router1, type **ping 10.x.2.2** and press **Enter**. The router prints five exclamation points and indicates that the success rate is 100%.

35. Type **telnet 10.1.2.2** and press **Enter**. The router indicates that the destination is unreachable and the prompt returns. Repeat several times.

36. On Router2, type **show access-list** and press **Enter**. How many matches are there in the first line of access list 100?

_____

37. Now you will remove the access list from interface Fast Ethernet 0/0 on Router 2. Type **config term** and press **Enter**.

38. Type **int fast 0/0** and press **Enter**.

39. Type **no ip access-group 100 in** and press **Enter**.

40. Press **Ctl-Z** to exit configuration mode.

41. On Router1, type **telnet 10.1.2.2** and press **Enter**. The Password: prompt appears, indicating that you can now access Router3 through telnet.

42. Now you will recreate this access list as a named access list. On Router2, type **config term** and press **Enter**.

43. Type **ip access-list extended CCNPLab** and press **Enter**.

44. Type **deny tcp 10.x.1.0 0.0.0.255 host 10.x.2.2 eq 23** and press **Enter**.

45. Type **permit ip any any** and press **Enter**.

46. Type **exit** and press **Enter**.

47. Type **int fast 0/0** and press **Enter**.

48. Type **ip access-group CCNPLab in** and press **Enter**.

49. Press **Ctl-Z** to exit configuration mode.

50. On Router1, repeat Steps 34 through 36 to test the named access list.

Certification Objective

Objective for Cisco Exam 640–603: Routing

➤ Select and configure the different ways to control routing update traffic

Review Questions

1. What comes at the end of both numbered standard and numbered extended access lists?

   a. an implicit deny all statement

   b. an implicit permit all statement

   c. nothing

   d. an implicit deny all statement for standard access lists, and an implicit permit all statement for extended access lists

2. Which of the following access list statements would block IP packets sent from 172.30.25.129 to 10.1.1.1?

   a. Router#access–list 19 deny 10.1.1.1 0.255.255.255

   b. Router#access–list 119 deny 172.30.0.0 0.0.255.255 10.0.0.0 0.0.0.255

   c. Router#access–list 119 deny 172.30.0.0 0.0.255.255 host 10.0.0.0

   d. Router#access–list 19 deny 172.30.0.0 0.0.255.255 10.1.1.0 0.0.0.255

3. Which of the following access list statements would block IP packets sent from 172.30.25.129 with a source port of TCP port 111 to 10.1.1.1?

   a. Router#access–list 19 deny 172.30.25.29

   b. Router#access–list 119 deny tcp host 172.30.25.129 eq 111 10.0.0.0 0.255.255.255

   c. Router#access–list 119 deny 172.30.25.129 eq 111 host 10.0.0.0 0.255.255.255

   d. Router#access–list 119 deny tcp host 172.30.25.129 10.0.0.0 0.255.255.255 eq 111

4. How is a named access list different from a numbered access list? (Choose all that apply.)

   a. Named access lists may not work in all the same situations as numbered access lists.

   b. You may delete statements from a named access list.

   c. You may change the order of statements in a named access list.

   d. Named access lists do not have an implicit denial at the end.

5. What does the **log** keyword do when configured in an extended access list?

   a. The router sends syslog messages to a server whenever that line in the access list is matched.

    b. The router drops packets matching that line and saves the number of times the line was matched in a log file on the router.

    c. The router saves the number of times the line was matched and displays it when the **show access-list** command is run.

    d. The router saves the number of times the line was matched and displays it when the **show counters** command is run.

LAB 6.2 CONFIGURING A ROUTE FILTER

Objective

In this lab, you will learn how to configure standard and extended IP access lists.

Materials Required

This lab will require the following:

➤ Three Cisco routers with the interfaces, IP addresses, and cabling, as shown in Figure 6-2

➤ EIGRP configured on each router to advertise network 10.0.0.0 in autonomous system 65000

➤ Known telnet and enable passwords for the routers

➤ A rollover console cable

➤ A laptop or a PC running a terminal emulation program such as Hyperterminal

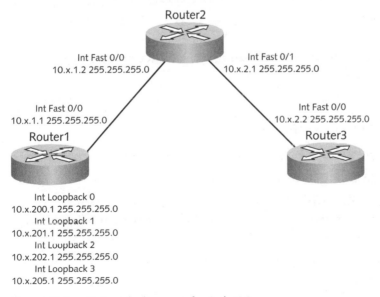

Router2
Int Fast 0/0
10.x.1.2 255.255.255.0

Int Fast 0/1
10.x.2.1 255.255.255.0

Int Fast 0/0
10.x.1.1 255.255.255.0
Router1

Int Fast 0/0
10.x.2.2 255.255.255.0
Router3

Int Loopback 0
10.x.200.1 255.255.255.0
Int Loopback 1
10.x.201.1 255.255.255.0
Int Loopback 2
10.x.202.1 255.255.255.0
Int Loopback 3
10.x.205.1 255.255.255.0

Figure 6-2 Network diagram for Lab 6.2

Estimated completion time: **10 minutes**

Activity Background

Route filters give you greater control over the routing tables on your routers. Route filters allow you to control the routes coming into or going out of a router's interfaces. This can be useful when you need to prevent routing update traffic over a WAN link, when you want to eliminate excess redundant paths, or when you need to fine-tune the redistribution of routes from one protocol into another (which will be covered in more detail in the next chapter).

A route filter is an access list applied to a routing process with the **distribute-list** command. In addition to specifying an access list to match routes to be filtered, you can also specify whether incoming or outgoing routing updates will be filtered with the **in** and **out** keywords. You may specify both an incoming and an outgoing route filter for a routing protocol. You can also configure the router to filter routes for a specific interface.

ACTIVITY

1. Power on the routers and the PC or laptop and open the terminal emulation program.

2. Plug the RJ-45 end of the console cable into the console port of Router2. Attach the other end of the console cable to the serial port on the laptop or PC. You may need to press **Enter** to bring up the Router2> prompt.

3. Type **show ip route** and press **Enter**. You see routes for each of the loopback interfaces on Router1 in Router2's routing table.

4. On Router1, type **enable** and press **Enter**. The router prompt changes to Router1#.

5. Type **config term** and press **Enter**. The router prompt changes to Router1(config)#.

6. Now you will create a route filter to prevent Router1 from advertising the routes from its loopback interfaces. Type **access-list 10 deny 10.*x*.200.0 0.0.7.255** and press **Enter**.

7. Type **access-list 10 permit any** and press **Enter**.

8. Type **router eigrp 65000** and press **Enter**.

9. Type **distribute-list 10 out** and press **Enter**. This configures the router to filter outgoing routes for EIGRP in autonomous system 65000 on all interfaces, using standard access list 10.

10. Press **Ctl-Z** to exit configuration mode.

11. Type **show ip protocol** and press **Enter**. The router prints information about EIGRP on this router, including the number or name of the outgoing route filter (called update filter lists in the command output).

12. On Router2, type **enable** and press **Enter**.

13. Type **clear ip route *** and press **Enter**. This will clear all IP routes from Router2's routing table, and force Router2 to rebuild it.

14. Type **show ip route** and press **Enter**. The router does not show routes for Router1's loopback interfaces.

15. Now you will configure the route filter so that it only applies to Router1's Fast Ethernet 0/0 interface. On Router1, type **config term** and press **Enter**.

16. Type **router eigrp 65000** and press **Enter**.

17. Type **distribute-list 10 out fast 0/0** and press **Enter**. This configures the router to filter outgoing routes that are leaving through interface Fast Ethernet 0/0.

18. On Router2, type **clear ip route *** and press **Enter**.

19. Type **show ip route** and press **Enter**. The command output does not include routes for Router1's loopback interfaces.

Certification Objective

Objective for Cisco Exam 640-603: Routing

➤ Select and configure the different ways to control routing update traffic

Review Questions

1. In which of the following situations might route filtering be useful? (Choose all that apply.)

   a. to reduce an excessive number of redundant paths

   b. to stop or minimize the routing update traffic crossing a WAN

   c. to prevent problems during redistribution

   d. to lower the frequency of routing updates over a WAN

2. Which of the following sets of commands could be used to filter routes 207.128.16.0/24 and 207.128.17.0/24 in outgoing routing updates while letting all other routes go through?

   a. Router(config)#access-list 15 deny 207.128.16.0 0.0.1.255

   Router(config)#access-list 15 permit any

   Router(config)#router eigrp 100

   Router(config-router)#distribute-list 15 out

     b. Router(config)#access-list 15 deny 207.128.16.0 0.0.1.255

        Router(config)#access-list 15 permit any

        Router(config)#router eigrp 100

        Router(config-router)#distribute-list 15 in

     c. Router(config)#access-list 15 permit 207.128.16.0 0.0.1.255

        Router(config)#access-list 15 deny any

        Router(config)#router eigrp 100

        Router(config-router)#distribute-list 15 out

     d. Router(config)#access-list 15 permit 207.128.16.0 0.0.1.255

        Router(config)#access-list 15 deny any

        Router(config)#router eigrp 100

        Router(config-router)#distribute-list 100 in

3. Which of the following sets of commands would allow routes for 172.16.0.0/24, 172.16.1.0/24, 172.16.2.0/24, and 172.16.3.0/24, and filter all others in incoming routing updates?

     a. Router(config)#access-list 15 deny 172.16.0.0 0.0.3.255

        Router(config)#access-list 15 permit any

        Router(config)#router eigrp 100

        Router(config-router)#distribute-list 15 out

     b. Router(config)#access-list 15 deny 172.16.0.0 0.0.3.255

        Router(config)#access-list 15 permit any

        Router(config)#router eigrp 100

        Router(config-router)#distribute-list 15 in

     c. Router(config)#access-list 15 permit 172.16.0.0 0.0.3.255

        Router(config)#access-list 15 deny any

        Router(config)#router eigrp 100

        Router(config-router)#distribute-list 15 out

     d. Router(config)#access-list 15 permit 172.16.0.0 0.0.3.255

        Router(config)#access-list 15 deny any

        Router(config)#router eigrp 100

        Router(config-router)#distribute-list 15 in

4. Which of the following commands would apply access list 10 as a route filter on routing updates coming into interface Serial 0/0?

     a. Router(config-router)#distribute-list 10 in

     b. Router(config-router)#distribute-list 10 out

c. Router(config-router)#distribute-list 10 in serial 0/0

d. Router(config-router)#distribute-list 10 out serial 0/0

5. Which of the following commands can you use to show the route filters applied to a routing protocol?

a. show ip protocol

b. show ip route

c. show access-list

d. show route-filter

Lab 6.3 Configuring Passive Interfaces

Objective

In this lab, you will learn how to configure passive interfaces.

Materials Required

This lab will require the following:

➤ Three Cisco routers with the interfaces, IP addresses, and cabling, as shown in Figure 6-3

➤ RIP configured on each router to advertise network 10.0.0.0

➤ Known telnet and enable passwords for the routers

➤ A rollover console cable

➤ A laptop or a PC running a terminal emulation program such as Hyperterminal

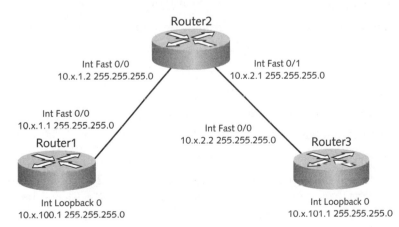

Figure 6-3   Network diagram for Lab 6.3

Estimated completion time: **20 minutes**

Activity Background

A passive interface is defined as an interface that receives routing updates, but does not send routing updates.. In some routing protocols, you may use a passive interface to deactivate the routing protocol for an interface. Passive interfaces are often useful when using redistribution (which you will learn about in the next chapter), or on networks with multiple redundant paths.

The behavior of a passive interface varies somewhat depending on the routing protocol in question. In EIGRP, a passive interface does not send hello packets. As a result, a passive interface in EIGRP prevents two routers from becoming neighbors. OSPF treats a passive interface as a stub network, and does not send or receive routing updates through it.

Often passive interfaces are used with other techniques to manipulate routing tables. For instance, passive interfaces might be used with static routes on particular routers in order to minimize the number of routes in the routing table on a particular router. You might also use a passive interface with static routes in order to prevent routing update traffic from crossing a slow WAN link. Additionally, passive interfaces may be used with redistribution.

ACTIVITY

1. Power on the routers and the PC or laptop and open the terminal emulation program.

2. Plug the RJ-45 end of the console cable into the console port of Router1. Attach the other end of the console cable to the serial port on the laptop or PC. You may need to press **Enter** to bring up the Router1> prompt.

3. Type **show ip route** and press **Enter**. You see routes for all networks, including the loopback interfaces configured on Router1 and Router3.

4. Type **enable** and press **Enter**. The router prompt changes to Router1#.

5. Type **config term** and press **Enter**. The router prompt changes to Router1(config)#.

6. Type **router rip** and press **Enter**.

7. Type **passive-interface fast 0/0** and press **Enter**. This interface can now receive routing updates from Router2, but will no longer send them to Router2.

8. Press **Ctl-Z** to exit configuration mode.

9. Now you will try to ping Router3. Type **ping 10.*x*.1.2** and press **Enter**. The router prints five exclamation points and indicates a 100% success rate.

10. Type **debug ip rip** and press **Enter**. Watch the debugging output for two minutes. Where does RIP send routing updates? From which interfaces does it receive routing updates?

_____

11. Type **undebug all** and press **Enter**.

12. On Router2, type **enable** and press **Enter**.

13. Type **debug ip rip** and press **Enter**. Watch the debugging output for two minutes. Does Router2 receive any routing updates from Router1?

_____

14. Type **undebug all** and press **Enter**.

15. Now you will configure a loopback interface on Router2 and see if Router1 learns it. Type **config term** and press **Enter**.

16. Type **int lo 0** and press **Enter**.

17. Type **ip address 10.x.102.1 255.255.255.0** and press **Enter**.

18. Press **Ctl-Z** to exit configuration mode.

19. Wait 30 seconds. On Router1, type **show ip route** and press **Enter**. You see a route for the loopback interface you just configured on Router2. If not, wait 30 seconds and repeat this step until you do see this route.

20. On Router2, type **show ip route** and press **Enter**. The route to 10.x.100.0/24 has an unreachable metric, or is missing from the routing table.

21. Now you will configure a passive interface in EIGRP. On Router 3, type **enable** and press **Enter**.

22. Type **config term** and press **Enter**.

23. Type **no router rip** and press **Enter**.

24. Type **router eigrp 65000** and press **Enter**.

25. Type **network 10.0.0.0** and press **Enter**.

26. Press **Ctl-Z** to exit configuration mode.

27. Repeat Steps 22 through 26 on Router1 and Router2.

28. On Router3, type **show ip route** and press **Enter**. You see routes for the links connecting the routers and for all the loopback interfaces on each router.

29. On Router1, type **config term** and press **Enter**.

30. Type **router eigrp 65000** and press **Enter**.

31. Type **passive-interface fast 0/0** and press **Enter**.

32. Press **Ctl-Z** to exit configuration mode.

33. Type **show ip route** and press **Enter**. The routing table now only shows connected interfaces.

6

34. Type **ping 10.x.101.1** and press **Enter**. The router prints five dots and indicates that the success rate is 0%.

35. Type **show ip eigrp neighbors** and press **Enter**. The command output does not show any EIGRP neighbors.

36. Now you will configure default routes on Router1 and Router2 so that all the routers can reach each other. Type **config term** and press **Enter**.

37. Type **ip route 0.0.0.0 0.0.0.0 10.x.1.2** and press **Enter**.

38. Press **Ctl-Z** to exit configuration mode.

39. Repeat Steps 36 through 38 on Router2.

40. On Router3, type **config term** and press **Enter**.

41. Type **ip route 0.0.0.0 0.0.0.0 10.x.2.1** and press **Enter**.

42. Press **Ctl-Z** to exit configuration mode.

43. On Router1, type **ping 10.x.101.1** and press **Enter**. The router prints five exclamation points and indicates that the success rate is 100%.

44. On Router3, type **ping 10.x.100.1** and press **Enter**. The router prints five exclamation points and indicates that the success rate is 100%.

Certification Objective

Objective for Cisco Exam 640–603: Routing

➤ Select and configure the different ways to control routing update traffic

Review Questions

1. What are some of the potential advantages of passive interfaces? (Choose all that apply.)

    a. In some routing protocols, interfaces can learn routes without advertising them.

    b. Passive interfaces are the only way to prevent individual interfaces from running OSPF without turning off OSPF for a whole classful network.

    c. Passive interfaces are the only way to prevent individual interfaces from running EIGRP or RIP without turning them off for a whole classful network.

    d. You can prevent routing update traffic from crossing a WAN.

2. What happens when you configure a passive interface on a router running EIGRP?

    a. The router will learn routes from its neighbors through that interface, but will not use it to send routing updates.

    b. The router will treat that interface as a stub network for EIGRP.

    c. The router will be unable to become neighbors with any routers sharing a network with that interface.

    d. The router will send routing updates out that interface, but will not receive them.

3. What happens when you configure a passive interface on a router running OSPF?

   a. The router will learn routes from its neighbors through that interface, but will not use it to send routing updates.

   b. The router will send hello packets out that interface, but will not form an adjacency with any other routers on network attached to it.

   c. The router will send link-state advertisements out that interface, but will not receive them.

   d. The router will treat that interface as a stub network, and will not send or receive routing updates through it.

4. What happens when you configure a passive interface on a router running RIP?

   a. The router will learn routes from its neighbors through that interface, but will not use it to send routing updates.

   b. The router will treat that interface as a stub network for EIGRP.

   c. The router will be unable to become neighbors with any routers sharing a network with that interface.

   d. The router will send routing updates out that interface, but will not receive them.

5. Which command can you use to find whether or not passive interfaces have been configured for a particular routing protocol?

   a. show ip passive-interfaces

   b. show ip interface

   c. show ip protocol

   d. show ip route

LAB 6.4 CONFIGURING ADMINISTRATIVE DISTANCE

Objective

In this lab, you will learn how to configure administrative distance.

Materials Required

This lab will require the following:

> Three Cisco routers with the interfaces, IP addresses, and cabling, as shown previously in Figure 6-3

> RIP configured on each router to advertise network 10.0.0.0

> Known telnet and enable passwords for the routers

> A rollover console cable

> A laptop or a PC running a terminal emulation program such as Hyperterminal

Estimated completion time: **20 minutes**

Activity Background

Administrative distance is another tool you can use to control the routes appearing in the routing tables of your routers. Cisco routers use administrative distance to choose between different sources of routing information. For instance, a router might learn the same route from both OSPF and RIP. By default, OSPF routes have an administrative distance of 110, and RIP routers have an administrative distance of 120. Since Cisco routers choose the source of routing information with the lowest administrative distance, the router would choose the route learned from OSPF. In a Cisco router's routing table, the administrative distance appears immediately after the route (and before the metric).

However, you can configure the administrative distance a router will give to routes learned from a routing protocol with the **distance** command. For instance, you can configure a router to give routes learned from OSPF an administrative distance of 50. As a result, the router would select an OSPF route over an identical EIGRP route with the default internal administrative distance of 90. The administrative distance configured can be any value from 10 to 255 (administrative distances below 10 are reserved). You can also configure the router to apply the new administrative distance to a specific neighbor by supplying an address and address mask. You can filter the routes whose administrative distance is being changed by supplying an access list number or name. For EIGRP, you must configure the administrative distance for both internal and external EIGRP routes. For instance, you would configure an administrative distance of 100 for internal routes and 120 for external routes with the **distance eigrp 100 120** command in router configuration mode.

One final use of administrative distance is to make floating static routes. Floating static routes are often used as backup routes. By default, connected routes and static routes through an interface have an administrative distance of 0, while static routes through a neighbor's IP address have an administrative distance of 1. As a result, a static route with the default administrative distance will always be chosen over a route learned dynamically. A floating static route, however, is configured to have a high administrative distance. As a result, a route from another source is preferred over the floating static route. However, if the route from the other source fails, then the floating static route is added to the routing table. For instance, suppose you configured a floating static route with an administrative distance of 170. If OSPF supplied a route to the same destination, the OSPF route is preferred since its default administrative distance is 110. However, if the OSPF route is removed from the routing table, then the floating static route is added.

ACTIVITY

1. Power on the routers and the PC or laptop and open the terminal emulation program.

2. Plug the RJ-45 end of the console cable into the console port of Router1. Attach the other end of the console cable to the serial port on the laptop or PC. You may need to press **Enter** to bring up the Router1> prompt.

3. Type **show ip route** and press **Enter**. All routes in the routing table are either connected or were learned through RIP. What is the administrative distance of the RIP routes?

_____

4. Type **enable** and press **Enter**. The router prompt changes to Router1#.

5. Type **config term** and press **Enter**. The router prompt changes to Router1(config)#.

6. Type **router eigrp 65000** and press **Enter**.

7. Type **distance eigrp 80 160** and press **Enter**. This configures the administrative distance for internal and external EIGRP routes slightly lower than the defaults of 90 and 170, respectively.

8. Type **network 10.0.0.0** and press **Enter**.

9. Press **Ctl-Z** to exit configuration mode.

10. Type **clear ip route *** and press **Enter**. This clears the routing table and forces the router to rebuild it.

11. Log onto Router2 and Router3 and repeat Steps 4 through 10.

12. On Router3, type **show ip route** and press **Enter**. All the routes are either connected or learned through EIGRP. What is the administrative distance of the EIGRP routes?

_____

13. On Router2, type **config term** and press **Enter**.

14. Type **int loop 1** and press **Enter**.

15. Type **ip address 192.168.1.1 255.255.255.0** and press **Enter**.

16. Type **router eigrp 65000** and press **Enter**.

17. Type **network 192.168.1.0** and press **Enter**.

18. Press **Ctl-Z** to exit configuration mode.

19. On Router1, type **config term** and press **Enter**.

20. Type **access-list 4 deny 192.168.0.0 0.0.255.255** and press **Enter**.

21. Type **access-list 4 permit any** and press **Enter**.

22. Type **router rip** and press **Enter**.

23. Type **distance 10 10.x.1.2 0.0.0.0 4** and press **Enter**. This configures Router1 to apply the new administrative distance to its neighbor 10.x.1.2 and to filter the routes altered with access list 4, including the 192.168.1.0/24 route advertised by Router2.

6

24. Press **Ctl-Z** to exit configuration mode.

25. Type **clear ip route *** and press **Enter**.

26. Type **show ip protocol** and press **Enter**. The router prints information about the routing protocols running on this router, including their administrative distances.

27. On Router2, type **config term** and press **Enter**.

28. Type **router rip** and press **Enter**.

29. Type **distance 10** and press **Enter**.

30. Press **Ctl-Z** to exit configuration mode.

31. Type **clear ip route *** and press **Enter**.

32. Repeat Steps 26 through 30 on Router3.

33. On Router3, type **show ip route** and press **Enter**. What is the administrative distance for the RIP routes now?

---

34. Now you will configure a floating static route on Router1. Type **config term** and press **Enter**.

35. Type **ip route 0.0.0.0 0.0.0.0 loop 0** and press **Enter**. This configures a route which would forward packets for all destinations through interface Loopback 0.

36. Type **ip route 0.0.0.0 0.0.0.0 10.x.1.2 170**. and press **Enter**. This configures a static route to the next hop address of 10.x.1.2 with an administrative distance of 170.

37. Press **Ctl-Z** to exit configuration mode.

38. Type **show ip route** and press **Enter**. What is the administrative distance of the default route currently in the routing table?

---

39. Type **config term** and press **Enter**.

40. Type **no int loop 0** and press **Enter**. You have now removed the primary default route from the routing table.

41. Press **Ctl-Z** to exit configuration mode.

42. Type **show ip route** and press **Enter**. What is the administrative distance of the backup route with a next hop of 10.x.1.2?

Certification Objective

Objective for Cisco Exam 640-603: Routing

➤ Select and configure the different ways to control routing update traffic

Review Questions

1. What effect does administrative distance have on a router's route selection?

   a. The router adjusts the metrics of its routes based on the administrative distance.

   b. The router chooses routes from the source with the highest administrative distance.

   c. The router chooses routes from the source with the lowest administrative distance.

   d. The router chooses routes from the neighbor with the best administrative distance.

2. Which of the following sources of routing information would be chosen by a router? Assume that the route received from all sources is identical.

   a. a static route through 10.1.1.1

   b. a static route through interface Serial 0/0

   c. a route learned through RIP with the default administrative distance

   d. a route learned through OSPF

3. Which of the following commands would configure an administrative distance of 70 for RIP from a neighboring router with an IP address of 172.16.1.1?

   a. Router(config-router)#distance 70

   b. Router(config-router)#distance rip 70

   c. Router(config-router)#distance 70 172.16.1.1 0.0.0.0

   d. Router(config-router)#neighbor 172.16.1.1 distance 70

4. Which of the following commands would configure an administrative distance of 100 for EIGRP internal routes and 200 for EIGRP external routes?

   a. Router(config-router)#distance eigrp 200 100

   b. Router(config-router)#distance 100 200

   c. Router(config-router)#eigrp distance 100 200

   d. Router(config-router)#distance eigrp 100 200

5. Which of the following commands would configure a floating static route to be a backup to an OSPF route? The default administrative distance for OSPF is 110.

   a. Router(config-router)# ip route 172.16.1.1 255.255.255.0 distance 120

   b. Router(config-router)#ip route 172.16.1.1 255.255.255.0 70

   c. Router(config-router)# ip route 172.16.1.1 255.255.255.0 100

   d. Router(config-router)# ip route 172.16.1.1 255.255.255.0 170

LAB 6.5 CONFIGURING POLICY-BASED ROUTING

Objective

In this lab, you will learn how to configure policy-based routing using route maps.

Materials Required

This lab will require the following:

➤ Three Cisco routers with the interfaces, IP addresses and cabling, as shown in Figure 6-4

➤ EIGRP (autonomous system 65000) enabled on each router to advertise network 10.0.0.0, and on Router1 network 172.16.0.0

➤ Known telnet and enable passwords for the routers

➤ A rollover console cable

➤ A laptop or a PC running a terminal emulation program such as Hyperterminal

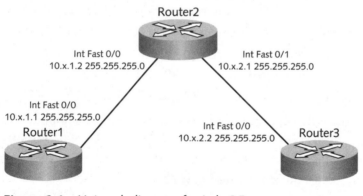

Figure 6-4   Network diagram for Lab 6.5

Estimated completion time: **20 minutes**

Activity Background

Route maps allow you to perform policy-based routing. You can use a route map to set routing policy-based packet characteristics. For instance, you can use a route map to forward packets through different routes depending on their source address, source port, size, or protocol. You can also use route maps to filter routes during redistribution, and for other purposes.

A route map is quite similar to an access list. However, route maps are more complex, and they may also modify the packet after a match. They consist of a series of statements applied to packets coming into an interface. Like an access list, each statement permits or denies a packet. The effect when a packet matches a deny statement varies depending on the use of the route map. Like an access list, there is also an implicit denial at the end of the route map. However, each statement in a route map has a sequence number. Each statement in the route map is executed in order, beginning with the lowest sequence number. After a statement in the route map is matched, no further execution is performed. Unlike an access list, you may replace a statement in a route map. If you leave sufficient space between each sequence number, you may also insert other statements in between the existing statements of a route map.

A statement typically consists of one or more match commands, followed by one or more set commands. If a statement does not contain a match statement, all packets match it. You can match packets specified in an access list with the **match ip address** *access-list* command. If you specify multiple access lists in this command, the packet will match the route map statement if it matches any one of the access lists. You may also specify multiple match commands, in which case the packet will match the sequence if it matches each match command. Other possible match commands include **match length** *minimum-size maximum-size*, which you can use to match packet size, and **match interface** *interface-name interface-number*, which you can use to match the next hop of the route. Possible set commands include **set interface** *interface-name interface-number*, which you can use to change the outgoing interface, and **set ip precedence** *precedence-value* and **set ip tos** *tos-value*, which you can use to set various quality of service values.

After building the route map, you must apply the route map to an interface with the **ip policy route-map** *route-map-name* command in interface configuration mode. The route map will be applied to packets coming into this interface.

When using route maps to perform policy routing on an interface, you should keep in mind that they may have an effect on performance. The router must examine every packet coming into the interface and must use the slowest packet switching method. However, route maps, when used for other purposes (such as during redistribution), typically do not have any effect on performance.

ACTIVITY

1. Power on the routers and the PC or laptop and open the terminal emulation program.

2. Plug the RJ-45 end of the console cable into the console port of Router2. Attach the other end of the console cable to the serial port on the laptop or PC. You may need to press **Enter** to bring up the Router2> prompt.

3. Type **enable** and press **Enter**. The router prompt changes to Router2#.

4. Type **config term** and press **Enter**. The router prompt changes to Router2(config)#.

5. Now you will create a series of access lists to match packets that might come into Router1's Fast Ethernet 0/0 interface. Type **access-list 125 permit tcp any any eq 23** and press **Enter**. This will match any TCP packet with a destination port of 23, or telnet. Because of the implicit denial at the end of the access list, remember that no other packets will be matched.

6. Type **access-list 140 permit icmp any any** and press **Enter**.

7. Type **route-map Lab permit 5** and press **Enter**. The router prompt changes to Router2(config-route-map)#.

8. Type **match ip address 125** and press **Enter**. This statement will match any packet matching access list 125.

9. Type **set interface null 0** and press **Enter**. This will send any packet matched by the match statement you configured in the previous step to the null interface, thereby discarding it.

10. Type **route-map Lab permit 10** and press **Enter**.

11. Type **match length 500 2147483647** and press **Enter**. This will match any packet whose length is between 500 and 2147483647 bytes.

12. Type **match ip address 140** and press **Enter**. Now a packet must both match access list 140 and have a length between 500 and 2147483647 bytes in order to be matched by this statement in the route map.

13. Type **set interface null 0** and press **Enter**.

14. Type **exit** and press **Enter**.

15. Type **int fast 0/0** and press **Enter**.

16. Type **ip policy route-map Lab** and press **Enter**. Route-map Lab will now be applied to packets coming into interface Fast Ethernet 0/0.

17. Press **Ctl-Z** to exit configuration mode.

18. Type **show route-map** and press **Enter**. This shows the route map and whether or not any packets matched any of the statements.

19. Type **show ip int fast 0/0** and press **Enter**. The router prints information about IP on interface Fast Ethernet 0/0, indicating that policy routing is enabled using route-map Lab.

20. Now you will test each statement in the route map, starting with sequence number 5. On Router1, type **telnet 10.x.2.2** and press **Enter**. The router prints that the destination is unreachable.

21. On Router2, type **show route-map Lab** and press **Enter**. The router prints the route-map Lab. How many matches are there for sequence number 5?

22. To show that the route map only applies to packets coming into Router1's Fast Ethernet 0/0 interface, you will attempt to telnet from Router3 to Router1. On Router3, type **telnet 10.x.1.1** and press **Enter**. The Password: prompt appears.

23. Log onto Router1 with the telnet password.

24. Type **exit** and press **Enter**.

25. Now you will test sequence number 10. On Router1, type **ping 10.x.2.2** and press **Enter**. This will send five 100-byte ICMP packets to Router3. The router prints five exclamation points and indicates that the success rate is 100%.

26. Type **enable** and press **Enter**.

27. Now you will attempt to ping Router3 with a larger packet size. Type **ping** and press **Enter**. The prompt changes to Protocol [ip]:.

28. Press **Enter**. The prompt changes to Target IP address:. prompt.

29. Type **10.x.2.2** and press **Enter**.

30. Press **Enter** until the prompt reads Datagram size [100]:.

31. Type **5000** and press **Enter**. Note that this value refers to the size of the entire ICMP packet, while the length you configured the packet to match in Step 13 refers to the Layer 3 portion of the packet.

32. Type **Enter** until the router prints that it is sending five 5000-byte ICMP packets. The router prints a combination of U's and dots and indicates that the success rate is 0%.

33. On Router2, type **show route-map Lab** and press **Enter**. The router prints the route-map Lab. How many matches are there for sequence number 10?

Certification Objectives

Objectives for Cisco Exam 640-603: Routing

➤ Configure policy-based routing using route maps

➤ Configure policy-based routing and verify proper operation

Review Questions

1. Which of the following are possible uses for a route map? (Choose all that apply.)

   a. have World Wide Web traffic use a different link than other traffic

   b. set precedence values for IP packets, and other values related to quality of service

   c. filter routes during redistribution

   d. change the default route in the routing table based on criteria in the packet

2. Which of the following sets of match statements in a route map would match packets with a size of 1500 bytes, which are matched by access list 100 and not matched by access list 130?

   a. match ip address 100

      match length 2000 30000

   b. match ip address 130

      match length 1000 5000

   c. match ip address 100

      match ip address 130

   d. match ip address 100 130

      match length 1000 5000

3. Which of the following is true about route map sequence numbers? (Choose all that apply.)

   a. All numbering is automatic.

   b. Statements are executed in order beginning with the lowest sequence number.

   c. Assuming you left room between sequence numbers, you may add statements between existing statements.

   d. You may not delete route map statements without deleting the entire route map.

4. Route-map Filter is applied to interface Serial 0/0. Which of the following packets would be processed by this route map?

   a. packets arriving at interface Serial 0/0

   b. packets arriving at any interface

   c. packets exiting through interface Serial 0/0

   d. packets arriving at interface Fast Ethernet 0/0 and exiting through interface Serial 0/0

5. Which of the following sets of commands would cause TCP packets with a destination port of 80 (World Wide Web) to use interface Serial 0/0 as their next hop?

   a. access-list 100 permit tcp any any eq 80

      route-map permit WWW 5

      match ip 100

      match tcp 80

      set interface serial 0/0

b. access-list 100 permit tcp any any

   match ip 100

   set interface serial 0/0

c. access-list 100 permit tcp any eq 80 any

   match ip 100

   set interface serial 0/0

d. access-list 100 permit tcp any any eq 80

   match ip 100

   set interface serial 0/0

6

CHAPTER SEVEN

REDISTRIBUTION

Labs included in this chapter

➤ Lab 7.1 Redistributing RIP into EIGRP

➤ Lab 7.2 One-Way Redistribution from RIP into OSPF Without a Default Route

➤ Lab 7.3 Migration from IGRP to EIGRP

➤ Lab 7.4 Two-Way Redistribution Between OSPF and EIGRP

➤ Lab 7.5 Two-Way Redistribution Between OSPF and EIGRP at Multiple Points

Cisco CCNP Exam #640-603 Objectives	
Objective	Lab
Configure route redistribution in a network that *does not* have redundant paths between dissimilar routing processes	7.1, 7.2, 7.3, 7.4
Configure route redistribution in a network that *has* redundant paths between dissimilar routing processes	7.5
Resolve path selection problems that result in a redistributed network	7.1, 7.2, 7.4, 7.5
Verify route redistribution	7.1, 7.2, 7.3, 7.4, 7.5
Configure redistribution between different routing domains and verify proper operation	7.1, 7.2, 7.3, 7.4, 7.5

LAB 7.1 REDISTRIBUTING RIP INTO EIGRP

Objective

In this lab, you will learn how to perform one-way redistribution from RIP into EIGRP.

Materials Required

This lab will require the following:

➤ Four Cisco routers with the interfaces, IP addresses, and cabling, as shown in Figure 7-1, and the interfaces attached to the DCE ends of the serial cables configured with a clock rate of 64000

➤ RIP configured on Router1 and Router2 to advertise network 10.0.0.0

➤ EIGRP configured on Router3 and Router4 to advertise network 10.0.0.0 in autonomous system 65000

➤ Known telnet and enable passwords for the routers

➤ A rollover console cable

➤ A laptop or a PC running a terminal emulation program such as Hyperterminal

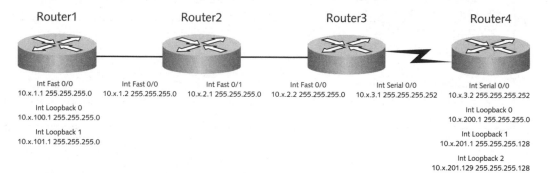

Figure 7-1   Network diagram for Lab 7.1

Estimated completion time: **20 minutes**

Activity Background

While the use of two or more routing protocols is generally not ideal, it is often necessary for a variety of reasons. These reasons can include use of legacy equipment that do not support your primary routing protocol, the merger of autonomous systems running different routing protocols, or migration between two routing protocols. Redistribution allows you to take routes learned by one routing protocol and propagate them into another routing protocol.

On Cisco routers, you may redistribute between any two routing protocols as long as they have the same underlying protocol stack. For instance, you may redistribute between EIGRP and OSPF, or any two IP routing protocols, but you may not redistribute between an IP routing protocol such as OSPF and a routing protocol used with the Internetwork Packet Exchange (IPX) protocol stack. You may also redistribute static or connected routes into a routing protocol.

While often useful or necessary, redistribution can cause serious problems. Without careful planning, redistribution may cause routing loops. This is because redistribution circumvents a routing protocol's normal methods of avoiding routing loops. Routing loops may also result when one routing protocol learns routes from a second, and then advertises those routes back to the second routing protocol. Additionally, poor path selection may result. Routing protocol metrics typically are not easily translatable. You may set a default metric or even individual metrics for routes redistributed between routing protocols, but either routing protocol is usually more efficient at assigning a reasonable metric. With some routing protocols (such as RIP), a poorly chosen default metric may result in unreachable routes. Finally, problems can result when one protocol understands VLSM and the other does not. Redistributing routes with VLSMs from OSPF into RIP, for instance, would prevent RIP from understanding the routes. However, careful planning can prevent these problems.

To configure redistribution, first you must decide which routing protocol will be the backbone protocol and which will be the edge protocol. You must then configure both routing protocols on the edge router, or the router at the border point between the two routing domains. (Generally, you should not run more than one routing protocol on a router, except on those routers where you plan to configure redistribution.) Then you must use the **redistribute** command to propagate routes from the edge protocol into the backbone protocol. In order for routers using the edge protocol to reach destinations in the backbone protocol's routing domain, you may propagate a default route, propagate a handful of static routes, or redistribute routes.

In practice, configuring redistribution is often much more complex. For instance, you may need to redistribute routes in both directions, or on multiple edge routers. Often you will also want to filter the routing information passed between the two routing protocols with one of the techniques discussed in Chapter 6. In general, the more you can simplify your redistribution scenarios, the more potential problems you can eliminate. For instance, propagating a default route into the edge protocol, when possible, instead of redistributing in both directions can eliminate many problems associated with redistribution.

ACTIVITY

1. Power on the routers and the PC or laptop and open the terminal emulation program.

2. Plug the RJ-45 end of the console cable into the console port of Router1. Attach the other end of the console cable to the serial port on the laptop or PC. You may need to press **Enter** to bring up the Router1> prompt.

3. Type **show ip route** and press **Enter**. You only see routes that are directly connected to Router1, or that were learned through RIP.

4. On Router4, type **show ip route** and press **Enter**. You only see routes that are directly connected to Router4, or that were learned through EIGRP.

5. Now you will redistribute routes between the two routing protocols. First you will activate two-way redistribution to see some of the problems that may occur. On Router2, type **enable** and press **Enter**. The router prompt changes to Router2#.

6. Type **config term** and press **Enter**. The router prompt changes to Router2(config)#.

7. Type **router eigrp 65000** and press **Enter**.

8. Type **passive-interface fast 0/0** and press **Enter**. This deactivates EIGRP on interface Fast Ethernet 0/0, which is connected to Router1 running RIP.

9. Type **network 10.0.0.0** and press **Enter**.

10. Type **redistribute rip metric 64 100 100 100 1500** and press **Enter**. This command redistributes RIP routes into EIGRP and sets the default metric.

11. Type **exit** and press **Enter**.

12. Type **router rip** and press **Enter**.

13. Type **passive-interface fast 0/1** and press **Enter**. This deactivates RIP on interface Fast Ethernet 0/1, which is connected to Router3 running EIGRP.

14. Type **redistribute eigrp 65000 metric 5** and press **Enter**. This command redistributes EIGRP routes into RIP and sets the default metric.

15. Press **Ctl-Z** to exit configuration mode.

16. Type **show ip route** and press **Enter**. You see all routes present on the four routers.

17. Type **show ip route eigrp** and press **Enter**. You see all routes learned from EIGRP.

18. Type **show ip route rip** and press **Enter**. You see all routes learned from RIP.

19. On Router4, type **show ip route** and press **Enter**. You see routes to all possible destinations on the four routers.

20. Type **ping 10.x.100.1** and press **Enter**. The router prints five dots and indicates that the success rate is 0%.

21. On Router1, type **show ip route** and press **Enter**. Which routes that you saw in Step 16 are missing?

22. Type **ping 10.x.3.1** and press **Enter**. The router prints five dots and indicates that the success rate is 0%.

23. Type **ping 10.x.201.129** and press **Enter**. The router prints five dots and indicates that the success rate is 0%.

24. Type **enable** and press **Enter**.

25. Type **debug ip rip** and press **Enter**. Debugging output appears. Within a minute, you see debugging output showing the routes that Router1 is receiving from and sending to Router2. Which of the routes that you saw in Step 16 are missing?

_____

26. Type **undebug all** and press **Enter**.

27. So that Router1 will be able to reach all possible networks on Router3 and Router4, you will now configure a default route on Router2 and redistribute it. On Router2, type **config term** and press **Enter**.

28. Type **ip route 0.0.0.0 0.0.0.0 10.x.2.2** and press **Enter**.

29. Type **router rip** and press **Enter**.

30. Type **no redistribute eigrp 65000** and press **Enter**. This stops RIP from redistributing EIGRP routes. Default routes are automatically redistributed by RIP, so no further configuration is required.

31. Press **Ctl-Z** to exit configuration mode.

32. Type **show ip route static** and press **Enter**. The router prints a list of static routes, which includes the default route.

33. On Router1, type **show ip route** and press **Enter**. You now see a default route. According to the routing table, where did Router1 learn about the default route?

_____

34. Type **ping 10.x.3.1** and press **Enter**. The router prints five exclamation points and indicates that the success rate is 100%.

35. Type **ping 10.x.201.129** and press **Enter**. The router prints five exclamation points and indicates that the success rate is 100%.

Certification Objectives

Objectives for Cisco Exam 640-603: Routing

➤ Configure route redistribution in a network that *does not* have redundant paths between dissimilar routing processes

➤ Resolve path selection problems that result in a redistributed network

➤ Verify route redistribution

➤ Configure redistribution between different routing domains and verify proper operation

Review Questions

1. Which of the following are potential problems caused by redistribution? (Choose all that apply.)

   a. routing loops

   b. poor path selection

   c. incompatible metrics

   d. incompatible protocol stacks

2. How can propagating a default route into the edge routing protocol help in redistributing routes?

   a. Routers in the edge protocol can use the default route to reach destinations in the backbone routing protocol without requiring two-way redistribution.

   b. The default route can be redistributed into both routing protocols.

   c. A default route makes two-way redistribution more efficient.

   d. The default route acts as a backup route in case a specific route is missing.

3. Which of the following best describes the requirements for redistribution on Cisco routers?

   a. two routing protocols using any protocol stack

   b. two routing protocols using the same protocol stack

   c. two routing protocols, or a routing protocol and a static or connected route, using any same protocol stack

   d. two routing protocols, or a routing protocol and a static or connected route, using the same protocol stack

4. Why might redistribution result in poor path selection?

   a. Redistribution removes all metric information for both routing protocols.

   b. Redistribution relies on default routes, which may not use the best path.

   c. Redistribution removes metric information for redistributed routes.

   d. Redistribution can only use the metrics learned from the redistributed routes.

5. Which of the following commands would redistribute routes from RIP into EIGRP in autonomous system 100?

   a. Router(config-router)#redistribute router rip

   b. Router(config-router)#redistribute rip 100

   c. Router(config-router)#redistribute rip

   d. Router(config-router)#redistribute rip eigrp 100

LAB 7.2 ONE-WAY REDISTRIBUTION FROM RIP INTO OSPF WITHOUT A DEFAULT ROUTE

Objective

In this lab, you will learn how to redistribute routes between RIP and OSPF without using a default route to allow the RIP routing domain to communicate with the OSPF routing domain.

Materials Required

This lab will require the following:

> ➤ Four Cisco routers with the interfaces, IP addresses, and cabling, as shown in Figure 7-1, and the interfaces attached to the DCE ends of the serial cables configured with a clock rate of 64000

> ➤ RIP configured on Router1 and Router2 to advertise network 10.0.0.0

> ➤ OSPF configured with process number 1 on Router3 and Router4 to advertise all interfaces with addresses in 10.0.0.0/8 in Area 0

> ➤ Known telnet and enable passwords for the routers

> ➤ A rollover console cable

> ➤ A laptop or a PC running a terminal emulation program such as Hyperterminal

Estimated completion time: **20 minutes**

Activity Background

Using one-way redistribution in one direction and a default route in the other is a reasonably safe way to redistribute routes between two routing protocols. When a routing domain already contains a default route, however, you may not use a second default route in order to reach destinations in the other routing domain. One option is to create static routes on the border router. You would then redistribute these static routes. Another option is two-way redistribution between the two routing protocols, which will be covered in Lab 7.4.

Any static routes used on the border router should summarize routes as much as possible. This is especially true if the routes summarized use VLSMs, as RIP will not be able to understand them. To summarize the routes in a static route, you can configure a static route to a null interface. The router will discard packets that match the static route, but that do not match a more specific route in the routing table. This is similar to what the router itself does automatically when you configure route summarization for a routing protocol on the router. However, you should make sure that these static routes are not introduced back into the routing domain containing the original routes.

When redistributing routes into OSPF, you should keep two things in mind. First, the **subnets** keyword controls whether or not subnets are redistributed into OSPF. Without this keyword, only major networks will be redistributed. Second, you may choose the type of metric used for redistributed routes. OSPF advertises two types of external routes, type 1 and type 2. The metric for type 1 external routes, indicated by E1 in the routing table, is calculated by adding the cost of the external link to the cost of each internal link along the path to the external link. This is useful when an OSPF autonomous system has multiple paths to another autonomous system. The metric for type 2 external routes, indicated by E2 in the routing table, is the cost of the external link. You should use type 2 external routes when an OSPF autonomous system has only one path to an external autonomous system. Type 2 external routes are preferred over type 1 routes, and are the default used by Cisco routers.

ACTIVITY

1. Power on the routers and the PC or laptop and open the terminal emulation program.

2. Plug the RJ-45 end of the console cable into the console port of Router1. Attach the other end of the console cable to the serial port on the laptop or PC. You may need to press **Enter** to bring up the Router1> prompt.

3. First you will configure a default route for RIP on Router1. Type **enable** and press **Enter**.

4. Type **config term** and press **Enter**.

5. Type **ip route 0.0.0.0 0.0.0.0 loop 0** and press **Enter**. This creates a default route that sends all packets for destinations without specific routes in the routing table to interface Loopback 0. Default routes are automatically redistributed by RIP, so no further configuration is required.

6. Press **Ctl-Z** to exit configuration mode.

7. On Router4, repeat Steps 3 and 4.

8. Type **ip route 0.0.0.0 0.0.0.0 loop 0** and press **Enter**.

9. Type **router ospf 1** and press **Enter**.

10. Type **default-information originate** and press **Enter**.

11. Press **Ctl-Z** to exit configuration mode.

12. Now you will redistribute routes between the two routing protocols. On Router2, repeat Steps 3 and 4.

13. Type **router ospf 1** and press **Enter**.

14. Type **network 10.*x*.2.1 0.0.0.0 area 0** and press **Enter**. This ensures that OSPF is only activated on interface Fast Ethernet 0/1, which borders the OSPF routing domain.

15. Type **redistribute rip metric 200 metric-type 2 subnets** and press **Enter**. You have now configured OSPF to redistribute all RIP routes (including subnets) into OSPF with a default cost of 200 and a type 2 external metric. (This is the default type of metric, and does not normally require explicit configuration.)

16. Type **exit** and press **Enter**.

17. Type **ip route 10.*x*.3.0 255.255.255.0 null 0** and press **Enter**. This creates a static route to 10.x.3.0/24 to the null interface, and is necessary because RIP will not understand the 10.x.3.0/30 network.

18. Type **ip route 10.*x*.201.0 255.255.255.0 null 0** and press **Enter**.

19. Now you will configure RIP so that it does not unnecessarily send updates out its Fast Ethernet 0/1 interface. Type **router rip** and press **Enter**.

20. Type **passive-interface fast 0/1** and press **Enter**.

21. Type **redistribute static** and press **Enter**.

22. Press **Ctl-Z** to exit configuration mode.

23. Type **show ip route** and press **Enter**. You see routes for all destinations within both the RIP and OSPF routing domains, as well as the static and default routes.

24. On Router1, type **show ip route** and press **Enter**. The routing table contains routes learned from the RIP routing domain, as well as the redistributed static routes.

25. Type **ping 10.*x*.201.129** and press **Enter**. The router prints five exclamation points and indicates that the success rate was 100%.

26. Type **ping 10.*x*.3.2** and press **Enter**. The router prints five exclamation points and indicates that the success rate was 100%.

27. On Router3, type **show ip route** and press **Enter**. The router prints a list of all routes learned through both RIP and OSPF, including the static routes you redistributed into RIP in Step 21. Which router is the next hop for the routes to 10.x.200.0/24 and 10.x.201/24? Which router should be the next hop for these routes?

---

28. On Router2, type **config term** and press **Enter**.

29. Type **access-list 1 deny 10.*x*.3.0 0.0.0.255** and press **Enter**.

30. Type **access-list 1 deny 10.*x*.201.0 0.0.0.255** and press **Enter**.

31. Type **access-list 1 permit any** and press **Enter**. Access list 1 now denies the static routes redistributed back into OSPF, while permitting all other routes.

32. Type **router ospf 1** and press **Enter**.

33. Type **distribute-list 1 out rip** and press **Enter**. This command filters redistributed routes from RIP that match access list 1.

34. Press **Ctl-Z** to exit configuration mode.

35. Type **show ip protocols** and press **Enter**. The router prints information about the IP routing protocols, including that redistributed RIP is filtered by access list 1, and that OSPF is redistributing both OSPF and RIP. (Note that the output of this command always indicates that a routing protocol is redistributing itself.)

36. On Router3, type **show ip route** and press **Enter**. You no longer see the routes for the static routes configured earlier in Router3's routing table.

Certification Objectives

Objectives for Cisco Exam 640-603: Routing

➤ Configure route redistribution in a network that *does not* have redundant paths between dissimilar routing processes

➤ Resolve path selection problems that result in a redistributed network

➤ Verify route redistribution

➤ Configure redistribution between different routing domains and verify proper operation

Review Questions

1. Which of the following commands would redistribute routes from RIP into OSPF with a default cost of 500, and advertise the redistributed routes as type 1 external routes?

   a. Router(config-router)#redistribute rip metric 500 external 1

   b. Router(config-router)#redistribute rip cost 500 metric-type 1

   c. Router(config-router)#redistribute rip cost 500 external 1

   d. Router(config-router)#redistribute rip metric 500 metric-type 1

2. The routing table on Router1 contains a static route for 10.172.16.0/20 to interface Null 0, which was redistributed into OSPF. Which of the following is true about this route? (Choose all that apply.)

   a. Other OSPF routers see this route as an internal OSPF route.

   b. Other OSPF routers see this route as an external OSPF route.

   c. Other OSPF routers discard packets sent to destinations matching this route unless they have a more specific route in their routing table.

   d. Router1 discards packets sent to destinations matching this route unless it has a more specific route in its routing table.

3. Which of the following commands would apply access list 15 as a route filter when redistributing routes from RIP into OSPF?

   a. Router(config-router)#distribute-list 15 in rip

   b. Router(config-router)#route-filter 15 rip out

   c. Router(config-router)#distribute-list 15 rip out

   d. Router(config-router)#distribute-list 15 out rip

4. Which of the following commands is necessary to redistribute a default route into RIP?

   a. Router(config-router)#redistribute static

   b. Router(config-router)#redistribute default

   c. Router(config-router)#default-information originate

   d. Default routes are redistributed into RIP by default.

5. What effect does the subnets keyword to the redistribute command have on routes redistributed into OSPF?

   a. It allows the redistribution of subnets into OSPF.

   b. It prevents the redistribution of subnets into OSPF.

   c. It allows OSPF to redistribute routes from classless routing protocols.

   d. It allows OSPF to redistribute routes from classful routing protocols.

LAB 7.3 MIGRATION FROM IGRP TO EIGRP

Objective

In this lab, you will learn how to use redistribution to migrate between IGRP and EIGRP.

Materials Required

This lab will require the following:

➤ Four Cisco routers with the interfaces, IP addresses, and cabling, as shown in Figure 7-2, and the interfaces attached to the DCE ends of the serial cables configured with a clock rate of 64000

➤ IGRP configured on all four routers to advertise network 10.0.0.0 in autonomous system 65000

➤ Known telnet and enable passwords for the routers

➤ A rollover console cable

➤ A laptop or a PC running a terminal emulation program such as Hyperterminal

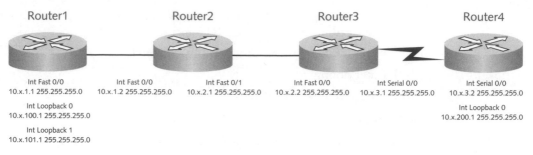

Figure 7-2   Network diagram for Lab 7.3

Estimated completion time: **20 minutes**

Activity Background

Another use of redistribution is for migration between two routing protocols. On today's networks, you may not have the luxury to bring down any part of an autonomous system when making changes. Migrating between two routing protocols requires careful planning and a phased approach. One possible plan is to configure the new routing protocol on one section of the autonomous system at a time, redistributing between the new routing protocol and the old until the next section can be converted.

Converting from IGRP to EIGRP is a relatively simple method. If configured to use the same autonomous system, IGRP and EIGRP automatically redistribute routes. Each routing protocol is proprietary to Cisco, and the metrics for each protocol are nearly identical. The metric for an EIGRP route is equivalent to the IGRP metric multiplied by 256. As a result, conversion between EIGRP and IGRP metrics is simple. However, EIGRP is a classless routing protocol that fully supports VLSM, while IGRP is a classful routing protocol that does not understand VLSM. As a result, IGRP cannot understand all the routes that EIGRP could potentially redistribute. If EIGRP attempts to redistribute such a route into IGRP, IGRP will not add the route to its routing table.

If the two routing protocols use different autonomous system numbers, however, you must manually configure redistribution. This is also true if you need to redistribute routes between the same routing protocol configured with different autonomous system numbers. For instance, you would need to configure redistribution in order for EIGRP in autonomous system 65000 to exchange routes with EIGRP in autonomous system 1.

ACTIVITY

1. Power on the routers and the PC or laptop and open the terminal emulation program.

2. Plug the RJ-45 end of the console cable into the console port of Router1. Attach the other end of the console cable to the serial port on the laptop or PC. You may need to press **Enter** to bring up the Router1> prompt.

3. On Router1, type **enable** and press **Enter**.

4. Type **config term** and press **Enter**.

5. First you will configure EIGRP on this router. Type **router eigrp 65000** and press **Enter**. Now you must configure EIGRP on a neighboring router so that EIGRP will be able to learn routes.

6. Type **network 10.0.0.0** and press **Enter**.

7. Press **Ctl-Z** to exit configuration mode.

8. On Router2, repeat Steps 3 and 4.

9. Type **router eigrp 65000** and press **Enter**.

10. Type **network 10.0.0.0** and press **Enter**.

11. Press **Ctl-Z** to exit configuration mode.

12. Type **show ip protocols** and press **Enter**. The router prints information about each IP routing protocol running on Router2. What protocols are IGRP and EIGRP redistributing?

_____

13. Type **show ip route** and press **Enter**. Which routes were learned from EIGRP?

_____

14. On Router1, repeat the previous step. Which routes were learned from EIGRP?

_____

15. Type **config term** and press **Enter**.

16. Type **no router igrp 65000** and press **Enter**.

17. Press **Ctl-Z** to exit configuration mode.

18. Now you will verify that the network still has end-to-end connectivity. On Router1, type **ping 10.x.200.1** and press **Enter**. The router prints five exclamation points and indicates that the success rate was 100%.

19. On Router4, type **ping 10.x.100.1** and press **Enter**. The router prints five exclamation points and indicates that the success rate was 100%.

20. On Router1, type **show ip route** and press **Enter**. Do you see the same routes that you saw in Step 13?

_____

21. On Router3, repeat Steps 3 and 4.

22. Type **router eigrp 65000** and press **Enter**.

23. Type **network 10.0.0.0** and press **Enter**.

24. Press **Ctl-Z** to exit configuration mode.

25. On Router2, type **config term** and press **Enter**.

26. Type **no router igrp 65000** and press **Enter**.

27. Press **Ctl-Z** to exit configuration mode.

28. Repeat Steps 18 and 19 to confirm that the network still has end-to-end connectivity.

29. On Router4, type **config term** and press **Enter**.

30. Type **router eigrp 65000** and press **Enter**.

31. Type **network 10.0.0.0** and press **Enter**.

32. Press **Ctl-Z** to exit configuration mode.

33. On Router3, type **config term** and press **Enter**.

34. Type **no router igrp 65000** and press **Enter**.

35. Press **Ctl-Z** to exit configuration mode.

36. Repeat Steps 18 and 19 to confirm that the network still has end-to-end connectivity.

37. On Router4, type **config term** and press **Enter**.

38. Type **no router igrp 65000** and press **Enter**.

39. Press **Ctl-Z** to exit configuration mode.

40. Repeat Steps 18 and 19 to confirm that the network still has end-to-end connectivity.

Certification Objectives

Objectives for Cisco Exam 640-603: Routing

➤ Configure route redistribution in a network that *does not* have redundant paths between dissimilar routing processes

➤ Verify route redistribution

➤ Configure redistribution between different routing domains and verify proper operation

Review Questions

1. Which of the following is the best explanation for why IGRP and EIGRP can automatically redistribute routes between each other?

    a. Both protocols are proprietary to Cisco, and they have incompatible metrics.

    b. Both protocols are based on Internet standards, and they have compatible metrics.

c. Both protocols are proprietary to Cisco, and they have compatible metrics.

d. Both protocols are distance vector routing protocols, and they have compatible metrics.

2. The EIGRP routing table on Router1 contains the route 10.172.192.16/29. If Router1 is the border router between EIGRP and IGRP routing domains, what will happen to this route when it is redistributed into IGRP?

a. IGRP will automatically convert it into a classful route.

b. IGRP will convert the subnet mask into the appropriate classful subnet mask.

c. IGRP will not add the route to its routing table.

d. IGRP will discard packets sent to that route.

3. Which of the following commands would you use to determine whether or not a routing protocol is redistributing another routing protocol?

a. show ip route

b. show ip protocols

c. show ip eigrp

d. show ip information

4. Which of the following commands would redistribute routes from IGRP in autonomous system 100 into EIGRP in autonomous system 200?

a. Router(config-router)#redistribute igrp 200 metric 128 100 100 100 1500

b. Router(config-router)#redistribute igrp 100 metric 128 100 100 100 1500

c. Router(config-router)#redistribute igrp

d. None, since redistribution between IGRP and EIGRP is performed by default.

5. Router1 is configured with IGRP in autonomous system 100 and Router2 is configured with EIGRP in autonomous system 100. What would you need to do in order to configure redistribution between the two routing protocols?

a. Nothing, since redistribution occurs automatically between the two routing protocols.

b. Redistribution occurs automatically after you configure them with different autonomous system numbers.

c. Redistribution occurs automatically after you configure EIGRP on Router1 or IGRP on Router2.

d. Redistribution occurs after you configure EIGRP on Router1 or IGRP on Router2, and use the redistribute command.

LAB 7.4 TWO-WAY REDISTRIBUTION BETWEEN OSPF AND EIGRP

Objective

In this lab, you will learn how to perform two-way redistribution between OSPF and EIGRP.

Materials Required

This lab will require the following:

➤ Four Cisco routers with the interfaces, IP addresses, and cabling, as shown in Figure 7-3, and the interfaces attached to the DCE ends of the serial cables configured with a clock rate of 64000

➤ EIGRP configured on Router1 and Router2 to advertise network 10.0.0.0 in autonomous system 65000

➤ OSPF configured on Router3 and Router4 to advertise all interfaces with addresses in 10.0.0.0/8

➤ No access lists configured on either router

➤ Known telnet and enable passwords for the routers

➤ A rollover console cable

➤ A laptop or a PC running a terminal emulation program such as Hyperterminal

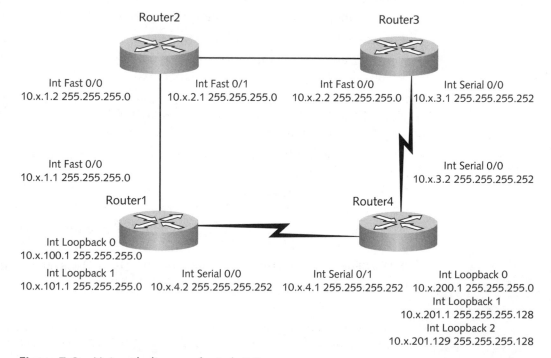

Figure 7-3   Network diagram for Lab 7.5

Estimated completion time: **20 minutes**

Activity Background

Two-way redistribution increases the odds of a routing loop or another problem. It is possible for one routing domain to learn a route from another routing domain, and then redistribute it back to the routing domain that originally advertised it. As redistribution removes the metric and other information used by the protocol to avoid routing loops, a routing domain might use the redistributed route instead of its own route. A routing loop may result.

One technique used to minimize the potential for routing loops is to set a high seed metric. A seed metric is the default metric given to redistributed routes. Redistributed routes with high metrics are not chosen over the original routes if redistributed back into the original routing protocol.

You can configure a default metric with either the **default-metric** command or the **metric** keyword to the **redistribute** command. The **default-metric** command sets a default metric for all redistributed routes. The **metric** keyword to the **redistribute** command, on the other hand, allows you to set a different default metric for multiple redistributed protocols.

Filtering routes is another technique used to prevent routing loops. By filtering the routes you redistribute from one routing protocol to the other, you can both tightly control the routes redistributed, and prevent routes from being reintroduced back into the routing domain where they originated.

When redistributing OSPF routes into another protocol, you have the option of selecting the type of routes to redistribute. You can match internal routes or external routes. This is configured with the **match internal** or **match external** keywords for the redistribute command. You can also match external type 1 or external type 2 routers with the **match external 1** or **match external 2** keywords. The default is to match all OSPF routes.

ACTIVITY

1. Power on the routers and the PC or laptop and open the terminal emulation program.

2. Plug the RJ-45 end of the console cable into the console port of Router1. Attach the other end of the console cable to the serial port on the laptop or PC. You may need to press **Enter** to bring up the Router1> prompt.

3. Type **enable** and press **Enter**. The router prompt changes to Router1#.

4. Type **config term** and press **Enter**. The router prompt changes to Router1(config)#.

5. Now you will configure an access list to filter the routes redistributed into EIGRP. Type **access-list 1 permit 10.*x*.4.0 0.0.0.3** and press **Enter**.

6. Type **access–list 1 permit 10.*x*.200.0 0.0.1.255** and press **Enter**. The implicit denial at the end of the access list prevents other routes from being redistributed.

7. Now you will configure an access list to filter the routes redistributed into OSPF. Type **access–list 2 permit 10.*x*.1.0 0.0.0.255** and press **Enter**.

8. Type **access–list 2 permit 10.*x*.100.0 0.0.1.255** and press **Enter**.

9. Type **router eigrp 65000** and press **Enter**.

10. Type **redistribute ospf 1 match internal** and press **Enter**. This redistributes routes from OSPF process 1 into EIGRP, matching only internal OSPF routes.

11. Type **default-metric 64 100 100 100 1500** and press **Enter**. This sets the default metric for routes redistributed into EIGRP.

12. Type **distribute–list 1 out ospf 1** and press **Enter**. This applies access list 1 as a route filter to OSPF routes redistributed into EIGRP autonomous system 65000.

13. Type **exit** and press **Enter**.

14. Type **router ospf 1** and press **Enter**.

15. Type **network 10.*x*.4.2 0.0.0.0 area 0** and press **Enter**. This activates OSPF on Router1's Serial 0/0 interface.

16. Type **redistribute eigrp 65000 metric 200 subnets** and press **Enter**. This redistributes routes (including subnets) from EIGRP autonomous system 65000 with a high seed metric.

17. Type **distribute–list 2 out eigrp 65000** and press **Enter**. This applies access list 2 as a route filter to EIGRP routes redistributed into OSPF process 1.

18. Press **Ctl–Z** to exit configuration mode.

19. On Router2, type **show ip route** and press **Enter**. Do you see all the routes you expect to see?

_____

20. Type **ping 10.1.3.1** and press **Enter**. The router prints five exclamation points and indicates that the success rate is 100%.

21. Type **trace 10.*x*.3.1** and press **Enter**. The router traces the path to 10.x.3.1.

22. Repeat Steps 20 and 21 with 10.x.100.1.

23. On Router4, type **show ip route** and press **Enter**. Do you see the routes you expect to see?

_____

24. Repeat Steps 20 and 21 with 10.x.1.1.

25. Repeat Steps 20 and 21 with 10.x.201.129.

26. Now you will demonstrate that the route filters are only redistributing the desired routes. On Router4, type **config term** and press **Enter**.

27. Type **int loop 3** and press **Enter**.

28. Type **ip address 172.16.1.1 255.255.255.0** and press **Enter**.

29. Type **exit** and press **Enter**.

30. Type **router ospf 1** and press **Enter**.

31. Type **network 172.16.1.0 0.0.0.255 area 0** and press **Enter**.

32. Press **Ctl-Z** to exit configuration mode.

33. On Router2, type **show ip route** and press **Enter**. Do you see a route for 172.16.1.0/24 in the EIGRP routing domain?

_____

34. Type **config term** and press **Enter**.

35. Type **int loop 0** and press **Enter**.

36. Type **ip address 192.168.154.1 255.255.255.0** and press **Enter**.

37. Type **exit** and press **Enter**.

38. Type **router eigrp 65000** and press **Enter**.

39. Type **network 192.168.154.0** and press **Enter**.

40. On Router 4, type **show ip route**. Do you see a route for 192.168.154.0/24 in Router4's routing table in the OSPF routing domain?

_____

Certification Objectives

Objectives for Cisco Exam 640-603: Routing

➤ Configure route redistribution in a network that *does not* have redundant paths between dissimilar routing processes

➤ Resolve path selection problems that result in a redistributed network

➤ Verify route redistribution

➤ Configure redistribution between different routing domains and verify proper operation

Review Questions

1. Which of the following commands would redistribute only external type 1 routes from OSPF into EIGRP?

    a. Router(config-router)#redistribute ospf 1 metric 500 match external 1

    b. Router(config-router)#redistribute ospf 1 metric 64 255 255 255 1500 match external 1

   c. Router(config-router)#redistribute ospf 1 metric 64 255 255 255 1500 match metric-type 1

   d. Router(config-router)#redistribute ospf 1 metric 64 255 255 255 1500 match external

2. Which of the following commands would set a default metric for all routing protocols redistributed into EIGRP autonomous system 100?

   a. Router(config-router)#redistribute eigrp 100 metric 64 100 100 100 1500

   b. Router(config-router)#default-metric eigrp 64 100 100 100 1500

   c. Router(config-router)#default-metric 64 100 100 100 1500

   d. Router(config-router)#redistribute ospf 1 metric 64 100 100 100 1500

3. You are redistributing EIGRP in autonomous system 100 and RIP into OSPF. Which of the following sets of commands would set a metric of 500 for redistributed EIGRP routes and a metric of 1000 for redistributed RIP routes?

   a. Router(config-router)#default-metric 500 1000

   b. Router(config-router)#redistribute eigrp 100 metric 500
     Router(config-router)#redistribute rip metric 1000

   c. Router(config-router)#redistribute eigrp metric 500 rip metric 1000

   d. Router(config-router)#redistribute eigrp 1 default-metric 500
     Router(config-router)#redistribute rip 1 default-metric 1000

4. What is the potential benefit of using a high seed metric?

   a. prevents incompatible metrics from interfering with redistribution

   b. decreases the administrative distance of the backbone routing protocol

   c. prevents routes originating from one routing protocol from being put in the routing table if they are re-learned by that routing protocol

   d. prevents routes from being learned by the other routing protocol

5. Router1 runs EIGRP in autonomous system 100, and redistributes OSPF routes. Which of the following sets of commands would you use to redistribute routes from OSPF into EIGRP so that only routes that are subnets of 172.20.0.0/18 are redistributed?

   a. Router1(config)#access-list 1 permit 172.20.0.0 0.0.3.255
     Router1(config)#router ospf 1
     Router1(config-router)#redistribute eigrp 100 metric 400
     Router1(config-router)#distribute-list 1 out eigrp

   b. Router1(config)#access-list 1 permit 172.20.0.0 0.0.3.255
     Router1(config)#router eigrp 100
     Router1(config-router)#redistribute ospf 1 metric 64 100 100 100 1500
     Router1(config-router)#distribute-list 1 out ospf

    c. Router1(config)#access-list 1 deny 172.20.0.0 0.0.3.255

       Router1(config)#access-list 1 permit any

       Router1(config)#router ospf 1

       Router1(config-router)#redistribute eigrp 100 metric 400

       Router1(config-router)#distribute-list 1 out eigrp

    d. Router1(config)#access-list 1 deny 172.20.0.0 0.0.3.255

       Router1(config)#access-list 1 permit any

       Router1(config)#router eigrp 100

       Router1(config-router)#redistribute ospf 1 metric 64 100 100 100 1500

       Router1(config-router)#distribute-list 1 out eigrp

7

LAB 7.5 TWO-WAY REDISTRIBUTION BETWEEN OSPF AND EIGRP AT MULTIPLE POINTS

Objective

In this lab, you will learn how to perform two-way redistribution between OSPF and EIGRP at multiple points.

Materials Required

This lab will require the following:

➤ Four Cisco routers with the interfaces, IP addresses, and cabling, as shown in Figure 7-3, and the interfaces attached to the DCE ends of the serial cables configured with a clock rate of 64000

➤ EIGRP configured on Router1 and Router2 to advertise network 10.0.0.0 in autonomous system 65000

➤ OSPF configured on Router3 and Router4 to advertise all interfaces with addresses in 10.0.0.0/8

➤ No access lists configured on either router

➤ Known telnet and enable passwords for the routers

➤ A rollover console cable

➤ A laptop or a PC running a terminal emulation program such as Hyperterminal

Estimated completion time: **20 minutes**

Activity Background

As the complexity of redistribution scenarios increases, the odds of routing loops and other problems also increase. Careful filtering of routing information becomes even more important.

Route maps are another tool that you can use to help avoid routing problems during redistribution. In addition to filtering unwanted routes, you can also use a route map to set metrics. In this way, you can set different metrics for different groups of routes. The **metric** keyword for the **set** command allows you to either set a metric value (such as 200 for OSPF metrics), or increase or decrease the metric (such as −200 or +200). For OSPF, you can also use the **metric-type** keyword for the **set** command to set the type of metric (external type 1 or external type 2).

To filter routes with a route map, you can match them with a **deny** statement in the route map. The routes matched will not be processed further by the route map, and will not be redistributed. Alternately, if the routes are not matched by one of the statements in the route map, they will be denied by the implicit denial at the end of the route map. If you do not wish routes otherwise unmatched by statements in a route map to be filtered, you should implicitly match them with the final statement in the route map.

ACTIVITY

1. Power on the routers and the PC or laptop and open the terminal emulation program.

2. Plug the RJ-45 end of the console cable into the console port of Router3. Attach the other end of the console cable to the serial port on the laptop or PC. You may need to press **Enter** to bring up the Router3> prompt.

3. Type **enable** and press **Enter**. The router prompt changes to Router3#.

4. Type **config term** and press **Enter**. The router prompt changes to Router3(config)#.

5. Now you will configure a route map to filter and set metrics for routes redistributed into OSPF. You start by creating two access lists to match routes to be redistributed into OSPF. Type **access-list 1 permit 10.*x*.1.0 0.0.0.255** and press **Enter**.

6. Type **access-list 2 permit 10.*x*.100.0 0.0.1.255** and press **Enter**.

7. Type **route-map OSPF permit 5** and press **Enter**. The router prompt changes to Router3(config-route-map)#.

8. Type **match ip address 1** and press **Enter**. This matches the 10.x.1.0/24 route specified by access list 1.

9. Type **set metric 500** and press **Enter**. This sets the OSPF metric to 500.

10. Type **set metric-type type-1** and press **Enter**. This configures the router to redistribute this route as an external type 2 route.

11. Type **route-map OSPF permit 10** and press **Enter**.

12. Type **match ip address 2** and press **Enter**. This matches any route matched by access list 2.

13. Type **set metric 1000** and press **Enter**. This configures the metric on routes matched by access list 1 to be 1000, 500 higher than the metric you configured in Step 9.

14. Type **set metric-type type-1** and press **Enter**.

15. Type **exit** and press **Enter**. All other routes will be denied because of the implicit denial at the end of the route map, and will not be redistributed.

16. Now you will create a similar route map for EIGRP, beginning with the access lists to match routes to be redistributed into EIGRP. Type **access-list 3 permit 10.x.3.0 0.0.0.3** and press **Enter**.

17. Type **access-list 4 permit 10.x.200.0 0.0.1.255** and press **Enter**.

18. Type **route-map EIGRP permit 5** and press **Enter**.

19. Type **match ip address 3** and press **Enter**.

20. Type **set metric 128 100 100 100 1500** and press **Enter**.

21. Type **route-map EIGRP permit 10** and press **Enter**.

22. Type **match ip address 4** and press **Enter**.

23. Type **set metric 64 100 100 100 1500** and press **Enter**.

24. Type **exit** and press **Enter**.

25. Type **router eigrp 65000** and press **Enter**.

26. Type **network 10.0.0.0** and press **Enter**.

27. Type **passive-interface serial 0/0** and press **Enter**.

28. Type **redistribute ospf 1 route-map EIGRP** and press **Enter**.

29. Type **exit** and press **Enter**.

30. Type **router ospf 1** and press **Enter**.

31. Type **redistribute eigrp 65000 route-map OSPF subnets** and press **Enter**.

32. Press **Ctl-Z** to exit configuration mode.

33. Type **show ip protocols** and press **Enter**. The router prints information about the IP routing protocols on the router. Note that it does not print any information about the route map you applied to the redistributed routes.

7

34. Type **show running-config** and press **Enter**. Press the **space bar** until the router's complete configuration appears. This command is the only way to see that the route map has been applied to redistributed routes.

35. Repeat Steps 3 through 29 on Router1.

36. Type **router ospf 1** and press **Enter**.

37. Type **network 10.*x*.4.2 0.0.0.0 area 0** and press **Enter**.

38. Type **redistribute eigrp 65000 route-map OSPF subnets** and press **Enter**.

39. Press **Ctl-Z** to exit configuration mode.

40. On Router4, type **show ip route** and press **Enter**. According to the routing table, what type of routes are 10.x.1.0/24, 10.x.100.0/24, and 10.x.101.0/24? Is the value of the metric for routes 10.x.100.0/24 and 10.x.101.0/24 500 higher than the metric of route 10.x.1.0/24?

41. Type **ping 10.*x*.1.1** and press **Enter**. The router prints five exclamation points and indicates that the success rate is 100%.

42. Type **trace 10.*x*.1.1** and press **Enter**. The router traces the path to 10.x.1.1.

43. Repeat Steps 41 and 42 with 10.x.100.1.

44. On Router2, type **show ip route** and press **Enter**. How do the metrics for the routes to 10.x.3.0/30, 10.x.200.0/24, 10.x.201.0/25, and 10.x.201.129/25 compare?

45. Repeat Steps 41 and 42 for 10.x.3.1.

46. Repeat Steps 41 and 42 for 10.x.201.129.

47. Now you will demonstrate that the route filters are only redistributing the desired routes. On Router4, type **config term** and press **Enter**.

48. Type **int loop 3** and press **Enter**.

49. Type **ip address 172.16.1.1 255.255.255.0** and press **Enter**.

50. Type **exit** and press **Enter**.

51. Type **router ospf 1** and press **Enter**.

52. Type **network 172.16.1.0 0.0.0.255 area 0** and press **Enter**.

53. Press **Ctl-Z** to exit configuration mode.

54. On Router2, type **show ip route** and press **Enter**. Do you see a route for 172.16.1.0/24 in the EIGRP routing domain?

Certification Objectives

Objectives for Cisco Exam 640-603: Routing

➤ Configure route redistribution in a network that *has* redundant paths between dissimilar routing processes

➤ Resolve path selection problems that result in a redistributed network

➤ Verify route redistribution

➤ Configure redistribution between different routing domains and verify proper operation

Review Questions

1. What is the potential advantage of using a route map during redistribution?

   a. Route maps work just like access lists, but are easier to configure.

   b. Route maps allow you to change routes based on the source address or other characteristics of packets.

   c. Route maps allow you to filter routes and set metrics for individual groups of redistributed routes.

   d. Route maps allow you to filter routes more efficiently than route filters.

2. Which of the following sets of commands would redistribute OSPF into EIGRP and apply a route map named RedistributeOSPF?

   a. Router(config-router)#redistribute ospf 1 route-map RedistibuteOSPF

   b. Router(config-router)#redistribute ospf 1
      Router(config-router)#route-map RedistributeOSPF

   c. Router(config-router)#redistribute ospf 1 route-map out RedistributeOSPF

   d. Router(config-router)#redistribute ospf 1
      Router(config-router)#route-map out RedistributeOSPF

3. Which command can you use to see that a route map has been applied to redistributed routes?

   a. show ip protocols

   b. show ip eigrp

   c. show ip ospf

   d. show running-config

4. You are redistributing EIGRP in autonomous system 100 into OSPF. Which of the following route maps would (when applied during redistribution) give routes matched by access list 1 a metric of 200, filter routes matched by access list 2, and allow all other routes to be redistributed with a metric of 500?

   a. Router(config)#route-map Redistribute deny 5
      Router(config-route-map)#match ip address 1

Router(config-route-map)#no redistribute eigrp 100

Router(config-route-map)#route-map Redistribute permit 10

Router(config-route-map)#match ip address 2

Router(config-route-map)#set metric 200

Router(config-route-map)#route-map Redistribute permit 15

Router(config-route-map)#set metric 500

b. Router(config)#route-map Redistribute deny 5

Router(config-route-map)#match ip address 1

Router(config-route-map)#route-map Redistribute permit 10

Router(config-route-map)#match ip address 2

Router(config-route-map)#set metric 200

Router(config-route-map)#set metric 500

c. Router(config)#route-map Redistribute deny 5

Router(config-route-map)#match ip address 1

Router(config-route-map)#route-map Redistribute permit 10

Router(config-route-map)#match ip address 2

Router(config-route-map)#set metric 200

d. Router(config)#route-map Redistribute deny 5

Router(config-route-map)#match ip address 1

Router(config-route-map)#route-map Redistribute permit 10

Router(config-route-map)#match ip address 2

Router(config-route-map)#set metric 200

Router(config-route-map)#route-map Redistribute permit 15

Router(config-route-map)#set metric 500

5. You are redistributing OSPF into EIGRP autonomous system 100. Which of the following route maps would (when applied during redistribution) allow redistribution for routes matched by access list 1 without specifically setting a metric, apply a metric to routes matched by access list 2, and deny all other routes?

a. Router(config)#route-map Redistribute deny 5

Router(config-route-map)#match ip address 1

Router(config-route-map)#route-map Redistribute permit 10

Router(config-route-map)#match ip address 2

Router(config-route-map)#set metric 64 100 100 100 1500

Router(config-route-map)#route-map Redistribute permit 15

b. Router(config)#route-map Redistribute deny 5

Router(config-route-map)#match ip address 1

Router(config-route-map)#route-map Redistribute permit 10
Router(config-route-map)#match ip address 2
Router(config-route-map)#set metric 64 100 100 100 1500
Router(config-route-map)#route-map Redistribute deny 15
Router(config-route-map)#match ip address any

c. Router(config)#route-map Redistribute deny 5
Router(config-route-map)#match ip address 1
Router(config-route-map)#route-map Redistribute permit 10
Router(config-route-map)#match ip address 2
Router(config-route-map)#set metric 64 100 100 100 1500
Router(config-route-map)#route-map Redistribute deny 15

d. Router(config)#route-map Redistribute permit 5
Router(config-route-map)#match ip address 1
Router(config-route-map)#route-map Redistribute permit 10
Router(config-route-map)#match ip address 2
Router(config-route-map)#set metric 64 100 100 100 1500
Router(config-route-map)#route-map Redistribute deny 15
Router(config-route-map)#set deny all

7

CONFIGURING AND TROUBLESHOOTING BGP

Labs included in this chapter

➤ Lab 8.1 Configuring BGP

➤ Lab 8.2 Synchronization and IBGP

➤ Lab 8.3 Configuring Route Summarization in BGP

➤ Lab 8.4 Using Default Routes to Avoid BGP

➤ Lab 8.5 Configuring Other BGP Parameters

Cisco CCNP Exam #640-603 Objectives	
Objective	Lab
Describe BGP features and operation	8.1, 8.2, 8.3, 8.4, 8.5
Describe how to connect to another autonomous system using an alternative to BGP, static routes	8.4
Explain how BGP policy-based routing functions within an autonomous system	8.1
Explain how BGP peering functions	8.1
Describe BGP communities and peer groups	8.1
Describe and configure external and internal BGP	8.1, 8.2, 8.3, 8.4, 8.5
Describe BGP synchronization	8.2
Configure a BGP environment and verify proper operation	8.1, 8.2, 8.3, 8.5

LAB 8.1 CONFIGURING BGP

Objective

In this lab, you will learn how to configure BGP and describe its features and operations.

Materials Required

This lab will require the following:

➤ Three Cisco routers with the interfaces, IP addresses, and cabling, as shown in Figure 8-1, and the interfaces attached to the DCE ends of the serial cables configured with a clock rate of 64000

➤ No routing protocol configured on any of the routers

➤ Known telnet and enable passwords for the routers

➤ A rollover console cable

➤ A laptop or a PC running a terminal emulation program such as Hyperterminal

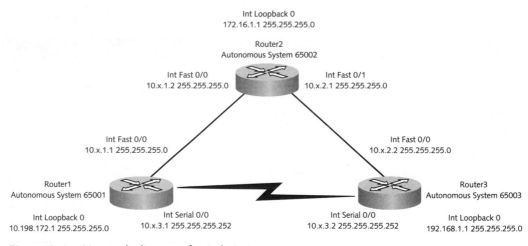

Figure 8-1   Network diagram for Lab 8-1

Estimated completion time: **20 minutes**

Activity Background

Previously, you learned about routing protocols designed for use within an autonomous system, or interior gateway protocols (IGP). Border Gateway Protocol (BGP), however, is an exterior gateway protocol (EGP), intended to connect different autonomous systems together at multiple points. BGP is also used to control policy over packets sent through, from, or to an autonomous system.

BGP is based on a distance vector routing protocol. However, instead of using the hop count to prevent routing loops, BGP routers look at the autonomous system (AS) path. If an AS appears more than once in an AS path, the router assumes the route is a loop.

Because BGP neighbors are often in different autonomous systems controlled by different organizations, BGP has no mechanism for dynamic discovery of neighbors. As a result, each neighbor (or peer) must be configured manually. When configuring BGP peers on a router, you must also configure the AS number of each peer.

In order to communicate, BGP peers use TCP port 179. If two peers cannot make a TCP connection, they cannot become neighbors. While this may seem obvious, you may sometimes need to manually configure a route between two peers so that they can communicate. BGP routers send several types of messages, including open messages to initiate BGP sessions, keepalive messages to verify that a session is still alive, update messages to withdraw or announce routes advertised, and notification messages to announce an error.

BGP peer relationships start out in the Idle state. When attempting to establish a TCP connection with a peer, the router enters either the Active or Connect state. Typically, a router with a peer relationship that transitions from the Active to Connect state is having difficulty establishing a TCP connection with its peer. After sending an open message, a BGP router enters the OpenSent state and waits for an open message from the peer. If it receives it, it goes to the OpenConfirm state. In this state, the router waits for a keepalive message from the other router. If it receives it, it enters the Established state and the peer relationship begins. At nearly any point along the way, if the router encounters an error, it sends a notification message to its peer and goes back into the Idle state. BGP peers do not exchange update messages unless they are in the Established state.

In order to allow network administrators to use BGP for policy routing, BGP routers send a great deal of information about a route in their updates. In addition to the prefix of the route and its length, which allow BGP to fully support Classless Interdomain Routing (CIDR), BGP sends a variety of path attributes, which further describe a route. These attributes may be well-known (recognized by all BGP implementations), or optional (not required to be recognized by all BGP implementations). They may also be mandatory or discretionary (which determines whether or not they are required), or they may be transitive or non-transitive (which determines whether or not a router will pass along an unused attribute). Some of the well-known mandatory attributes that are used to describe all routes used by BGP include the AS path, the next hop, and the origin. The local preference, used by a router to determine the exit to an AS, is a well-known discretionary attribute, while the multi-exit discriminator (sometimes called the BGP metric) is an optional, non-transitive attribute used to influence the path into an AS. The community attribute, used to select groups of routes for filtering or other processing, is an example of a optional transitive attribute. Path attribute information is stored in the router's BGP table.

When configuring BGP, you should keep in mind that routes are not automatically added to BGP. You must configure them manually with the **network** command. In order for a route to be advertised by BGP, it must already exist in the router's routing table. If a route has not been learned through some other source (such as a dynamic routing protocol, a static route, or a connected route), then the router will not advertise the route through BGP. Finally, if you do not specify a subnet mask when configuring a route, BGP will use the classful network mask. If this is not the desired mask, you should manually configure the mask with the **mask** keyword. For instance, to configure a router to advertise the 172.30.16.0/20 network, you would use the **network 172.30.16.0 mask 255.255.240.0** command in router configuration mode. The network and subnet mask configured must exactly match the route in the router's routing table. The command given above would not match 172.30.16.0/24, and the route would not be advertised by BGP.

ACTIVITY

1. Power on the routers and the PC or laptop and open the terminal emulation program.

2. Plug the RJ-45 end of the console cable into the console port of Router1. Attach the other end of the console cable to the serial port on the laptop or PC. You may need to press **Enter** to bring up the Router1> prompt.

3. Type **enable** and press **Enter**. The router prompt changes to Router1#.

4. Type **config term** and press **Enter**.

5. Type **router bgp 65001** and press **Enter**.

6. Type **neighbor 10.x.1.2 remote-as 65002** and press **Enter**. This configures Router2 as an EBGP peer.

7. Type **neighbor 10.x.3.2 remote-as 65003** and press **Enter**. This configures Router3 as an EBGP peer.

8. Type **network 10.198.172.0 mask 255.255.255.0** and press **Enter**.

9. Type **network 10.x.1.0 mask 255.255.255.0** and press **Enter**. This is necessary because while Router1 and Router2 already have this route in their routing tables, Router3 does not, and therefore must learn it through BGP.

10. Press **Ctl-Z** to exit configuration mode.

11. Type **show ip bgp neighbors** and press **Enter**. The router prints information about Router1's BGP neighbors. Router2 and Router3 are in either the Active or Idle state, and the number of connections established is zero.

12. On Router2, type **ping 10.198.172.1** and press **Enter**. The router prints five dots and indicates that the success rate was 0%.

13. Repeat Steps 3 and 4.

14. Type **router bgp 65002** and press **Enter**.

15. Type **neighbor 10.x.1.1 remote-as 65001** and press **Enter**.

16. Type **neighbor 10.x.2.2 remote-as 65003** and press **Enter**.

17. Type **network 172.16.1.0 mask 255.255.255.0** and press **Enter**.

18. Type **network 10.x.2.0 mask 255.255.255.0** and press **Enter**.

19. Press **Ctl-Z** to exit configuration mode.

20. Type **show ip bgp neighbors** and press **Enter**. Router1 should now be in the Established state, and Router3 in the Active state. If Router1 is not in the Established state, wait 30 seconds and repeat this step until it is.

21. Type **show ip route** and press **Enter**. The route to 10.198.172.0/24 appears in the routing table.

22. Type **ping 10.198.172.1** and press **Enter**. The router prints five exclamation points and indicates that the success rate was 100%.

23. Type **show ip bgp** and press **Enter**. The router prints information about the BGP process running on Router2, including the routes it knows about from BGP, and information about them (including path attributes).

24. On Router3, repeat Steps 3 and 4.

25. Type **router bgp 65003** and press **Enter**.

26. Type **neighbor 10.x.2.1 remote-as 65002** and press **Enter**. The IP address of Router2's Fast Ethernet 0/1 interface is used because it is on a connected interface and Router3 already has a route to it.

27. Type **neighbor 10.x.3.1 remote-as 65001** and press **Enter**.

28. Type **network 192.168.1.0 mask 255.255.255.0** and press **Enter**.

29. Type **network 10.x.3.0 mask 255.255.255.252** and press **Enter**.

30. Press **Ctl-Z** to exit configuration mode.

31. Type **show ip bgp neighbors** and press **Enter**. Both neighbors should be in the Established state. If this is not true, wait 30 seconds and repeat this step until it is true.

32. Type **show ip bgp** and press **Enter**. The router prints detailed information about the BGP process running on this router.

33. Type **show ip bgp 10.198.172.0** and press **Enter**. The router prints information about the 10.198.172.0/24 route in the router's BGP table, including the possible AS paths, the best AS path, and the local preference.

34. Now you will attempt to add a route that does not exist in the routing table. Type **config term** and press **Enter**.

35. Type **router bgp 65003** and press **Enter**.

36. Type **network 192.168.254.0 mask 255.255.255.0** and press **Enter**.

37. Press **Ctl-Z** to exit configuration mode.

38. Type **show ip bgp 192.168.254.0** and press **Enter**. The router prints that the network is not in the table.

8

39. Type **config term** and press **Enter**.

40. Type **int loop 1** and press **Enter**.

41. Type **ip address 192.168.254.1 255.255.255.0** and press **Enter**.

42. Press **Ctl–Z** to exit configuration mode.

43. Type **show ip bgp 192.168.254.0** and press **Enter**. The router prints detailed information about the route.

44. Type **debug ip bgp** and press **Enter**.

45. Type **clear ip bgp *** and press **Enter**. This clears and resets Router3's BGP connections with each of its neighbors. (Do this only if absolutely necessary, since this significantly impacts routing on any network using BGP.) Debugging output appears, showing the states as each neighbor forms a new peer relationship with Router3.

46. Type **undebug all** and press **Enter**.

Certification Objectives

Objectives for Cisco Exam 640-603: Routing

➤ Describe BGP features and operation

➤ Explain how BGP policy-based routing functions within an autonomous system

➤ Explain how BGP peering functions

➤ Describe BGP communities and peer groups

➤ Describe and configure external and internal BGP

➤ Configure a BGP environment and verify proper operation

Review Questions

1. Which of the following commands would configure 10.198.14.1 in AS 65535 as a BGP peer?

    a. Router(config-router)#neighbor 10.198.14.1 bgp-peer 65535

    b. Router(config-router)#neighbor 10.198.14.1 remote-as 65535

    c. Router(config-router)#neighbor 10.198.14.1 65535

    d. Router(config-router)#neighbor 10.198.14.1 as 65535

2. In which state can two BGP peers exchange update messages?

    a. Idle

    b. Active

    c. OpenConfirm

    d. Established

3. Which of the following commands will print information about BGP routes, including path attributes?

   a. show ip bgp route

   b. debug ip bgp

   c. show ip bgp

   d. show ip route bgp

4. How do BGP routers determine whether or not a path is likely to be a routing loop?

   a. Routes with increasing hop counts are likely to be routing loops.

   b. Routes with increasing metrics are likely to be routing loops.

   c. Routes with AS paths that include the same AS more than once are likely to be routing loops.

   d. Routes with AS paths that include the same router more than once are likely to be routing loops.

5. You configured a route to be advertised by BGP, but the router's peers (all in the Established state) did not receive the message in an update. What are possible reasons for this? (Choose all that apply.)

   a. The route did not exist in the router's routing table prior to being advertised.

   b. The route is in the router's routing table but is not reachable.

   c. The router was unable to begin a BGP session with its peers.

   d. The network number and subnet mask configured did not match the route in the routing table.

LAB 8.2 SYNCHRONIZATION AND IBGP

Objective

In this lab, you will learn how to configure IBGP and describe its features and operations.

Materials Required

This lab will require the following:

➤ Three Cisco routers with the interfaces, IP addresses, and cabling, as shown in Figure 8-2, and the interfaces attached to the DCE ends of the serial cables configured with a clock rate of 64000

➤ No routing protocol configured on any of the routers

➤ Known telnet and enable passwords for the routers

➤ A rollover console cable

➤ A laptop or a PC running a terminal emulation program such as Hyperterminal

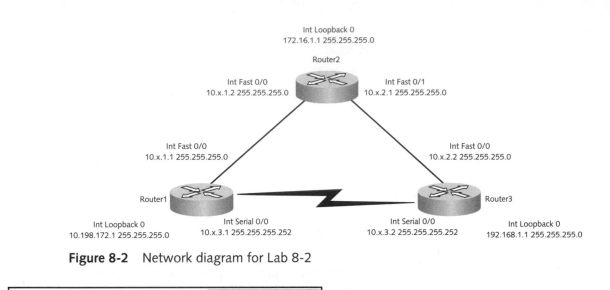

Figure 8-2   Network diagram for Lab 8-2

Estimated completion time: **20 minutes**

Activity Background

You may configure two different types of BGP peer relationships. These are External BGP (EBGP), which you configured in Lab 8.1, and Internal BGP (IBGP). The AS numbers configured on a router determine whether or not a peer is an IBGP peer or an EBGP peer. If the AS number configured matches the router's own AS number, then the peer is an IBGP peer. Otherwise, it is an EBGP peer.

While in most ways IBGP peer relationships are similar to EBGP peer relationships, one important difference is synchronization. Synchronization helps determine whether or not an IBGP peer will exchange a route with its IBGP peers. If an IBGP peer learns a route from another IBGP peer, it will not add that route to its routing table or advertise it until it appears from another source, such as a dynamic routing protocol. An IBGP peer will, however, use and advertise the routes it receives from its EBGP peers.

Synchronization is intended to prevent black holes. If a router running IBGP learns of a route that has not been propagated by the IGP running in the autonomous system, the router may not be able to reach that destination yet. For instance, the next hop router may not be an IBGP peer, and will not have a route to the destination network. If the IBGP peer advertised this route to either external or internal BGP peers, then it would be advertising a route to a destination it could not reach. Unreachable routes are known as black hole routes.

You can disable synchronization by running the **no synchronization** command in router configuration mode. You may safely disable synchronization if traffic from other autonomous systems does not pass through your AS, if all the routers in the autonomous system are running BGP, or if all of the routers in the transit path through your AS are running BGP. An Internet Service Provider, for instance, might run IBGP on all of the routers in its transit path, and would therefore disable synchronization. Synchronization is typically on by default.

ACTIVITY

1. Power on the routers and the PC or laptop and open the terminal emulation program.

2. Plug the RJ-45 end of the console cable into the console port of Router1. Attach the other end of the console cable to the serial port on the laptop or PC. You may need to press **Enter** to bring up the Router1> prompt.

3. Type **enable** and press **Enter**. The router prompt changes to Router1#.

4. Type **config term** and press **Enter**. The router prompt changes to Router1(config)#.

5. Type **router bgp 65000** and press **Enter**.

6. Type **neighbor 10.*x*.1.2 remote-as 65000** and press **Enter**. Since the AS configured on this router and for neighbor 10.x.1.2 match, this command configures Router2 as an IBGP peer.

7. Type **neighbor 10.*x*.3.2 remote-as 65000** and press **Enter**.

8. Type **network 10.198.172.0 mask 255.255.255.0** and press **Enter**.

9. Type **network 10.*x*.1.0 mask 255.255.255.0** and press **Enter**.

10. Press **Ctl-Z** to exit configuration mode.

11. Repeat Steps 3 and 4 on Router2.

12. Type **router bgp 65000** and press **Enter**.

13. Type **neighbor 10.*x*.1.1 remote-as 65000** and press **Enter**.

14. Type **neighbor 10.*x*.2.2 remote-as 65000** and press **Enter**.

15. Type **network 172.16.1.0 mask 255.255.255.0** and press **Enter**.

16. Type **network 10.*x*.2.0 mask 255.255.255.0** and press **Enter**.

17. Press **Ctl-Z** to exit configuration mode.

18. Repeat Steps 3 and 4 on Router3.

19. Type **router bgp 65000** and press **Enter**.

20. Type **neighbor 10.*x*.3.1 remote-as 65000** and press **Enter**.

21. Type **neighbor 10.*x*.2.1 remote-as 65000** and press **Enter**.

22. Type **network 192.168.1.0 mask 255.255.255.0** and press **Enter**.

23. Type **network 10.*x*.3.0 mask 255.255.255.252** and press **Enter**.

24. Press **Ctl-Z** to exit configuration mode.

25. Type **show ip bgp neighbors** and press **Enter**. Both Router1 and Router2 should be in the Established state. If they are not, wait 30 seconds and repeat this step until they are.

26. Type **show ip bgp** and press **Enter**. The router prints information about the BGP process running on this router, and the routes learned through BGP. Which routes were learned through IBGP?

_____

27. Type **show ip route** and press **Enter**. Which routes that you saw in the previous steps are missing from Router3's routing table?

_____

28. Type **config term** and press **Enter**.

29. Type **router bgp 65000** and press **Enter**.

30. Type **no synchronization** and press **Enter**.

31. Press **Ctl-Z** to exit configuration mode.

32. Type **show ip route** and press **Enter**. The routing table now contains routes learned through IBGP. If not, wait 30 seconds and repeat this step until it does.

33. Repeat Steps 28 through 32 on Router1 and Router2.

Certification Objectives

Objectives for Cisco Exam 640-603: Routing

➤ Describe BGP features and operation

➤ Describe and configure external and internal BGP

➤ Describe BGP synchronization

➤ Configure a BGP environment and verify proper operation

Review Questions

1. A router running IBGP learns a route from one of its IBGP peers. If synchronization is enabled, what must be true before the router can advertise this route?

   a. The router must be running both IBGP and EBGP.

   b. The route must already be in the router's routing table from another source.

   c. The router must have also learned the route from a dynamic routing protocol.

   d. The route must also be a static route in the router's routing table.

2. Which of the following commands would disable synchronization on a router?

   a. Router(config-router)#no synchronization

   b. Router(config-router)#no bgp synchronization

    c. Router(config-router)#synchronization off

    d. Router(config-router)#no ibgp-synchronization

3. How does a router determine whether a particular BGP session is IBGP or EBGP?

    a. by looking for the neighbor ibgp command

    b. by comparing the AS number of the router with the AS number of the peer

    c. by comparing the AS number of the router with the AS number of all peers

    d. by comparing the AS number of the IGP running on the router with the AS number of the peer

4. Under which of the following circumstances can you safely disable synchronization? (Choose all that apply.)

    a. All routers in the AS run IBGP.

    b. All routers in the transit path run IBGP.

    c. Other autonomous systems do not send traffic through your AS.

    d. All routers in your AS run the same IGP.

5. What is the potential benefit of synchronization?

    a. It prevents IBGP routers from advertising routes they cannot reach.

    b. It keeps the routing table of routers running IBGP synchronized.

    c. It prevents EBGP routers from advertising routes they cannot reach.

    d. It speeds up BGP updates.

LAB 8.3 CONFIGURING ROUTE SUMMARIZATION AND BGP

Objective

In this lab, you will learn how to configure route summarization in BGP.

Materials Required

This lab will require the following:

➤ Three Cisco routers with the interfaces, IP addresses, and cabling, as shown in Figure 8-3, and the interfaces attached to the DCE ends of the serial cables configured with a clock rate of 64000

➤ No routing protocol configured on any of the routers

➤ Known telnet and enable passwords for the routers

➤ A rollover console cable

➤ A laptop or a PC running a terminal emulation program such as Hyperterminal

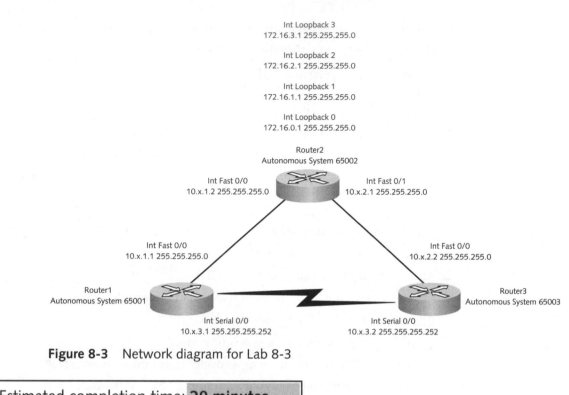

Figure 8-3   Network diagram for Lab 8-3

Estimated completion time: **20 minutes**

Activity Background

BGP fully supports VLSM and CIDR. For each route, BGP sends both the prefix and the length of the prefix. For instance, for a route to the172.21.32.0 network with a subnet mask of 255.255.240.0, BGP would include the prefix (172.21.32.0) and its length (20 bits).

Similar to the way that a route must already be in a router's routing table before it can be advertised by BGP, at least some of the routes summarized in an aggregate address in BGP must be in the router's BGP table. If these routes are not advertised by BGP or learned through BGP, then you will be unable to summarize them. The command used to summarize routes in BGP is **aggregate-address *ip-address subnet-mask***. By default, Cisco routers will advertise both the aggregate address and the individual routes that were summarized. However, you can configure Cisco routers to only advertise the aggregate address with the **summary-only** keyword.

You may also summarize routes from within different autonomous systems. By default, a router will indicate that the aggregate address came from your autonomous system. It will set the atomic aggregate path attribute in order to indicate that this is a summarized route, and that the AS path may be incomplete. However, you may also use the **as-set** keyword. This includes the entire set of AS numbers of the routes summarized by your aggregate address in BGP updates. You may use both the **summary-only** and the **as-set** keywords together.

You should always be very careful to advertise only networks that you can reach. A typo when configuring an aggregate address might lead you to advertise summarized routes that do not belong to you. On the Internet, this may result in black hole routes, with many people unable to reach hosts on these networks.

BGP's support of CIDR allows you to aggregate routes, as needed. Because of the large size of the Internet BGP routing table, route summarization is encouraged as much as possible. One factor that reduces the amount of route summarization on the Internet is multihoming, or having multiple connections to the Internet. You will learn more about multihoming in Chapter 9.

ACTIVITY

1. Power on the routers and the PC or laptop and open the terminal emulation program.

2. Plug the RJ-45 end of the console cable into the console port of Router1. Attach the other end of the console cable to the serial port on the laptop or PC. You may need to press **Enter** to bring up the Router1> prompt.

3. Type **enable** and press **Enter**. The router prompt changes to Router1#.

4. Type **config term** and press **Enter**. The router prompt changes to Router1(config)#.

5. Type **router bgp 65001** and press **Enter**.

6. Type **neighbor 10.x.1.2 remote-as 65002** and press **Enter**.

7. Press **Ctl-Z** to exit configuration mode.

8. Repeat Steps 3 and 4 on Router2.

9. Type **router bgp 65002** and press **Enter**.

10. Type **neighbor 10.x.1.1 remote-as 65001** and press **Enter**.

11. Type **aggregate-address 172.16.0.0 255.255.252.0** and press **Enter**. The aggregate address and subnet mask will summarize the routes on Router2's loopback interfaces.

12. Press **Ctl-Z** to exit configuration mode.

13. Type **show ip bgp neighbors** and press **Enter**. Router1 should be in the Established state. If not, wait 30 seconds and repeat this step until it does.

14. Type **show ip bgp** and press **Enter**. The Router2# prompt returns without printing any information. No routes are advertised through BGP.

15. On Router1, type **show ip route** and press **Enter**. Does the routing table contain the aggregate address you configured in Step 11, or any routes learned through BGP?

16. On Router1, type **show running-config** and press **Enter**. Do you see the aggregate address you configured in Step 11?

_____

17. Now you will add routes for each of Router2's loopback interfaces into the BGP routing table. On Router2, type **config term** and press **Enter**.

18. Type **router bgp 65002** and press **Enter**.

19. Type **network 172.16.0.0 mask 255.255.255.0** and press **Enter**.

20. Repeat the previous step with the networks 172.16.1.0, 172.16.2.0, and 172.16.3.0. Use the same subnet mask each time.

21. Type **aggregate-address 172.16.0.0 255.255.252.0** and press **Enter**.

22. Press **Ctl-Z** to exit configuration mode.

23. Type **clear ip bgp 65001** and press **Enter**. This resets Router2's BGP session with Router1.

24. Type **show ip bgp neighbor** and press **Enter**. Router1 should be in the Established state. If not, wait 30 seconds and repeat this step until it is.

25. On Router1, type **show ip route** and press **Enter**. Which routes do you see that are advertised by BGP?

_____

26. Type **show ip bgp** and press **Enter**. How many routes that you saw in the previous step are advertised by BGP?

_____

27. Now you will configure the aggregate address on Router2 so that it advertises only the aggregate address. Type **config term** and press **Enter**.

28. Type **router bgp 65002** and press **Enter**.

29. Type **aggregate-address 172.16.0.0 255.255.252.0 summary-only as-set** and press **Enter**. This command configures the router to advertise only the summarized route, and to include AS information for each route included within the aggregate.

30. Press **Ctl-Z** to exit configuration mode.

31. Type **clear ip bgp 65001** and press **Enter**.

32. Type **show ip bgp neighbor** and press **Enter**. Router1 should be in the Established state. If not, wait 30 seconds and repeat this step until it is.

33. On Router1, type **show ip route** and press **Enter**. How many of the routes that you saw in Step 25 are in Router1's routing table now?

_____

34. Type **show ip bgp** and press **Enter**. You see the aggregate address advertised by BGP, and none of the individual routes.

Certification Objectives

Objectives for Cisco Exam 640-603: Routing

➤ Describe BGP features and operation

➤ Describe and configure external and internal BGP

➤ Configure a BGP environment and verify proper operation

Review Questions

1. Which of the following must be true before a route can be aggregated in BGP?

   a. At least some of the routes summarized must already have been learned from an IGP, BGP, or another source.

   b. At least some of the routes summarized must already have been learned or advertised by BGP.

   c. All the routes summarized must already have been learned or advertised by BGP.

   d. BGP places no restrictions on the routes you can aggregate.

2. Which of the following commands would summarize the routes 172.16.0.0/16, 172.17.0.0/16, 172.18.0.0/16, and 172.19.0.0/16, and advertise both the aggregate address and the individual routes?

   a. Router(config-router)#aggregate-address 172.16.0.0 255.252.0.0 no-summary

   b. Router(config-router)#aggregate-address 172.16.0.0 255.252.0.0 summary-only

   c. Router(config-router)#aggregate-address 172.16.0.0 255.252.0.0

   d. Router(config-router)#bgp aggregate-address 172.16.0.0 255.252.0.0

3. What effect does the as-set keyword have when configuring an aggregate address in BGP?

   a. It prevents the advertisement of the individual routes summarized.

   b. It removes all AS path information about the individual routes summarized.

   c. It includes the autonomous systems of each individual route summarized in the AS path information.

   d. It configures the router to advertise the aggregate address as an individual route originating with itself.

8

4. What is the possible effect of advertising a summary route that includes routes that do not belong to your autonomous system?

a. It reduces the size of the Internet BGP routing table.

b. It may create a black hole route.

c. It increases the number of paths to these destinations.

d. It prevents other routes from summarizing those routes.

5. Which of the following commands would configure a router to advertise an aggregate address for 10.172.0.0/21, without advertising any of the individual routes, while including the AS of each of the individual routes in the updates?

a. Router(config-router)#aggregate-address 10.172.0.0 255.255.248.0

b. Router(config-router)#aggregate-address 10.172.0.0 255.255.248.0 summary-only

c. Router(config-router)#aggregate-address 10.172.0.0 255.255.248.0 summary-only as-path full

d. Router(config-router)#aggregate-address 10.172.0.0 255.255.248.0 summary-only as-set

LAB 8.4 USING DEFAULT ROUTES TO AVOID BGP

Objective

In this lab, you will learn how to avoid using BGP through the use of static and default routes.

Materials Required

This lab will require the following:

➤ Four Cisco routers with the interfaces, IP addresses, and cabling, as shown in Figure 8-4, with the interfaces attached to the DCE ends of the serial cables configured with a clock rate of 64000

➤ OSPF with process number 1 configured with all interfaces in Area 0 on Router1 and Router4

➤ EIGRP in autonomous system 65000 configured to advertise network 10.0.0.0 on Router2 and Router3, and network 192.168.154.0 on Router2

➤ Known telnet and enable passwords for the routers

➤ A rollover console cable

➤ A laptop or a PC running a terminal emulation program such as Hyperterminal

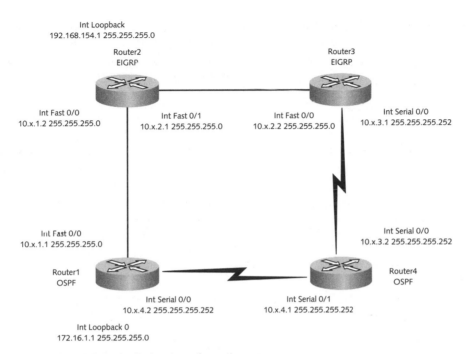

Int Loopback
192.168.154.1 255.255.255.0

Router2
EIGRP

Router3
EIGRP

Int Fast 0/0
10.x.1.2 255.255.255.0

Int Fast 0/1
10.x.2.1 255.255.255.0

Int Fast 0/0
10.x.2.2 255.255.255.0

Int Serial 0/0
10.x.3.1 255.255.255.252

Int Fast 0/0
10.x.1.1 255.255.255.0

Int Serial 0/0
10.x.3.2 255.255.255.252

Router1
OSPF

Router4
OSPF

Int Serial 0/0
10.x.4.2 255.255.255.252

Int Serial 0/1
10.x.4.1 255.255.255.252

Int Loopback 0
172.16.1.1 255.255.255.0

Figure 8-4   Network diagram for Lab 8-4

Estimated completion time: 20 minutes

Activity Background

In the previous labs in this chapter, you learned how to configure BGP. However, using BGP is not always desirable. First, successful use of BGP requires a fair amount of knowledge. You should not recommend BGP to your customers if they do not have a solid understanding of BGP. Second, BGP can use a lot of resources. You should not use BGP if you do not have routers with enough memory to hold the BPG routing table (which contains over 110, 000 routes at the time of this writing), or routers without sufficiently powerful processors to handle nearly constant updates from their peers. Because of their frequency, BGP updates also use a lot of bandwidth, so you should not use BGP if you have low bandwidth connections to external autonomous systems. Finally, in many situations, BGP will not provide any benefit. For instance, BGP is not useful if you have only one connection to an external autonomous system, or if you do not need to set routing policy.

You can avoid the use of BGP through the use of static and default routes. These routes can then be redistributed into your IGP. While the use of default routes often results in poor path selection, they do avoid the drawbacks of using BGP. Each routing protocol handles default routes in a slightly different way. In RIP, for instance, a default route is automatically redistributed. In OSPF, you may propagate a default route with the

default-information originate command. You can use the **always** keyword so that OSPF continues to advertise this route even when the router is unable to reach the next hop for the default route. In EIGRP, the most efficient way to propagate a default route is to configure one with the **ip route 0.0.0.0 0.0.0.0** command, and then redistribute static routes.

Multiple connections to another autonomous system or to the Internet may be handled without using BGP by using a floating static route. As you learned in Chapter 6, a floating static route has an administrative distance set higher than a different route to the same destination learned through another source. To use a floating static route as a backup default route, simply configure a default route with a high administrative distance. When the primary default route fails, the router will use the floating route. This technique does not allow you to use load balancing, as the backup route will not be used unless the primary route fails.

ACTIVITY

1. Power on the routers and the PC or laptop and open the terminal emulation program.

2. Plug the RJ-45 end of the console cable into the console port of Router4. Attach the other end of the console cable to the serial port on the laptop or PC. You may need to press **Enter** to bring up the Router4> prompt.

3. Type **enable** and press **Enter**. The router prompt changes to Router4#.

4. Type **config term** and press **Enter**. The router prompt changes to Router4(config)#.

5. Now you will configure a default route on Router4 with a next hop of Router3. Type **ip route 0.0.0.0 0.0.0.0 10.x.3.1** and press **Enter**.

6. Type **router ospf 1** and press **Enter**.

7. Now you will propagate this default route throughout the OSPF autonomous system. Type **default-information originate** and press **Enter**.

8. Press **Ctl-Z** to exit configuration mode.

9. On Router1, type **show ip route**. A default route to 0.0.0.0/0 is listed in Router1's routing table. What type of route is this?

_____

10. On Router3, repeat Steps 3 and 4.

11. Now you will configure a default route on Router3 with a next hop of Router4. Type **ip route 0.0.0.0 0.0.0.0 10.x.3.2** and press **Enter**.

12. Type **router eigrp 65000** and press **Enter**.

13. Type **no auto-summary** and press **Enter**. This prevents the router from automatically summarizing routes and dropping packets destined for subnets of 10.0.0.0/8 without more specific routes in the routing table.

14. Type **redistribute static** and press **Enter**.

15. Press **Ctl-Z** to exit configuration mode.

16. On Router2, repeat Steps 3 and 4.

17. Type **router eigrp 65000** and press **Enter**.

18. Type **no auto-summary** and press **Enter**.

19. Press **Ctl-Z** to exit configuration mode.

20. Type **show ip route** and press **Enter**. A default route is listed in Router2's routing table. What type of route is this?

_____

21. Now you will test end-to-end connectivity. On Router1, type **ping 192.168.154.1** and press **Enter**. The router prints five exclamation points and indicates that the success rate is 100%.

22. Type **trace 192.168.154.1** and press **Enter**. The router traces the path to 192.168.154.1. What path do packets to this address use? Is this the best possible path?

_____

23. On Router2, type **ping 172.16.1.1** and press **Enter**. The router prints five exclamation points and indicates that the success rate is 100%.

24. Type **trace 172.16.1.1** and press **Enter**. The router traces the path to 172.16.1.1. What path do packets to this destination use?

_____

25. Now you will configure floating static default routes in case the link between Router3 and Router4 goes down. On Router1, type **config term** and press **Enter**.

26. Type **ip route 0.0.0.0 0.0.0.0 10.x.1.2 200** and press **Enter**. This configures a floating static default route with a next hop of Router2 and an administrative distance of 200.

27. Type **router ospf 1** and press **Enter**.

28. Type **default-information originate** and press **Enter**.

29. Press **Ctl-Z** to exit configuration mode.

30. Type **show ip route** and press **Enter**. What is the next hop for the default route in Router1's routing table?

_____

31. On Router2, type **config term** and press **Enter**.

32. Type **ip route 0.0.0.0 0.0.0.0 10.x.1.1 200** and press **Enter**. This configures a floating static default route with a next hop of Router1 and an administrative distance of 200.

33. Type **router eigrp 65000** and press **Enter**.

34. Type **redistribute static** and press **Enter**.

35. Press **Ctl-Z** to exit configuration mode.

36. Type **show ip route** and press **Enter**. What is the next hop for the default route in Router2's routing table?

    _____

37. Now you will shut down the link between Router3 and Router4. On Router3, type **config term** and press **Enter**.

38. Type **int s0/0** and press **Enter**.

39. Type **shut** and press **Enter**. Interface Serial 0/0 is now administratively down, and neither Router3 nor Router4 will be able to use the default route you configured earlier.

40. Press **Ctl-Z** to exit configuration mode.

41. Type **show ip route** and press **Enter**. What is the next hop for the default route on this router?

    _____

42. Type **ping 172.16.1.1** and press **Enter**. The router prints five exclamation points and indicates that the success rate is 100%.

43. Type **trace 172.16.1.1** and press **Enter**. The router traces the path to 172.16.1.1. What path do packets to this destination use?

    _____

44. Repeat Steps 42 and 43 on Router2.

45. On Router4, type **ping 192.168.154.1** and press **Enter**. The router prints five exclamation points and indicates that the success rate is 100%.

46. Type **trace 192.168.154.1** and press **Enter**. The router traces the path to 192.168.154.1. What path do packets to this address use?

    _____

47. Repeat Steps 45 and 46 on Router1.

Certification Objectives

Objectives for Cisco Exam 640-603: Routing

➤ Describe BGP features and operation

➤ Describe how to connect to another autonomous system using an alternative to BGP, static routes

➤ Describe and configure external and internal BGP

Review Questions

1. Which of the following are situations where you should not use BGP? (Choose all that apply.)

   a. You have only one connection to the Internet.

   b. You do not have extensive knowledge of BGP.

   c. Your routers have little memory and slow processors.

   d. You have low bandwidth connections to the Internet and to other autonomous systems.

2. Which of the following commands would propagate a default route throughout an OSPF autonomous system, regardless of whether or not the route is up?

   a. Router(config-router)#default-information originate

   b. Router(config)#ip route 0.0.0.0 0.0.0.0 10.1.2.1

   c. Router(config-router)#default-route propagate always

   d. Router(config-router)#default-information originate always

3. What is a drawback of configuring a floating static route as a backup Internet connection?

   a. You cannot perform load balancing with the primary Internet connection.

   b. The floating static route stays up at all times.

   c. increased routing table size

   d. more processing power necessary for dynamic updates

4. Which of the following sets of commands would configure a floating static route as a backup default route? The primary default route is an external EIGRP route with an administrative distance of 170.

   a. Router(config-router)#ip route 0.0.0.0 0.0.0.0 150

   b. Router(config-router)#ip route 0.0.0.0 0.0.0.0 10.1.2.1 150

   c. Router(config-router)#ip route 0.0.0.0 0.0.0.0 10.1.2.1

   d. Router(config-router)#ip route 0.0.0.0 0.0.0.0 10.1.2.1 200

5. Which of the following sets of commands would propagate a default route throughout EIGRP autonomous system 100?

   a. Router(config-router)#default-information originate

   b. Router(config-router)#default-route propagate

   c. Router(config-router)#redistribute static

   d. Router(config-router)#redistribute default

8

LAB 8.5 CONFIGURING OTHER BGP PARAMETERS

Objective

In this lab, you will learn how to configure other BGP parameters.

Materials Required

This lab will require the following:

> ➤ Three Cisco routers with the interfaces, IP addresses, and cabling, as shown in Figure 8-5

> ➤ EIGRP in autonomous system 65001 running on Router1 and Router2, configured to advertise networks 10.0.0.0 and 172.16.0.0, and with the **no auto-summary** command

> ➤ Known telnet and enable passwords for the routers

> ➤ A rollover console cable

> ➤ A laptop or a PC running a terminal emulation program such as Hyperterminal

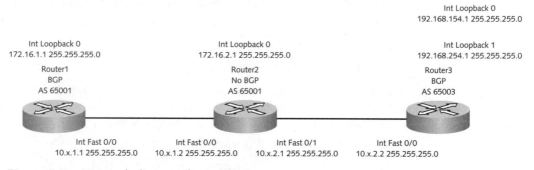

Figure 8-5   Network diagram for Lab 8-5

Estimated completion time: **20 minutes**

Activity Background

Because of BGP's lack of topology constraints, BGP is used in a wide variety of situations. However, in many circumstances, additional configuration may be needed in order for BGP to function properly.

For instance, by default on Cisco routers, EBGP peers must be adjacent to each other. Each EBGP packet has a time to live (TTL) value of 1. The TTL value is included in the IP packet header. Each time a router receives a packet, it decrements the TTL value by one before forwarding it onto the next hop. If a router decrements a packet's TTL value to 0, the router drops the packet. Since EBGP packets have a TTL of 1, they cannot travel more than one hop before the TTL expires and the router drops them. As a result, a Cisco router cannot make an EBGP connection with another router more than one hop away. However, you can increase the value of the TTL with the **neighbor** *ip-address* **ebgp-multihop** command. By default, this command configures the TTL value to be 254. You can also explicitly set a TTL value by placing it after the **ebgp-multihop** keyword. This command is unnecessary for IBGP, as the default TTL value for IBGP packets is 255.

Using a loopback address as the source of BGP updates also requires additional configuration. In an autonomous system with multiple paths, using a loopback interface as the source of update packets is more stable than using a physical interface, since the loopback interface will stay up as long as the router is up. Additionally, using a loopback interface is useful with load balancing. Unless you use the loopback interface as the source of updates, updates coming from multiple interfaces will also come with multiple source addresses and cause problems. You can configure BGP to use the loopback address as the source of updates with the **neighbor** *ip-address* **update-source loopback** command.

Another useful command is the **neighbor** *ip-address* **shutdown** command. Sometimes you may need to disable a peer relationship update to a particular peer for a period of time. This command allows you to disable BGP to a particular peer, without having to reconfigure the neighbor afterwards. Instead, you can simply use the **no neighbor** *ip-address* **shutdown** command to re-enable the peer relationship with that neighbor.

ACTIVITY

1. Power on the routers and the PC or laptop and open the terminal emulation program.

2. Plug the RJ-45 end of the console cable into the console port of Router2. Attach the other end of the console cable to the serial port on the laptop or PC. You may need to press **Enter** to bring up the Router2> prompt.

3. Type **enable** and press **Enter**. The router prompt changes to Router2#.

4. Type **config term** and press **Enter**. The router prompt changes to Router2(config)#.

5. First you will propagate a static route to the 192.168.154.0/24 network so that Router1 and Router2 are able to establish TCP connections with Router3's loopback address. Type **ip route 192.168.154.0 255.255.255.0 10.x.2.2** and press **Enter**.

6. Type **router eigrp 65001** and press **Enter**.

7. Type **redistribute static** and press **Enter**.

8. Press **Ctl-Z** to exit configuration mode.

9. On Router1, repeat Steps 3 and 4.

10. Type **router bgp 65001** and press **Enter**.

11. Type **neighbor 192.168.154.1 remote-as 65003** and press **Enter**.

12. Type **neighbor 192.168.154.1 update-source loopback 0** and press **Enter**.

13. Type **neighbor 192.168.154.1 ebgp-multihop** and press **Enter**. This configures Router1 to use the maximum TTL for BGP packets sent to neighbor 192.168.154.1. When they can make a TCP connection, Router1 and Router3 can now become EBGP peers even though the two routers are not directly connected.

14. Type **network 172.16.1.0 mask 255.255.255.0** and press **Enter**.

15. Type **network 172.16.2.0 mask 255.255.255.0** and press **Enter**.

16. Press **Ctl-Z** to exit configuration mode.

17. On Router3, repeat Steps 3 and 4.

18. Now you will configure a static route so that Router3 will be able to reach the loopback interfaces on Router1 and Router2. Type **ip route 172.16.0.0 255.255.252.0 10.x.2.1** and press **Enter**.

19. Type **ip route 10.x.1.0 255.255.255.0 10.x.2.1** and press **Enter**.

20. Type **router bgp 65003** and press **Enter**.

21. Type **neighbor 172.16.1.1 remote-as 65001** and press **Enter**.

22. Type **neighbor 172.16.1.1 update-source loopback 0** and press **Enter**.

23. Type **neighbor 172.16.1.1 ebgp-multihop** and press **Enter**.

24. Type **network 192.168.154.0 mask 255.255.255.0** and press **Enter**.

25. Type **network 192.168.254.0 mask 255.255.255.0** and press **Enter**.

26. Press **Ctl-Z** to exit configuration mode.

27. Type **show ip bgp neighbors** and press **Enter**. Router1 appears as a BGP neighbor.

28. Type **show ip bgp** and press **Enter**. The routes for the loopback interfaces on both Router1 and Router2 appear in the command output, as well as the routes for Router3's loopback interfaces and the route for 10.x.1.0/24.

29. Type **debug ip bgp events** and press **Enter**.

30. Type **config term** and press **Enter**.

31. Type **router bgp 65003** and press **Enter**.

32. Type **neighbor 172.16.1.1 shutdown** and press **Enter**. If the router prints debugging output while you are typing, press **Ctl-R** in order for the router to reprint the line you are typing. This shuts down Router3's BGP connection with Router1. Debugging output appears, indicating that the request was reset due to Admin Shutdown, and that the peer relationship with 172.16.1.1 went from Established to Idle.

33. Type **no neighbor 172.16.1.1 shutdown** and press **Enter**. You may need to hit **Enter** to get the Router3(config-router)# prompt. Debugging output indicates that Router3 is reestablishing a BGP connection with Router1, and that it is computing updates for its routing table.

34. Type **undebug all** and press **Enter**.

Certification Objectives

Objectives for Cisco Exam 640-603: Routing

➤ Describe BGP features and operation

➤ Describe and configure external and internal BGP

➤ Configure a BGP environment and verify proper operation

Review Questions

1. Why isn't the **neighbor** *ip-address* **ebgp-multihop** command necessary with IBGP?

   a. IBGP peers must be in a full mesh.

   b. The TTL used by IBGP peers is set to 255 by default.

   c. The TTL used by IBGP peers is set to 0 by default.

   d. IBGP does not have a hop limit.

2. What does a router do when it decrements the TTL on a packet down to 0?

   a. It drops it.

   b. It forwards it onto the next hop as usual.

   c. It forwards it onto the next hop, reducing the TTL by one.

   d. It sends that packet to the next hop specified by the router's default route.

3. Which of the following commands would configure 172.25.172.1 as an EBGP peer more than one hop away?

   a. Router(config-router)#neighbor 172.25.172.1 ebgp-multihop 0

   b. Router(config-router)#ebg-multihop 172.25.172.1

   c. Router(config-router)#peer 172.25.172.1 ebgp-multihop

   d. Router(config-router)#neighbor 172.25.172.1 ebgp-multihop

4. Which of the following are reasons why you might choose to use a loopback address for the source of BGP updates? (Choose all that apply.)

   a. For load balancing over multiple links

   b. For greater stability in autonomous systems with multiple paths

   c. The loopback address is used for the BGP router ID.

   d. To prevent outages when the single link to a particular BGP peer fails

5. Which of the following commands would configure interface Loopback 0 as the source of routing updates for peer 172.25.172.1?

   a. Router(config-router)#neighbor 172.25.172.1 loopback 0

   b. Router(config-router)# peer 172.25.172.1 update-source loopback 0

   c. Router(config-router)# neighbor 172.25.172.1 update-source loopback 0

   d. Router(config-router)# neighbor 172.25.172.1 loopback 0 update-source

CHAPTER NINE

ADVANCED BGP

Labs included in this chapter

➤ Lab 9.1 Configuring Route Reflectors

➤ Lab 9.2 Controlling Routing Policy with Prefix Lists

➤ Lab 9.3 Multihoming

➤ Lab 9.4 Redistributing Routes into an IGP

➤ Lab 9.5 Routing Policy and Peer Groups

Cisco CCNP Exam #640-603 Objectives	
Objective	Lab
Describe the scalability problems associated with internal BGP	9.1
Explain and configure BGP route reflectors	9.1
Describe and configure policy control in BGP using prefix lists	9.2, 9.5
Describe methods to connect to multiple ISPs using BGP	9.3
Explain the use of redistribution between BGP and Interior Gateway Protocols (IGPs)	9.4
Configure a multihomed BGP environment and verify proper operation	9.3
Describe BGP communities and peer groups	9.5

LAB 9.1 CONFIGURING ROUTE REFLECTORS

Objective

In this lab, you will learn how to configure route reflectors.

Materials Required

This lab will require the following:

➤ Five Cisco routers with the interfaces, IP addresses, and cabling, as shown in Figure 9-1, and the interfaces connected to the DCE ends of the serial cables configured with a clock rate of 64000

➤ A switch or hub for the Fast Ethernet network connecting Router1, Router2 and Router3

➤ EIGRP in autonomous system 65000 configured on each router to advertise network 10.0.0.0

➤ Known telnet and enable passwords for the routers

➤ A rollover console cable

➤ A laptop or a PC running a terminal emulation program such as Hyperterminal

Estimated completion time: **30 minutes**

Activity Background

While External BGP (EBGP) is used throughout the Internet, IBGP can have scalability issues. These arise from the fact that IBGP peers must be in a full mesh. According to the BGP split horizon rule, routers cannot advertise routes they learned through IBGP to other IBGP peers. For instance, RouterA might learn a route from RouterB. RouterA would not propagate this route to RouterC. If RouterC did not have an IBGP session with RouterB, it would not learn about this route. Therefore, the only way to ensure that each IBGP peer learns all the routes that other IBGP peers know is for each IBGP router to have an IBGP session with every other IBGP router. In this case, a full mesh refers to the fact that each IBGP router must be configured as a neighbor for each other IBGP router. It does not mean that each router must have a physical connection or a permanent virtual circuit (PVC) to every other router.

While a full mesh is fine in smaller networks, in larger networks this can require many **neighbor** statements on each router, many individual IBGP sessions to maintain, and large amounts of update traffic. In a network with 20 IBGP peers, for instance, you would need to configure 190 IBGP **neighbor** statements on each router for 190 IBGP sessions.

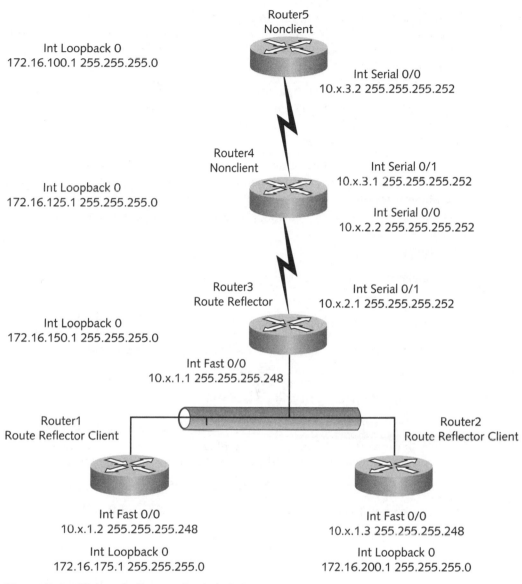

Figure 9-1 Network diagram for Lab 9-1

One technique to reduce the number of IBGP sessions necessary is the use of route reflectors. A route reflector is a router that is allowed to propagate routes it has learned through IBGP to its clients. Each route reflector peers with each of its clients. However, the clients do not need to become peers with each other. As a result, the total number of IBGP sessions needed becomes much smaller. In addition to reducing the number of IBGP sessions required (and also update traffic), route reflectors require minimum configuration, and do not need to be configured in the entire autonomous system.

In an autonomous system, you may configure multiple clusters consisting of a route reflector and its clients. You may also configure other IBGP peers that are not in a cluster. These routers are known as nonclients. Each cluster must be in a full mesh with the other clusters and with the nonclients.

You may also configure multiple route reflectors in the same client. In this case, you must configure the route reflectors with a cluster ID. When a route reflector receives an update, it uses the cluster ID (if present) to determine if the update arrived from another route reflector in the same cluster.

You must be careful, however, when configuring route reflectors. A misconfigured route reflector cluster may cause routing loops. One strategy to avoid routing loops is to follow the physical topology of the autonomous system when configuring route reflector clusters. For instance, avoid configuring clients that are not connected to their route reflectors.

ACTIVITY

1. Power on the routers and the PC or laptop and open the terminal emulation program.

2. Plug the RJ-45 end of the console cable into the console port of Router3. Attach the other end of the console cable to the serial port on the laptop or PC. You may need to press **Enter** to bring up the Router3> prompt.

3. Type **enable** and press **Enter**. The router prompt changes to Router3#.

4. Type **config term** and press **Enter**.

5. Type **router bgp 65000** and press **Enter**.

6. Now you will configure Router4 and Router5, the nonclients, as IBGP peers of Router3. Type **neighbor 10.x.2.2 remote-as 65000** and press **Enter**.

7. Type **neighbor 10.x.3.2 remote-as 65000** and press **Enter**.

8. Type **network 172.16.150.0 mask 255.255.255.0** and press **Enter**.

9. Type **no synchronization** and press **Enter**.

10. Press **Ctl-Z** to exit configuration mode.

11. Now you will configure Router3 as an IBGP peer on Router4 and Router5, but you will not configure Router4 and Router5 as IBGP peers. This will show what happens when IBGP peers are not configured in a full mesh. Repeat Steps 3 and 4 on Router4.

12. Type **router bgp 65000** and press **Enter**.

13. Type **neighbor 10.x.1.1 remote-as 65000** and press **Enter**.

14. Type **no synchronization** and press **Enter**.

15. Type **network 172.16.125.0 mask 255.255.255.0** and press **Enter**.

16. Press **Ctl-Z** to exit configuration mode.

17. Repeat Steps 11 through 14 on Router5.

18. Type **network 172.16.100.0 mask 255.255.255.0** and press **Enter**.

19. Press **Ctl-Z** to exit configuration mode.

20. On Router3, type **show ip bgp** and press **Enter**. If the router prompt returns without printing any information, wait 30 seconds and repeat this step until it the router prints information about the BGP table on this router. Which routes are advertised by BGP?

    _____

21. On Router4, repeat the previous step. Which routes were present on Router3, but do not appear on Router4?

    _____

22. Repeat Step 20 on Router5. Which routes were present on Router3, but do not appear on Router5?

    _____

23. Now you will allow Router3, Router4, and Router5 to learn IBGP routes from each other by creating a full mesh of IBGP sessions. On Router5, type **config term** and press **Enter**.

24. Type **router bgp 65000** and press **Enter**.

25. Type **neighbor 10.x.2.2 remote-as 65000** and press **Enter**.

26. Press **Ctl-Z** to exit configuration mode.

27. Type **clear ip bgp *** and press **Enter**.

28. Repeat Steps 23 through 27 on Router4, substituting the ip address 10.x.3.2 when you repeat Step 25.

29. On Router4, type **show ip bgp neighbor** and press **Enter**. If both neighbors are not in the established state, wait 30 seconds and repeat this step as needed.

30. Type **show ip bgp** and press **Enter**. You should see routes for each of the loop-back interfaces on Router3, Router4, and Router5 advertised by BGP.

31. Repeat the previous step on Router5.

32. Now you will configure Router3 as the route reflector. Repeat Steps 3 and 4 on Router3.

33. Type **router bgp 65000** and press **Enter**.

34. Type **neighbor 10.x.1.2 remote-as 65000** and press **Enter**.

35. Type **neighbor 10.x.1.2 route-reflector-client** and press **Enter**.

36. Type **neighbor 10.x.1.3 remote-as 65000** and press **Enter**.

37. Type **neighbor 10.x.1.3 route-reflector-client** and press **Enter**.

9

38. Press **Ctl-Z** to exit configuration mode.

39. On Router1, repeat Steps 3 and 4.

40. Type **router bgp 65000** and press **Enter**.

41. Type **neighbor 10.*x*.1.1 remote-as 65000** and press **Enter**.

42. Type **network 172.16.175.0 mask 255.255.255.0** and press **Enter**.

43. Press **Ctl-Z** to exit configuration mode.

44. On Router2, repeat Steps 39 through 41.

45. Type **network 172.16.200.0 mask 255.255.255.0** and press **Enter**.

46. Press **Ctl-Z** to exit configuration mode.

47. Type **show ip bgp** and press **Enter**. Routes for each of the five loopback interfaces advertised by BGP appear in the command output. If they do not, wait 30 seconds and repeat until they do.

48. To confirm that the routes are being advertised throughout the autonomous system, repeat the previous step on Router1, Router3, Router4, and Router5.

49. On Router3, type **show ip bgp neighbors** and press **Enter**. The output for Router1 and Router2 indicates that they are route-reflector clients.

50. On Router2, type **show ip bgp neighbors** and press **Enter**. The output does not indicate that Router3 is a route reflector.

Certification Objectives

Objectives for Cisco Exam 640-603: Routing

➤ Describe the scalability problems associated with internal BGP

➤ Explain and configure BGP route reflectors

Review Questions

1. Why does IBGP have scalability issues?

    a. Each IBGP router broadcasts its entire routing able every 60 seconds.

    b. The BGP table must be recalculated each time a link changes state.

    c. Each IBGP router must peer with every other IBGP router.

    d. Routing updates take longer in large IBGP networks.

2. What is the IBGP split horizon rule?

    a. A BGP router cannot advertise routes it learns from one interface back out that interface.

    b. A BGP router cannot advertise routes back to the peer from which it learned them.

    c. A BGP router cannot advertise routes back to the AS from which it learned them.

    d. An IBGP router must have a peer relationship with every other IBGP router in the autonomous system.

3. Besides configuring the route reflector as a peer of each route reflector client, what additional configuration is required on the client? (Assume the IP address of the route reflector is 172.16.1.1.)

    a. Router(config-router)#neighbor 172.16.1.1 route-reflector-client

    b. Router(config-router)#neighbor 172.16.1.1 route reflector

    c. Router(config-router)#route-reflector 172.16.1.1

    d. none

4. When on the route reflector, which of the following commands would configure a router with an IP address of 192.168.154.1 as a route reflector client?

    a. Router(config-router)#neighbor 192.168.154.1 route-reflector-client

    b. Router(config-router)# neighbor 192.168.154.1 route reflector

    c. Router(config-router)#route-reflector client 192.168.154.1

    d. Router(config-router)#neighbor 192.168.154.1 client

5. Which of the following is true about the peer relationships between route reflectors, their clients, and nonclients?

    a. Each route reflector, each client and each nonclient must be in a full mesh.

    b. Each route reflector must be in a full mesh with other route reflectors and nonclients, but does not need to peer with clients.

    c. Each route reflector must be in a full mesh with other route reflectors and nonclients, and must also peer with each client.

    d. Each route reflector must peer with each client, but cannot peer with nonclients.

LAB 9.2 CONTROLLING ROUTING POLICY WITH PREFIX LISTS

Objective

In this lab, you will learn how to configure routing policy with prefix lists.

Materials Required

This lab will require the following:

➤ Three Cisco routers with the interfaces, IP addresses and cabling, as shown in Figure 9-2, and the interfaces connected to the DCE ends of the serial cables configured with a clock rate of 64000

➤ OSPF configured on each router to advertise all subnets of 10.0.0.0/8 in Area 0

➤ BGP configured on each router for the autonomous system indicated in Figure 9-2, with a separate network statement on each router advertising a route for its loopback interface, and each router configured to be neighbors with the other two routers

➤ Known telnet and enable passwords for the routers

➤ A rollover console cable

➤ A laptop or a PC running a terminal emulation program such as Hyperterminal

Int Loopback 0
172.16.0.1 255.255.240.0

Int Loopback 1
172.16.16.1 255.255.240.0

Int Loopback 2
172.16.32.1 255.255.252.0

Int Loopback 3
172.16.128.1 225.255.128.0

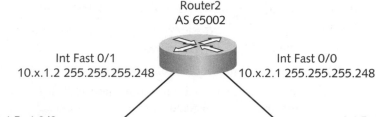

Router2
AS 65002

Int Fast 0/1
10.x.1.2 255.255.255.248

Int Fast 0/0
10.x.2.1 255.255.255.248

Int Fast 0/0
10.x.1.1 255.255.255.248

Int Fast 0/0
10.x.2.2 255.255.255.248

Router1
AS 65001

Router3
AS 65003

Int Serial 0/0
10.x.3.2 255.255.255.252

Int Serial 0/0
10.x.3.1 255.255.255.252

Int Loopback 0
172.17.0.1 255.255.224.0

Int Loopback 0
172.18.1.1 255.255.255.128

Int Loopback 1
172.17.32.1 255.255.224.0

Int Loopback 1
172.18.1.129 255.255.255.192

Int Loopback 2
172.17.64.1 255.255.252.0

Int Loopback 2
172.18.1.193 255.255.255.248

Int Loopback 3
172.17.128.1 255.255.128.0

Int Loopback 3
172.18.1.225 255.255.255.252

Figure 9-2   Network diagram for Lab 9-2

Estimated completion time: **20 minutes**

Activity Background

One of the mechanisms you can use to control routing policy on Cisco routers is prefix lists. A prefix list is an alternate to using a route filter or route map. Given the large number of routes that may be found on a BGP router, prefix lists offer better performance than route filters. Prefix lists also support incremental updates, which route filters do not. Finally, the prefix list syntax is easier to use for filtering routes than an access list, and it is more flexible. (Note that you cannot use a route filter and a prefix list at the same time.)

Like an access list, a router examines a prefix list a line at a time, and stops processing a route after it finds a match. Additionally, a prefix list has an implicit denial at the end. Like a route map, a prefix list has a sequence number. This allows you to add statements to a prefix list after you initially configure it. (You do not need to know the sequence number of a statement in order to delete it.) Unlike a route map, however, by default, prefix list statements are numbered automatically. The automatic numbering gives the first statement a sequence number of 5, the second 10, and so on, in increments of five. You may turn off automatic numbering with the **no ip prefix-list sequence-number** command in configuration mode.

Prefix lists consist of a series of **permit** or **deny** statements. Statements matched by a **deny** statement, or the implicit denial at the end of a prefix list, are filtered. Statements matched by a **permit** statement are not filtered. Prefix lists give you a variety of methods to match a route. You may directly match a route by including its prefix and prefix length in the statement. For instance, **ip prefix-list Filter permit 10.0.0.0/24** would match the route 10.0.0.0/24 and no other routes. You may match groups of routes with the **ge** (greater than) or **le** (less than) keywords. For instance, the statement **ip prefix-list Filter permit 10.0.0.0/8 ge 20** would match all routes that are subnets of 10.0.0.0/8 with prefixes 20 bits or longer. The statement **ip prefix-list Filter permit 10.0.0.0/8 le 16** would match all routes that are subnets of 10.0.0.0/8 with prefixes no more than 16 bits long. You may also use both keywords in the same statement. The statement **ip prefix-list Filter permit 10.0.0.0/8 ge 16 le 24** would match all routes that are subnets of 10.0.0.0/8 and which have prefixes equal to or between 16 and 24 bits in length.

In order to activate a prefix list, you use the **neighbor** *ip-address* **prefix-list** *prefix-list-name* command in router configuration mode. You must also reset the BGP session for the appropriate neighbor. While a hard reset with the **clear ip bgp** command will reset routing policy, this will seriously disrupt routing in a production network. For outgoing policy, you may use a soft reset. This causes the router to resend all its updates, and uses less resources than a hard reset. A soft reset is also possible with incoming routing policy. However, you must first configure a router with the **neighbor** *ip-address* **soft-reconfiguration inbound** command. This command causes the router to store a full copy of all BGP updates received from its neighbor. As a result, when you perform a soft inbound reset, the router goes through each update received from that neighbor and reapplies its routing policies to each route. In addition to requiring advance configuration, this command can require a large amount of memory on the router.

9

ACTIVITY

1. Power on the routers and the PC or laptop and open the terminal emulation program.

2. Plug the RJ-45 end of the console cable into the console port of Router1. Attach the other end of the console cable to the serial port on the laptop or PC. You may need to press **Enter** to bring up the Router1> prompt.

3. Type **enable** and press **Enter**. The router prompt changes to Router1#.

4. Type **config term** and press **Enter**.

5. Type **router bgp 65001** and press **Enter**.

6. Type **aggregate-address 172.17.0.0 255.255.0.0** and press **Enter**.

7. Press **Ctl-Z** to exit configuration mode.

8. Repeat Steps 3 through 4 on Router2.

9. Type **router bgp 65002** and press **Enter**.

10. Type **aggregate-address 172.16.0.0 255.255.0.0** and press **Enter**.

11. Press **Ctl-Z** to exit configuration mode.

12. Repeat Steps 3 and 4 on Router3.

13. Type **router bgp 65003** and press **Enter**.

14. Type **aggregate-address 172.18.0.0 255.255.0.0** and press **Enter**.

15. Press **Ctl-Z** to exit configuration mode.

16. Type **show ip bgp** and press **Enter**. You should see information about the BGP table on this router, including routes for all the loopback addresses on each router, and the aggregate addresses you configured earlier in this lab. If you do not, wait 30 seconds and repeat this step as needed. Note that the routes learned externally have two entries. One entry was learned from Router1 and the other from Router2. The best route is marked with a >.

17. Type **config term** and press **Enter**.

18. Now you will configure a prefix list to control the routes that Router3 advertises to Router1. Type **ip prefix-list OutToRouter1 permit 0.0.0.0/0 le 16** and press **Enter**. This prefix list permits all routes with any prefix, as long as the prefix is 16 bits or shorter. Since this will be the last statement in the prefix list, all other routes will be denied by the implicit denial at the end. Which BGP routes advertised by Router3 would be matched by this prefix list?

    _____

19. Type **router bgp 65003** and press **Enter**.

20. Type **neighbor 10.1.3.2 prefix-list OutToRouter1 out** and press **Enter**.

21. Press **Ctl-Z** to exit configuration mode.

22. On Router1, type **show ip bgp** and press **Enter**. In Router1's BGP table, you can still see two entries for each of Router3's loopback interfaces (one learned from Router1 and one learned from Router3).

23. Type **debug ip bgp updates** and press **Enter**.

24. On Router3, type **clear ip bgp 65001 soft out** and press **Enter**. This will do a soft outbound reset of the BGP session with Router1.

25. Quickly move to Router1. Debugging output appears, indicating that Router1 is receiving an update from Router3.

26. Type **undebug all** and press **Enter**.

27. Type **show ip bgp** and press **Enter**. How many entries are there for the routes advertised by Router3?

_____

28. On Router2, type **show ip bgp** and press **Enter**. How many entries are visible for the routes advertised by Router3?

_____

29. Type **debug ip bgp updates** and press **Enter**.

30. On Router3, type **config term** and press **Enter**.

31. Now you will configure a prefix list to control the BGP routes that Router3 advertises to Router2. Type **ip prefix-list OutToRouter2 permit 172.18.0.0/16** and press **Enter**. This will exactly match the route 172.18.0.0/16.

32. Type **ip prefix-list OutToRouter2 permit 172.18.0.0/16 ge 26 le 29** and press **Enter**. This will match routes in the 172.18.0.0/16 block with prefixes between 26 and 29 bits long. Which routes advertised by BGP would you expect this prefix list to match?

_____

33. Type **router bgp 65003** and press **Enter**.

34. Type **neighbor 10.1.2.1 prefix-list OutToRouter2 out** and press **Enter**.

35. Press **Ctl-Z** to exit configuration mode.

36. Type **clear ip bgp *** and press **Enter**.

37. Quickly move to Router2. Debugging output prints, indicating that Router2 is receiving an update from Router3. After the debugging output stops, type **show ip bgp** and press **Enter**. Now how many routes advertised by Router3 are present?

_____

38. Type **undebug all**.

39. On Router1, type **show ip bgp** and press **Enter**. How many routes advertised by Router3 are present?

_____

40. On Router3, type **show ip prefix-list** and press **Enter**. The router prints the prefix lists configured on the router and the number of times they were matched.

41. Type **clear ip prefix-list OutToRouter2** and press **Enter**. This clears the counters for prefix list OutToRouter2.

42. Type **show ip prefix-list OutToRouter2** and press **Enter**. The router prints sequence number 5 in the prefix list OutToRouter2.

43. Type **show ip prefix-list OutToRouter2 172.18.0.0/16 first-match** and press **Enter**. The router prints the first line in the prefix list matching that route.

44. Type **show ip prefix-list OutToRouter2 10.0.0.0/8 first-match** and press **Enter**. The router prompt returns without printing anything, since no line in the prefix list matches this route.

45. Type **config term** and press **Enter**.

46. Now you will create a prefix list named FilterIn, which will filter incoming routes that have prefixes longer than 20 bits. On Router3, type **ip prefix-list FilterIn permit 172.16.0.0/16 le 18** and press **Enter**. This will permit all routes from within the 172.16.0.0/16 block that have a prefix of 18 bits or fewer.

47. Type **ip prefix-list FilterIn permit 172.17.0.0/16 le 18** and press **Enter**. The implicit denial at the end of the prefix list will deny all other routes.

48. Type **router bgp 65003** and press **Enter**.

49. Type **neighbor 10.1.3.2 prefix-list FilterIn in** and press **Enter**.

50. Type **neighbor 10.1.2.1 prefix-list FilterIn in** and press **Enter**.

51. Press **Ctl–Z** to exit configuration mode.

52. Type **debug ip bgp updates** and press **Enter**.

53. Type **clear ip bgp *** and press **Enter**. This performs a hard reset on the BGP sessions with each of Router3's neighbors. Debugging output appears, indicating that the router is receiving updates from its neighbors. Some of the lines indicate that routes were DENIED due to distribute/prefix-list.

54. After the debugging output has stopped for 20 seconds, type **undebug all** and press **Enter**.

55. Type **show ip bgp** and press **Enter**. Which routes remain in Router3's BGP table, and what are their prefix lengths?

_____

Certification Objective

Objective for Cisco Exam 640-603: Routing

➤ Describe and configure policy control in BGP using prefix lists

Review Questions

1. Which of the following are advantages of using prefix lists over route filters? (Choose all that apply.)

   a. Prefix lists are more flexible.

   b. Prefix lists support incremental updates.

   c. Prefix list syntax is easier to use for filtering routes.

   d. Prefix lists offer better performance than route filters.

2. Which of the following is true about statements in prefix lists? (Choose all that apply.)

   a. Statements can only be added, not deleted.

   b. Each statement has a sequence number, which determines when that statement is executed.

   c. Statements are given sequence numbers automatically, by default.

   d. Each statement must have a match clause and a set clause.

3. Which of the following statements in a prefix list would filter the network 198.14.59.0/26?

   a. ip prefix-list deny 198.14.59.0/26 ge 28

   b. ip prefix-list permit 198.14.59.0/26

   c. ip prefix-list deny 198.14.59.0/26 ge 28 le 30

   d. ip prefix-list deny 198.14.59.0/26

4. Which of the following statements in a prefix list would filter subnets of 15.196.0.0/16 that have prefixes between 20 and 32 bits long?

   a. ip prefix-list deny 15.196.0.0/16

   b. ip prefix-list deny 15.196.0.0/16 ge 20 le 32

   c. ip prefix-list deny 15.196.0.0/16 le 20 ge 32

   d. ip prefix-list deny 15.196.0.0 ge 20 le 32

5. Which of the following commands would apply a prefix list named Outbound to BGP peer 172.16.1.1 for outbound updates?

   a. Router(config-router)#neighbor 172.16.1.1 prefix-list Outbound

   b. Router(config-router)# neighbor 172.16.1.1 prefix-list out Outbound

   c. Router(config-router)# neighbor 172.16.1.1 prefix-list Outbound out

   d. Router(config-router)# neighbor 172.16.1.1 prefix-list Outbound in

9

Lab 9.3 Multihoming

Objective

In this lab, you will learn how to configure multihoming for an autonomous system.

Materials Required

This lab will require the following:

➤ Five Cisco routers with the interfaces, IP addresses, and cabling, as shown in Figure 9-3, and the interfaces connected to the DCE ends of the serial cables configured with a clock rate of 64000

➤ OSPF configured on Router3, Router4, and Router5 to advertise all subnets of 10.0.0.0/8 in Area 0

➤ A route to 0.0.0.0/0 with a next hop of 10.x.2.1 configured on Router3, with the **default-information originate** command used to propagate the default route in OSPF

➤ A route to 0.0.0.0/0 with a next hop of 10.x.4.2 configured on Router4, with the **default-information originate** command used to propagate the default route in OSPF

➤ Known telnet and enable passwords for the routers

➤ A rollover console cable

➤ A laptop or a PC running a terminal emulation program such as Hyperterminal

Estimated completion time: **20 minutes**

Activity Background

A multihomed autonomous system has more than one BGP connection at a time. For instance, a multihomed autonomous system might connect to the Internet through two or more Internet service providers (ISPs). Multihoming offers two advantages. First, multihoming gives you redundant connections. If one of the connections fails, you can still use the second connection. Second, multihoming can give you better routes to destinations. For instance, the path to a particular destination through one ISP may require 10 hops, while the path through another ISP might only require seven. Multihoming allows you to find the shorter path.

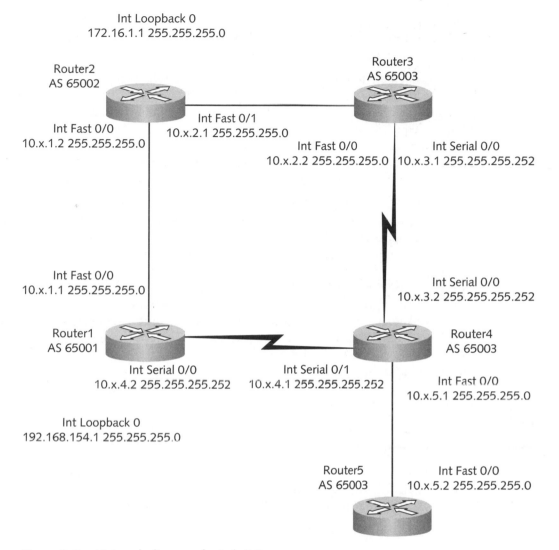

Figure 9-3   Network diagram for Lab 9-3

Typically, an ISP gives you three options for the number of routers your routers will learn. First, your routers might learn a default route from the ISP. As a result, your IGP would determine the path packets would take out of your AS. If your IGP is OSPF, you should configure the default routes as type 1 external routes. Second, your routers might learn default routes and customer or other local routes from the ISP. As a result, you have little control over path selection outside your AS. For destinations outside the AS without a more specific route, your IGP would determine the path out of the AS. This gives you better path selection for the ISP's other customers (which may or may not be important), while giving you little control over path selection to other destinations. Third, your routers might learn the entire BGP routing table from the ISP. This requires significantly more memory and processor power than the other two possibilities, but gives you the most control over path selection outside your AS. In each case, the ISP's routers would learn any routes advertised by your autonomous system.

In multihomed environments, a variety of tools are available to influence path selection. The local preference path attribute is a well-known discretionary path attribute included in IBGP peer updates. The local preference path attribute is not sent to EBGP peers. All else being equal, a route with a higher local preference is preferred. The default value for local preference on Cisco routers is 100. Local preference is typically used to influence paths leaving an autonomous system. You can configure a new default local preference with the **bgp default local-preference** command in router configuration mode. You can also change local preference values with route maps.

Another method to influence path selection is to configure the weight of a route. Weight is a Cisco proprietary path attribute. It is valid only on the router on which it was configured, and is not included in updates sent to other routers. As with the local preference attribute, routes with higher weights are preferred. The weight of a route may be any value between 0 and 65,535. By default, a router assigns a weight of 32,768 to routes it advertises, and a weight of 0 to routes originating elsewhere. Because the weight of a route is looked at first in the algorithm used to select routes, the weight of a route takes precedence over local preference. You can assign a weight to all routes learned from a particular neighbor with the **neighbor** *ip-address* **weight** command. You can also assign weights inside route maps.

ACTIVITY

1. Power on the routers and the PC or laptop and open the terminal emulation program.

2. Plug the RJ-45 end of the console cable into the console port of Router1. Attach the other end of the console cable to the serial port on the laptop or PC. You may need to press **Enter** to bring up the Router1> prompt.

3. First you will configure Router1 and Router2 as BGP peers with each other, and with the attached routers in AS 65003. Router1 and Router2 will function as the ISP routers. Type **enable** and press **Enter**. The router prompt changes to Router1#.

4. Type **config term** and press **Enter**.

5. Type **router bgp 65001** and press **Enter**.

6. Type **neighbor 10.*x*.1.2 remote-as 65002** and press **Enter**.

7. Type **neighbor 10.*x*.4.1 remote-as 65003** and press **Enter**.

8. Type **network 192.168.154.0 mask 255.255.255.0** and press **Enter**.

9. Press **Ctl-Z** to exit configuration mode.

10. Repeat Steps 3 and 4 on Router2.

11. Type **router bgp 65002** and press **Enter**.

12. Type **neighbor 10.x.1.1 remote-as 65001** and press **Enter**.

13. Type **neighbor 10.x.2.2 remote-as 65003** and press **Enter**.

14. Type **network 172.16.1.0 mask 255.255.255.0** and press **Enter**.

15. Type **network 10.x.1.0 mask 255.255.255.0** and press **Enter**.

16. Type **network 10.x.2.0 mask 255.255.255.0** and press **Enter**.

17. Press **Ctl-Z** to exit configuration mode.

18. Now you will configure Router3 and Router4 as IBGP peers, and as peers with the ISP router to which each is connected. Repeat Steps 3 and 4 on Router3.

19. Type **router bgp 65003** and press **Enter**.

20. Type **neighbor 10.x.3.2 remote-as 65003** and press **Enter**.

21. Type **neighbor 10.x.2.1 remote-as 65002** and press **Enter**.

22. Type **network 10.x.3.0 mask 255.255.255.252** and press **Enter**.

23. Type **no synchronization** and press **Enter**.

24. Press **Ctl-Z** to exit configuration mode.

25. Repeat Steps 3 and 4 on Router4.

26. Type **router bgp 65003** and press **Enter**.

27. Type **neighbor 10.x.3.1 remote-as 65003** and press **Enter**.

28. Type **neighbor 10.x.4.2 remote-as 65001** and press **Enter**.

29. Type **network 10.x.4.0 mask 255.255.255.252** and press **Enter**.

30. Type **network 10.x.5.0 mask 255.255.255.0** and press **Enter**.

31. Type **no synchronization** and press **Enter**.

32. Press **Ctl-Z** to exit configuration mode.

33. On Router5, type **trace 172.16.1.1** and press **Enter**. What path do packets to this destination take?

    _____

34. Type **trace 192.168.154.1** and press **Enter**. What path do packets to this destination take?

    _____

35. On Router4, type **show ip bgp** and press **Enter**. What is the local preference in the BGP table for routes that use Router3 as their next hop?

    _____

9

36. On Router3, type **config term** and press **Enter**.

37. Now you will see what effect changing the local preference can have on paths leaving the autonomous system. Type **router bgp 65003** and press **Enter**.

38. Type **bgp default local-preference 10000** and press **Enter**.

39. Press **Ctl-Z** to exit configuration mode.

40. On Router4, type **clear ip bgp 65003** and press **Enter**.

41. Type **show ip bgp** and press **Enter**. The routes should appear with a local preference of 10000. If not, wait 30 seconds and repeat this step as needed.

42. On Router5, repeat Steps 33 and 34. How do the paths taken to these destinations differ from those you found in Steps 33 and 34 (if at all)?

_____

43. On Router4, type **show ip bgp** and press **Enter**. What is the local preference in the BGP table for routes that use Router3 as their next hop?

_____

44. On Router4, type **config term** and press **Enter**.

45. Type **router bgp 65003** and press **Enter**.

46. Type **neighbor 10.x.4.2 weight 1000** and press **Enter**.

47. Press **Ctl-Z** to exit configuration mode.

48. Type **clear ip bgp *** and press **Enter**.

49. Type **show ip bgp** and press **Enter**. Routes for most destinations should appear in the BGP table with a weight of 1000. If not, wait 30 seconds and repeat this step as needed.

50. On Router5, repeat Steps 33 and 34. How do the paths taken to these destinations differ from those found in Step 33, 34 and 41 (if at all)?

_____

Certification Objectives

Objectives for Cisco Exam 640-603: Routing

➤ Describe methods to connect to multiple ISPs using BGP

➤ Configure a multihomed BGP environment and verify proper operation

Review Questions

1. Which of the following are reasons why you might want to use multihoming? (Choose all that apply.)

   a. Multihoming prevents network outages.

   b. Multihoming minimizes the possibility of network outages by creating redundant paths to other autonomous systems.

    c. Multihoming allows you to get better paths to other autonomous systems.

    d. Multihoming allows you to use default routes instead of BGP.

2. What effect does the local preference attribute have on a route?

    a. Routes into an autonomous system with higher local preferences are preferred.

    b. Routes leaving an autonomous system with higher local preferences are preferred.

    c. Routes with higher local preferences are preferred regardless of other attributes.

    d. Routes with higher local preferences are not removed from the routing table even when they are unreachable.

3. Which of the following is true about the weight attribute? (Choose all that apply.)

    a. The weight attribute is proprietary to Cisco.

    b. The weight attribute is only propagated within an autonomous system.

    c. The weight attribute takes precedence over the local preference.

    d. The weight attribute is not included in updates sent to other routers.

4. Which of the following commands would configure a default local preference value of 500?

    a. Router(config-router)#bgp default local-preference 500

    b. Router(config-router)#neighbor 172.16.1.1 local-preference 500

    c. Router(config-router)#bgp local-preference 500

    d. Router(config-router)#default local-preference 500

5. You are the network administrator for a multihomed AS. Users in your AS need to reach the networks of other customers of your ISPs. However, your routers have slow processors and relatively little memory. What routes should routers in your AS learn from your ISPs?

    a. only default routes

    b. default routes plus customer routers

    c. all routes, with customer routes filtered

    d. all routes

LAB 9.4 REDISTRIBUTING ROUTES INTO AN IGP

Objective

In this lab, you will learn how to redistribute routes between an IGP and BGP.

Materials Required

This lab will require the following:

- ➤ Three Cisco routers with the interfaces, IP addresses, and cabling, as shown in Figure 9-4, and the interfaces connected to the DCE ends of the serial cables configured with a clock rate of 64000

- ➤ OSPF configured on Router1 and Router2 to advertise all subnets of 10.0.0.0/8 in Area 0

- ➤ Known telnet and enable passwords for the routers

- ➤ A rollover console cable

- ➤ A laptop or a PC running a terminal emulation program such as Hyperterminal

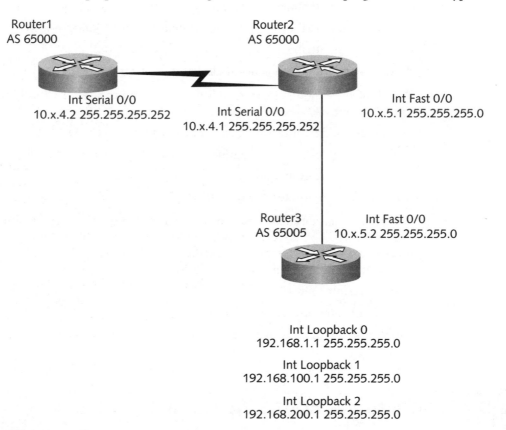

Figure 9-4   Network diagram for Lab 9-4

Estimated completion time: **20 minutes**

Activity Background

You may use one of three primary methods to introduce routes from your autonomous system's IGP into BGP. First, you may use the **network** command. Each route advertised with this command must exist in the router's routing table, and must be manually configured on the BGP router advertising it. Second, you may redistribute null routes summarizing existing routes into BGP. For instance, you might configure a router to redistribute a null route to 172.16.0.0/20. Other routers will send it packets bound for destinations in this network. If the router has a more specific route in its routing table, it uses it to forward packets. If it does not, it discards the packets. However, the router continues to advertise redistributed null routes even when all the summarized routes are down. Traffic may be dropped after many hops, and working alternate paths may not be used. An aggregate address, on the other hand, is not advertised when all the summarized routes are down. Third, you may redistribute routes from your IGP directly into BGP. While this is the simplest method, instability in your IGP will also cause instability in BGP. Instability in BGP will affect the ability of hosts in your autonomous system to reach hosts in other autonomous systems, and vice versa. Additionally, you must be careful to only redistribute routes from within your autonomous system. Redistribution of routes learned from BGP back into BGP could cause routing loops.

When redistributing routes from BGP back into an IGP, you also have several options depending on your needs and network topology. In many topologies, redistribution may not be necessary. For instance, you may propagate one or more default routes throughout an autonomous system. For an autonomous system using IBGP on all of its routers, such as an ISP, you may turn off synchronization and not use the IGP. In this way, the IBGP peers will learn routes from each other. In other circumstances, you may want to redistribute routes from BGP into the IGP. For instance, you may find it useful to redistribute routes to destinations in a bordering autonomous system when a default route would result in poor path selection. However, you typically need to do filtering on the routes introduced into the IGP. This is particularly true if your routers are receiving the full Internet BGP routing table, as the sheer number of routes received will make routing tables in your IGP too large.

ACTIVITY

1. Power on the routers and the PC or laptop and open the terminal emulation program.

2. Plug the RJ-45 end of the console cable into the console port of Router3. Attach the other end of the console cable to the serial port on the laptop or PC. You may need to press **Enter** to bring up the Router3> prompt.

3. Type **enable** and press **Enter**. The router prompt changes to Router3#.

4. Type **config term** and press **Enter**.

5. Type **router bgp 65005** and press **Enter**.

6. Type **neighbor 10.*x*.5.1 remote-as 65000** and press **Enter**.

7. Type **network 192.168.1.0 mask 255.255.255.0** and press **Enter**.

8. Repeat the previous step with the 192.168.100.0/24 and 192.168.200.0/24 networks.

9. Type **aggregate-address 192.168.0.0 255.255.0.0** and press **Enter**.

10. Press **Ctl-Z** to exit configuration mode.

11. On Router2, repeat Steps 3 and 4.

12. Type **ip subnet-zero** and press **Enter**. This command allows you to configure a network in the zero subnet, which you will do in the next step.

13. Type **ip route 10.0.0.0 255.255.248.0 null 0** and press **Enter**. This creates a null route summarizing the routes advertised by OSPF.

14. Type **router bgp 65000** and press **Enter**.

15. Type **neighbor 10.*x*.5.2 remote-as 65005** and press **Enter**.

16. Type **network 10.0.0.0 mask 255.255.248.0** and prss **Enter**. Now the null route you configured in Step 13 is advertised by BGP.

17. Press **Ctl-Z** to exit configuration mode.

18. On Router3, type **show ip route** and press **Enter**. You see a route to 10.0.0.0/21. If you do not, wait 30 seconds and repeat this step as needed.

19. Now you will redistribute routes learned from BGP back into the OSPF. On Router2, type **config term** and press **Enter**.

20. First you will filter the routes to be learned. Type **access-list 1 deny 192.168.100.0 0.0.0.255** and press **Enter**.

21. Type **access-list 1 deny 192.168.200.0 0.0.0.255** and press **Enter**.

22. Type **access-list 1 permit 192.168.0.0 0.0.255.255** and press **Enter**. Which routes do you expect this access list to permit, and which routes do you expect it to block?

---

23. Type **router ospf 1** and press **Enter**.

24. Type **redistribute bgp 65000 subnets** and press **Enter**. This command redistributes BGP routes (including subnets) into OSPF.

25. Type **distribute-list 1 out bgp 65000** and press **Enter**.

26. Press **Ctl-Z** to exit configuration mode.

27. On Router1, type **show ip route** and press **Enter**. Which routes has Router1 learned as external type 2 OSPF routes?

Certification Objective

Objective for Cisco Exam 640-603: Routing

➤ Explain the use of redistribution between BGP and IGP

Review Questions

1. What is a disadvantage of creating a null route summarizing routes in your IGP, and then redistributing static routes into BGP?

   a. Null routes are typically unstable.

   b. The null route remains in the routing table even when all the routes it summarizes are down.

   c. Packets sent to the null route are discarded.

   d. The null route disappears from the routing table when all the routes it summarizes are down.

2. Why does Cisco recommend manually configuring networks to be advertised by BGP over redistributing routes from an IGP?

   a. Redistributing routes from an IGP is less stable than manually configuring them.

   b. Redistributing routes is less efficient than manual configuration of the networks to be advertised.

   c. Redistributing routes requires more complex configuration than manual configuration of the networks to be advertised.

   d. Filtering of redistributed routes is less efficient than manual configuration of the networks to be advertised.

3. IBGP is running on all the routers in your autonomous system. In this case, which of the following is the best scenario for propagating routes learned from BGP into your IGP?

   a. redistributing routes from IBGP into the IGP without filtering

   b. propagating default routes into the IGP

   c. turning off synchronization without propagating routes into the IGP

   d. redistributing routes from IBGP into the IGP with filtering

4. Which of the following is a potential danger of redistributing routes between an IGP and BGP?

   a. Routing loops may result from instabilities in the IGP.

   b. Routing loops may result if routes learned through BGP are redistributed back into BGP.

   c. Instability in BGP may result in instability in the IGP.

   d. The router may not have the necessary memory or processor power to handle the additional updates from the IGP.

5. Which of the following commands would redistribute a null route into BGP?

    a. redistribute null

    b. redistribute static in

    c. redistribute static null

    d. redistribute static

Lab 9.5 Routing Policy and Peer Groups

Objective

In this lab, you will learn how to use peer groups to configure routing policy.

Materials Required

This lab will require the following:

➤ Three Cisco routers with the interfaces, IP addresses, and cabling, as shown in Figure 9-5

➤ Known telnet and enable passwords for the routers

➤ A rollover console cable

➤ A laptop or a PC running a terminal emulation program such as Hyperterminal

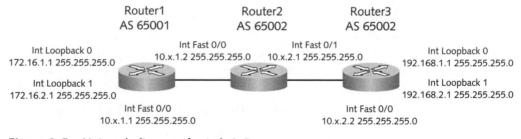

Figure 9-5   Network diagram for Lab 9-5

Estimated completion time: **20 minutes**

Activity Background

While BGP allows you a great deal of control over routing policy, configuring routing policies on multiple routers is time intensive and prone to mistakes. This is particularly true as the complexity of the configuration on each router increases. Additionally, multiple BGP peers with the same outbound routing policy will send duplicate updates, which is inefficient.

One approach to reducing the amount of configuration necessary and improving the efficiency of BGP updates is the use of peer groups. A peer group is a group of routers sharing the same routing policy. The peer group also sends a single routing update, which is more efficient than each peer group member sending its own update.

In order to configure a peer group, you must first configure the name of the peer group on the peer group leader with the **neighbor** *peer-group-name* **peer-group** command. Next, you must configure routing policy on the router, substituting the name of the peer group for the IP address of a BGP peer. Finally, you must add neighbors to the peer group with the **neighbor** *ip-address* **peer-group** *peer-group-name* command. At this point, you may optionally override peer group settings for certain neighbors for incoming updates. Because the peer group sends a single update for all members of the peer group, however, you cannot override peer group policies for outgoing updates. You may configure peer groups for both internal and external peers.

ACTIVITY

1. Power on the routers and the PC or laptop and open the terminal emulation program.

2. Plug the RJ-45 end of the console cable into the console port of Router3. Attach the other end of the console cable to the serial port on the laptop or PC. You may need to press **Enter** to bring up the Router3> prompt.

3. Type **enable** and press **Enter**. The router prompt changes to Router3#.

4. Type **config term** and press **Enter**.

5. Type **router bgp 65002** and press **Enter**.

6. Type **neighbor 10.*x*.2.1 remote-as 65002** and press **Enter**.

7. Type **network 192.168.1.0 mask 255.255.255.0** and press **Enter**.

8. Type **network 192.168.2.0 mask 255.255.255.0** and press **Enter**.

9. Type **aggregate-address 192.168.0.0 255.255.0.0** and press **Enter**.

10. Type **no synchronization** and press **Enter**.

11. Press **Ctl-Z** to exit configuration mode.

12. On Router1, repeat Steps 3 and 4.

13. Type **router bgp 65001** and press **Enter**.

14. Type **neighbor 10.*x*.1.2 remote-as 65002** and press **Enter**.

15. Type **network 172.16.1.0 mask 255.255.255.0** and press **Enter**.

16. Type **network 172.16.2.0 mask 255.255.255.0** and press **Enter**.

17. Type **aggregate-address 172.16.0.0 255.255.0.0** and press **Enter**.

9

18. Press **Ctl-Z** to exit configuration mode.

19. On Router2, repeat Steps 3 through 5.

20. Type **neighbor 10.*x*.2.2 remote-as 65002** and press **Enter**.

21. Type **neighbor 10.*x*.1.1 remote-as 65001** and press **Enter**.

22. Type **network 10.*x*.2.0 mask 255.255.255.0** and press **Enter**.

23. Type **network 10.*x*.1.0 mask 255.255.255.0** and press **Enter**.

24. Type **no synchronization** and press **Enter**.

25. Press **Ctl-Z** to exit configuration mode.

26. Type **show ip bgp** and press **Enter**. You see routes for all the networks and aggregate addresses you configured earlier. If you do not, wait 30 seconds and repeat this step as needed.

27. On Router1, type **show ip bgp** and press **Enter**. Which routes do you see in Router1's BGP table?

_____

28. On Router3, type **show ip bgp** and press **Enter**. Which routes do you see in Router3's BGP table?

_____

29. On Router2, type **config term** and press **Enter**.

30. Now you will configure routing policies and create peer groups for Router2's external and internal peers. Type **ip prefix-list InternalPrefixList deny 172.16.0.0/16 ge 17** and press **Enter**.

31. Type **ip prefix-list InternalPrefixList permit 0.0.0.0/0 le 24** and press **Enter**.

32. Type **access-list 1 deny 192.168.0.0 0.0.3.255** and press **Enter**.

33. Type **access-list 1 permit any** and press **Enter**.

34. Type **ip prefix-list ExternalPrefixList deny 192.168.0.0/16 ge 17** and press **Enter**. This statement filters subnets of 192.168.0.0/16 with prefixes of 17 bits or longer.

35. Type **ip prefix-list ExternalPrefixList permit 0.0.0.0/0 le 24** and press **Enter**. This statement allows all networks with prefixes of 24 bits or fewer.

36. Type **router bgp 65002** and press **Enter**.

37. First you will configure a peer group and routing policy for Router2's IBGP peer, Router3. Type **neighbor Internal peer-group** and press **Enter**. This command creates a peer group named Internal.

38. Type **neighbor 10.*x*.2.2 peer-group Internal** and press **Enter**. This adds Router3 to the peer group.

39. Type **neighbor Internal prefix-list InternalPrefixList out** and press **Enter**.

40. Now you will configure a peer group and routing policy for Router2's EBGP peer, Router1. Type **neighbor External peer-group** and press **Enter**.

41. Type **neighbor 10.x.1.1 peer-group External** and press **Enter**.

42. Type **neighbor External prefix-list ExternalPrefixList out** and press **Enter**.

43. Press **Ctl-Z** to exit configuration mode.

44. Type **clear ip bgp *** and press **Enter**.

45. Type **show ip bgp** and press **Enter**. You see all the routes you saw in Steps 27 and 28. If you do not, wait 30 seconds and repeat this step as needed.

46. On Router1, type **show ip bgp** and press **Enter**. Which routes do you now see in Router1's BGP table?

_____

47. On Router3, type **show ip bgp** and press **Enter**. Which routes do you now see in Router3's BGP table?

_____

Certification Objectives

Objectives for Cisco Exam 640-603: Routing

➤ Describe and configure policy control in BGP using prefix lists

➤ Describe BGP communities and peer groups

Review Questions

1. Which of the following are advantages of using peer groups to configure routing policy? (Choose all that apply.)

a. You do not need to configure as many neighbor statements.

b. You can configure routing policy on multiple routers at the same time.

c. The peer group sends one update, instead of one update for each member.

d. The peer group processes each update received, instead of each individual member.

2. When can you override configuration settings for an individual member of a peer group?

a. for outgoing updates

b. whenever necessary

c. for incoming updates

d. to change the weight attribute on routers in the peer group

3. Which of the following commands would configure a peer group named Inside?

a. Router(config-router)#neighbor Inside peer-group

b. Router(config-router)#peer-group Inside

c. Router(config-router)#bgp peer-group Inside

d. Router(config-router)#neighbor 10.1.1.1 peer-group inside

4. Which of the following commands would apply a prefix list named Filter to incoming routes from a peer group named Outside?

a. Router(config-router)#peer-group Outside prefix-list Filter in

b. Router(config-router)#bgp peer-group Outside prefix-list Filter in

c. Router(config-router)#neighbor Outside prefix-list Filter in

d. Router(config-router)#neighbor Outside prefix-list Filter

5. Which of the following commands would apply a route map named Local to outgoing routes sent by a peer group named Inside?

a. Router(config-router)#peer-group Inside route-map Local

b. Router(config-router)#peer-group Inside route-map Local out

c. Router(config-router)#bgp neighbor Inside route-map Local out

d. Router(config-router)#neighbor Inside route-map Local out